FEB 1 3 201

W9-CAZ-115

Pigs Can't Swim

Pigs Can't Swim

A MEMOIR

HELEN PEPPE

A Merloyd Lawrence Book
Da Capo Press

Editorial production by Lori Hobkirk at the Book Factory.

Cataloging-in-Publication data for this book is available from the Library of Congress.
ISBN: 978-0-306-82272-8 (hardcover)
ISBN: 978-0-306-82273-5 (e-book)

Published as a Merloyd Lawrence Book by Da Capo Press
A Member of the Perseus Books Group
www.dacapopress.com

Da Capo Press books are available at special discounts for bulk purchases in the U.S. by corporations, institutions, and other organizations. For more information, please contact the Special Markets Department at the Perseus Books Group, 2300 Chestnut Street, Suite 200, Philadelphia, PA 19103, or call (800) 810-4145, ext. 5000, or e-mail special.markets@perseusbooks .com.

10 9 8 7 6 5 4 3 2 1

I dedicate this book to my parents, who continue to be the best parents they can by supporting and understanding my decision to write Pigs Can't Swim, *despite their own emotional discomfort at what my child-self observed and thought. I have raised only two children, and there are many times I wish I could go back and do things differently. I don't want to imagine raising nine. I am grateful for how hard my parents worked and for how much they gave us when they had so little. There is nothing they wouldn't do to help any of their children just as there is nothing their children wouldn't do to help them. I couldn't have written* Pigs Can't Swim *without them.*

And to Eric Peppe, who continues to be my rocket man.

"It's better to be good than evil, but one achieves goodness at a terrific cost."

—STEPHEN KING

"And yet to every bad there is a worse."

—THOMAS HARDY

"The least I can do is speak out for those who cannot speak for themselves."

—JANE GOODALL

"I wish people would realize that animals are totally dependent on us, helpless, like children, a trust that is put upon us."

—JAMES HERRIOT

Contents

CONTENTS

Author's Note

I come from an unreal place, where the believable and the unbelievable wove into a reality that became my personal truth. This truth is a product of where I stood at the bottom of a large family, of what I saw and of what I thought as my siblings and parents wrought their own truths. They could not have seen exactly what I did, because I occupied the spot they would need to see it. Instead, they saw things I couldn't. They can't have thought what I thought because, despite DNA, my brain is my own. We all had different windows with different views and remember that which was important to us at the moment. I am convinced, probably a result of reading so many books about chimpanzees, that we remember mainly those things which we need to for survival. A child's brain is like flypaper that hangs from a barn ceiling: it doesn't get to choose which memories fly away free and which memories stick to death.

The characters in this book are real and not composites, but I altered features and names to protect identities. Some scenes are composites as childhood is overly long and overly repetitive, mostly the same, day after day. I did my best to recreate dialogue out of the mush of thousands of conversations, my own and others, that were, again, mostly the same. I cannot guarantee that any scene or any conversation is a replica. In truth, I can say to do so would be a lie, but I can guarantee with complete confidence that these scenes and conversations are what I see and, most significantly, what I feel, when I look at the view out my childhood window.

1

"What Were You Thinking?"

My brother, the blustery-and-favored one who was older by nine years, once said that skin and vinyl stick together like dollar bills to a stripper. I didn't know at the time what a stripper did or where the bills would stick, but I did know firsthand that vinyl car seats stuck to any skin that was bare. My blustery-and-favored brother's knowledge of girlie shows was limited to the Maine State Fair, thirty minutes from our house. This fair drew furtive- and guilty-looking males from behind their Rototillers, hoes, and rakes to the only type of event that featured the only type of dancers who had the power to make my mother behave like herself in public.

"I'll have no son of mine gawking at strippers. There's no need of women dancing around like that, and I have half a mind to tell them so myself," she snapped one late September evening between gritted teeth at the teenager she dragged across the parking lot by the ear. She'd already pinched both his cheeks, and he wore her disappointment on his face like misplaced blush. "They're nothing but tramps and hussies. Now get in the car before I wring your neck." She slapped at his chest and shoulders in stops and starts.

My mother was able to make a face of venomous contempt with only slight adjustments to her mouth and eyes. She could go from speaking to my father with a pleasant, approachable expression to speaking to her kids as if pleasure never existed. When she saw one of her children hadn't done the last thing she'd requested or, worse, said he did when he didn't, she changed more swiftly than Superman right before my eyes. In years to come I would study all women's faces to see if they had this superpower, and I would learn that not only did they have it—even the kindest-faced jolly females—but I had it too.

The youngest of nine, I often watched my siblings as they received their lessons. Never sorry for anything but getting caught, they tensed their muscles, tucked their chins to their chests, and hunched their shoulders as they endured, much like apes in a tropical downpour. From my spot on the perimeter of the family in the days when I was still cute and innocent, I wondered about "need" and "knowing better" each time my parents shouted things like "there's no need of that" and "you know better."

I'd feel darts of shame for wanting to see what went on behind the plywood walls that were painted with pictures of jutting-breasted women who dressed as Wonder Woman might if she were going swimming. What did these tramps and hussies do that caused men to line up and wait, that gave these women so much power? I'd learned shortly after birth that men didn't expect to wait for anything, especially their meals, their cigarettes, the bathroom, or the screwdriver they yelled for while holding pieces of metal or wood together. I wanted to know the difference between a hussy and a superhero, and I wanted to know why we sometimes found my father outside those walls, claiming when we'd found him that he'd gotten lost.

Later that night, after I got home and lay in my bed, as two of my sisters giggled nearby in their own beds about something they claimed I could never understand because I was too young, I considered how the dancers got money to stick to them. With an ever-growing desire for chocolate—Kit-Kats, Charleston Chews, Marathon Bars, and Reese's Peanut Butter Cups, I was desperate for cash. Did the strippers have to do anything for money? Was it uncomfortable?

SOMETIMES THE SEAT IN THE FAMILY CAR BURNED SO HOT I stood until the wind from the open windows cooled the sun-baked surfaces. When I had a choice, I'd make myself a pretend home in the carpeted way-back with books and a worn black blanket, and I'd let the curvy roads rock my body the fifteen miles from home into the City-of-the-Library, where we grocery shopped and bought hardware for farm and house repairs. This city landscape's most exciting point of interest was the waterfalls that fell with a wild rush of sound and splash into a boulder-filled river.

The City-of-the-Library and its sibling, the City-over-the-Bridge, were as different then as girlie-show strippers were from my mother. Disapproving of the French people who lived on one side of the City-over-the-Bridge and the dirty poor people who lived on the other, my parents crossed the river with repetitive judgments flowing from their mouths. I learned in my early years that there are three kinds of poor people: those who work but don't have money, those who don't have to work because the state gives them money, and those who work, have a little money, and pretend they are better than everyone else.

"You have all that you need. Think of the starving children in China and what have you," my father would say to his youngest three children as he walked through the grocery store munching on chocolate-covered peanuts.

During one King's department store errand I hid under a clothing rack and imagined how, after the workers left for the day, I'd sneak out and spend the night eating Reese's Peanut Butter cups and Humpty Dumpty potato chips. As I waited, I squeezed my eyes shut tight and journeyed through the deep space that was filled with shooting stars behind my lids. When my mother found me and whisper-yelled, "I've been calling and calling, searching everywhere. Where have you been? What were you thinking?" I'd been to a faraway place, escaping to where only I could go. It didn't occur to me to explain my ingenious candy plan. From watching my siblings I had already learned not to divulge information.

The next time I went to King's I experimented with hairspray when no one was looking, wanting to see if I could get my hair to stick straight out like Pippy Longstocking's braids. When I sprayed my eyes and screamed, with the sound beginning deep in my belly, I got the attention of the store manager, who stood with his chin down to his chest and his shoulders hunched while my mother berated him for placing the cans where children could reach them. She didn't ask me what I was thinking that day but instead rushed me to the bathroom. I learned that a person could be sometimes pardoned from the why-would-you-do-such-a-thing? tirade if she was physically hurt.

During most errands I waited in the car, with books and possibly my plush Cat in the Hat or stuffed Snoopy in my lap. If winter, my toes would freeze in my shoes, my cheeks and mouth would grow stiff, and my muscles would tremble. After what felt like hours, my mother might appear with a box of Milk Duds or Junior Mints, and I would feel a rush of love and be relieved that my siblings had chosen to stay home, because now I wouldn't have to share with anyone but my mother. My father had his own candy.

Returning from town to country, my father drove past trash-filled yards and maneuvered around dogs who sat in the middle of the road until our back tires caught their attention and they chased us. "Cussed dog," "Damn dog," "Stupid dog," and honking were as much a part of car rides as burning vinyl seats. The day we hit a dog and it lay in the road yiking into deadly silence was a day my brain decided to weave lifelike images of death into its fibers as if inspired to begin a new project. In school, teachers would say, "Memorize the multiplication table, memorize when to carry, when to borrow," and I'd want to so badly that I made my stomach sick with the stress of it. I would stare at the numbers, willing them into my brain, with the fear of the teacher yelling at me causing me to push myself. But the seconds of seeing chickens with their heads cut off, a cat thrown into the pond, a deer bleeding from a gunshot wound, or a dog dying in the road—those seconds I had no control over remembering and no control over forgetting, no matter how badly I wanted to.

If we'd purchased lumber in town that required the back window to be open, the wind would gust through and steal my breath. I experimented with surviving on as little air as possible. To hold my breath longer and longer seemed a skill worth honing. I would imagine from my place in the way-back what it would feel like to bounce out the window, and I pondered how far my parents would drive before they noticed. My mother might say, months later, as they drove toward home, "Remember, that's where we lost Helen. What could she have been thinking? I wonder whatever happened to her."

WHEN WE HAD NO CHORES SEVERAL SISTERS AND I WOULD sometimes walk to a man-made pond behind a long farmhouse. The water looked chocolate brown, like a stream out of *Charlie and the Chocolate Factory*, but tasted like rot, and I don't remember any of us ever touching or seeing the bottom. When I opened my eyes beneath the motionless water I saw nothing, not a sliver of light, not even the legs of my sisters and the boys they fondled. And I heard nothing, not even the frogs or the birds and snakes who sometimes ate them. There was nothing but the booming silence that had a faraway ring to it. Swimming furiously up and out with images of snarling monsters filling my mind, my heart thumped like a bass drum in my ears.

And once, there ahead of me, a parent stood big and solid, a mother to the male teenagers who were treading water with their shirts off, their naked chests shining with droplets above the murk. This mother gestured and screamed from the bank, and I was angry with myself for not seeing her first. I'm not sure how it came to be, possibly because I was the youngest, but I was the lookout, and now someone else's mother screamed at us over the opaque water.

"You're nothing but a bunch of dirty whores," she shouted so loudly that her voice cracked and her spit flew. "Get your damn clothes back on and your filthy bodies away from my boys."

Accused, cold sweat prickled over my chilled skin. My sister, the one my parents frequently threatened to send to the Opportunity

Farm for Boys, a country boarding school for homeless children, because she feared no one and nothing and couldn't be forced to pretend she did, might have splashed confidently out of the water, the word "Bitch" on her tongue. She might have smiled at the boys who understood the raise of her eyebrows and the curve of her mouth that meant, "Later." I didn't think the Opportunity Farm for Boys sounded like a place that would make either the boys or my sister miserable, and I wondered what kinds of opportunities these boys got when, from where I stood, to be male meant plenty of opportunity on its own.

2

Mac

WHENEVER I HEARD MY MOTHER SAY, "LITTLE PITCHERS HAVE big ears," I would grind my cavity-rich teeth in frustration. Especially when she said it to one of my siblings as if they were superior to me, part of an exclusive club. It was, it seemed, my family's intent to keep me uninformed and confused. I didn't know my parents' first names until first grade, thinking of them only as Mamma and Daddy or as Honey and Old Goat. My sisters would say, "Shhh, here she comes," and then giggle. In the beginning, to get back at them, I'd tattle if I discovered anything that could get them in trouble. My father knew this about me and would say, "You're hearing things. I didn't say anything." My mother would say, "Mind your Ps and Qs." In a group they'd say, "Little pitchers"—the code words for "Helen can hear us."

What they did tell me wouldn't stand any test. Santa never came down our chimney and out of the wood stove, his reindeer never stood on our barn roof. When I was sitting on the toilet one Christmas Eve, I heard my sisters call me a baby for believing he did. There was no tooth fairy and there has been no Apocalypse, although I waited for it, always expecting it, with the same apprehension a rabbit has when a hawk flies overhead. Was I going to be taken or not? My imagination never ran away with me because that's impossible. My mother never called me, no matter how many times my father said she did to get rid of me. As far as I can tell, the bogeyman my sister said lived in my closet was a lie because I never saw him. I can't see that weeding hundreds of rows of beans and corn built my character or that word problems about trains were necessary for me to succeed once I was in the real world. I learned no one who doesn't want to be proven a liar should ever say with conviction that an animal can't think, can't feel, or can't get in or out of something.

"Oh, he won't get out of there," my father said confidently, referring to a young pig he and my blustery brother had just locked in a barn pen. "Yup, that'll hold 'em," my brother agreed, kicking at a wall to test its strength. "It's fine." I stood there, barefoot, my toes digging into the hay that blended stubbornly with manure, and I watched the little pig jump and clamber at the plywood pen. I worried he'd get splinters in his delicate snout and thought if I fed him, he'd be happier. "I'll get him some bread," I said.

"He don't need nothin'," my father said. "He can wait until feeding time."

I walked out of the barn, following my brother and father. Minutes later we heard a crash and turned around to see the pig land on all four cloven hooves before running off toward the gardens. Broken glass and pieces of wood littered the ground. "Guess he didn't want to wait," I said before I raced after him to the accompaniment of "Did you see that?" and "Cussed pig."

THANKSGIVINGS WERE LOUD, SMOKY, AND SMELLY. ADULTS TALKED in voices that rose and fell over each other. Cigarette smoke and pungent onions made my eyes sting and water. Disliking the holiday for how my cousins and siblings banded together, leaving me alone with strange adults, I was thrilled when, one Thanksgiving, an uncle brought his small Labrador puppy, Mac.

"Smart as a whip," he said proudly, setting him down in the kitchen. I loved him unconditionally before his big paws hit the linoleum.

After dinner the adults sat at the Formica kitchen table with pie and coffee. I sat on my mother's lap, sipping her warm tea before sliding off her knees and down her shins to sit under the table with Mac. The aluminum legs mixed with the people legs, and big shoes formed a rectangle around me. I was secluded in a private cave. It was late afternoon and getting dark. I could hear the adults' voices as a distant rumble from somewhere above me. My attention was focused solely on the black puppy who sniffed at the floor around the occupied shoes. Inching forward on my bottom, I reached his side, and he stopped his hunt to stare at me. I looked into his large eyes and hugged him, feeling as if we were connected by living outside of all the activity. I said, "I love you," almost at the same time his teeth bit into the side of my nose and eyebrow. He might have growled. I screamed and was suddenly yanked backward up out of my cave into the harsh fluorescent light of the kitchen.

My mother held me so that I lay on my back across her knees. "Stop moving so that I can see your eye," she commanded, but in a worried tone that caused fresh fear. I squeezed my eyes shut, and blood ran onto my lid and down my forehead into my hair. It was warm and then cold when someone put a bag of ice on my face.

"I can't tell if he got her eye," my mother said. "There's too much blood."

An adult yelled, "Get that damned dog out of here!"

"I don't think he could have done that much damage. He's just a puppy," another male voice said, possibly my uncle. "Faces just bleed a lot."

"A bite is a bite," a woman said sternly, and no one bothered to argue with her logic.

"She'll be fine," my father said.

I could feel the pressure of people gathered around me. "Now stop all the noise and let me look," my mother said again, removing the ice.

I worked to stop the sound, but I couldn't stop gasping for air. I was embarrassed to have so many people staring at me. I wanted to know where Mac was, if he was still under the table, if he was scared of all the noise.

"I don't think he got her eye," my mother announced. "But it was close. Do you think she needs stitches?"

"Nah, it'll heal and never show," my father said, as if stitches and healing were the same thing.

"You should get her checked," an aunt said. "I'd get her checked if she were mine. You don't want to fool around with eyes."

"There's no need of all that," my father said. "I've had worse."

"Where's Mac?" I sniffled, wanting to hug him better.

"Don't you worry about the puppy. He'll be fine," my mother said, and pressed the ice tight against my forehead and nose.

A YEAR WISER THE FOLLOWING THANKSGIVING, I NOTICED THAT holidays meant killing extra animals. One day Tom was gobbling himself blue in the face when my parents eyed him, calculating how many people his unfeathered body would feed, and the next he was a centerpiece on the table, his chest stuffed with bread and onions. My siblings argued over who would get his legs and who would get his finest white and dark meat. The wishbone and neck were yet another fight. But to call meat by the name it bore in life was a sure way to get in more trouble than anyone wanted. "It's just pot roast," my mother would yell, slapping with whatever she had handy at the son or daughter who dared to say it was Suzie-Q or Tommy or Dewy or whoever.

I'd stare at the juicy meat on my plate in horror, remembering how the animal used to nuzzle my hands, lean into me, or lap and suck my fingers. I'd stare at the juicy meat and consider what the juice was and search for the veins and arteries I knew were there. I'd feel my stomach turn away from the possibility of incoming food, and the back of my throat would start to close in a gag. Suddenly all food would be suspect, even the cold, stringy tomatoes in my macaroni. I'd tell myself they weren't bloody—how could they possibly be?—but my brain would fill with the image of clots, and my throat would contract to prevent anything from entering my stomach.

"Don't think about it. Just eat!" my mother commanded, as if not thinking were a possibility.

THAT THANKSGIVING I WANTED TO STAY SEPARATE FROM THE adults' never-ending, never-interesting conversation. There were no animals under the table to keep me in the house. After the dishes were washed I ran after my cousins and siblings, lagging behind, unable to keep up with their long-legged speed. The day was cold and overcast, and I was minus both mittens and a hat when I saw everybody climb the splintery wooden gate to the sheep pasture. They dashed off toward the distant pine trees, screaming in their game to outrun Henry the ram, who would chase them with his head lowered, charging. From evening chores to morning chores he lived in a stall that was barely the size of him. We could hear him slamming his pen's front wall with his head from most anywhere on the farm. My blustery-and-favored brother would lift the door that slid up and down like a guillotine to let him in and out. My father often assured us: "Oh, Henry won't hurt you. He's all bluff. Just carry a hoe or a stick."

Not willing to be left, I climbed the gate, jumped down into the pasture, paused for a second from the landing sting in my ankles, and then began to run across the frozen uneven ground. On my way I stopped to pat two girl sheep who liked to be scratched on their wooly heads just above their black noses. Their wool was greasy but warm against my bare fingers. I could feel my nails fill with dirt. Each time my fingers slowed, Molly pushed against my hand, and I didn't want to disappoint her.

Suddenly she moved off with a nervous bleat, trotting like a fat lady in high heels. I looked away from her wide, wooly sides to see Henry racing toward me at an ungainly but surprisingly rapid gallop. I could hear chatter and laughter in the distance. I ran for the gate, reaching it at the same time Henry did. "Help!" I screamed, turning to yell for sisters who were too far away to hear. The ram got me hard in the stomach and backed up to charge again, head lowered. I don't know what my mouth did as his forehead hit me a second and a third time, as if I were his archenemy. I had no breath left to make noise and was certain I was going to die when a man yanked me up by my armpits, scraping my back on the gate's boards. He ran with me toward the house, my manure-covered shoes flopping against his legs.

Later, when I'd been pronounced "fine," could take a full breath, and had stopped hiccupping and twitching, I made a plan to start patting Henry in his stall like I did the ewes. I'd never spent much time with him because he was locked in his sheep-sized box separate from the other animals who lived in larger stalls I could open myself. When Henry died unexpectedly and my parents covered his grave with large rocks so that nothing could dig him up, my mother cried and said, "He wasn't like that nasty one we had. He was such a good-natured ram."

UNTIL I STARTED SCHOOL I RARELY SAW ADULTS WHO WEREN'T my parents unless the mailman happened to catch me outside or we visited one of my mother's many sisters and brothers. My father had several siblings, too, but they had a dark history and no teeth or need to see each other. If we went to town, I avoided people, searching instead for stray dogs to give a pat, a hug, or any scrap of food I had in my pocket. Often I was saved the trouble of searching, as they found me. "It's a wonder Helen doesn't get bitten or something worse," my mother said, forgetting, despite the grooved scar beside my eye, that I'd already *been* bitten. "She hugs the mangiest-looking creatures. I just don't get it."

"One of these times she'll be sorry," my father said. "Cussed strays."

The summer following the dog bite my mother told me and several of my siblings to get into the car; we were going to visit her brother. As soon as I realized this was the brother who owned Mac, I got in the way-back of the station wagon, where I rolled and ricocheted off the walls with my hair-twirling-pretty sister as the car wove hairpin curves and sped down hills. Once there, I raced out to find a large brown Labrador barking at the end of a chain. When he saw me, he stood on his hind legs and pawed the air with his front legs like the black stallion in one of my books. He made strangling and gasping sounds as he forced his neck to stretch to its limit. I stared at him, considering whether a Lab could change color from black to brown. I tried to pat the dog's blocky head without getting tripped by his chain or knocked over by one of his flailing legs. Finding nothing in his face that I could recognize as Mac, I ran to find my cousin who was the closest to me in age. She was on a play gym.

"Where's Mac?" I asked.

"Who's Mac?"

"Your dog," I said, confused she didn't know.

She frowned at me. "Oh, Mac. We put him down ages ago."

I felt a heaviness in my stomach like I might need to use her bathroom. Living where I did, how I did, I knew what putting down meant. "Why?" I asked. My mouth was dry.

"Because he bit you. How could you forget that? Now we have Duke."

I could hear Duke barking and whining in the distance. His whines pulled at my heart.

My fingers went to my eye and traced the scar. "But why did you do that? He didn't mean to bite me. My mother said he was fine."

"Fine and dead," my cousin said, swinging off the monkey bars to land near me. "Want to go in my room and play with my new doll?" Her room was beautiful with beautiful clothes, a beautiful bed, and beautiful dolls. I wondered why she didn't have books.

I followed my cousin out of the yard to sit with her on the plush carpet of her princess-like room. Duke clanked his chain behind me, and I followed her as though I didn't have a care beyond playing with dolls. It was as though "fine and dead" was the same as "fine and dandy" in a world where fine had no meaning at all.

3

Liar, Liar, Pants on Fire

IT WAS SATURDAY, AND MY STOMACH RUMBLED AS I FANTASIZED about taking the last piece of pink pie in the refrigerator. I wondered if I could get away with eating all of it, then decided I'd eat only half of it, then only a tiny slice so no one would notice. My parents' car had just disappeared around the bend in the dirt road for errands in town. I watched for an opportunity, waited for people, a mix of siblings, to go upstairs or outside or to the bathroom.

As soon as my parents had left, my sisters had slipped in an eight-track tape and begun dancing, and three of them were jumping around the living room and singing at the top of their lungs, "Cracklin' Rosie, you're a store-bought woman." I couldn't see them, but I could feel the house shake. "Like a guitar humming," the windows rattled. My sister-who-holds-grudges-longer-than-God was making cookies that she baked every Saturday, cookies that I liked for only about fifteen minutes after she took them out of the oven. She sang, "Play it now, play it now, play it now, my baby" while she shook her hips in front of the counter.

I didn't care about Neil Diamond or about dancing. I cared about pie. I tucked my legs around the cold metal rungs of the green vinyl chair where I sat and tried to look innocent as I drew horse and rabbit heads on butcher paper. I began to fume about why my mother made the pink pie only once a year. "Is pink pie hard to make?" I'd asked her four days before, leaning against the lower white cupboards, watching her.

"Not as hard as your father's apple pies," she'd answered as she'd boiled the pink syrup on the stove. "That crust never does what it's supposed to."

She baked apple pies year round. "Is pink pie expensive?"

"Not really. It's just Jell-O and sugar."

"Can you make more if everyone eats it?" I'd asked.

"No, it's just for Thanksgiving," she'd said, and I didn't dare to ask the next question that sat on my tongue: "Why?"

MY STOMACH RUMBLED LOUDER AND DEEPER, AND I THOUGHT I wouldn't be able to stand the hunger much longer. I pictured the pie sitting in the fridge beside the Jell-O filled with weird bits of fruit that I couldn't eat without gagging. I considered making up a reason for my baking sister to leave the room. Lies began to form in my head, one to get her to leave the room and another in case anyone noticed the missing food. Before I had time to decide on the best story, my blustery-and-favored brother slammed into the house shouting, "The barn's on fire!"

My sister-who-holds-grudges-longer-than-God turned off the mixer and said, "Oh stop being such a meatball. It isn't either," holding her spatula up in front of her. I eagerly eyed the chocolate chip dough that clung to the rubber. Then she looked out the window over the sink beside her and shouted, "Oh my God, it is!" She threw the spatula on the counter beside the dirty measuring cups and raced out the kitchen door, her long hair flying, leaving the dough and the pink pie unguarded.

I stayed in my chair until I heard her feet on the porch, and then I ran to the fridge. I found the pie instantly, as if it were a beacon of heavenly light, and I dug my fingers into the chilled pink firmness, stuffing it with pieces of sugary graham cracker crust into my mouth, chewing and swallowing so fast I could barely taste it. "Find us a dream that don't ask no questions, ba ba ba," my sisters shouted, and the house protested with each jump. I climbed onto the counter and scooped out a clump of raw cookie batter. My sister-who-holds-grudges-longer-than-God entered suddenly in a blast of cold air with a black rabbit hugged to her chest. I wondered if there was anything on my face and licked my lips as I pretended to look out the window.

"Stay inside and do not move!" she ordered when she saw me start to slide off the counter. It was as if she no longer cared about her cookies. I loved this sister but resented her bossiness. Someday I would be the one to boss people around. I could hardly wait for my turn. She often locked the three of us youngest girls out of the house when our mother was away so that she could watch *Somerset* without hearing anyone titter. I didn't understand why she disliked laughing but was okay with fists pounding on the door and shouts of "I'm gonna tell!" Sometimes I hid behind the brown rocking chair in the living room where she couldn't find me, and I flipped through my mother's encyclopedias, searching for pictures of naked people.

She rushed out again, and I jumped down to sit on the floor and soothe Blackie, whose eyes were wide and round and whose muscles were tight with the need to flee. I picked him up and cuddled his soft trembling body in my arms. His long ears were cold beneath my fingers. I noticed six oval-shaped pellets on the linoleum that reminded me of the chocolate peanuts my father got when he watched my mother grocery shop. I hoped that a fire was a good enough reason for animal poop in the house. It was getting cold in the kitchen, so I took him farther away from the entry to the room that had a black-and-white television in it, some plants, and my mother's sewing machine. I sat on the brown scratchy carpet and shivered. No one bothered to shut any doors, and I could hear my mother's voice in my head, "How hard is it to close a door? What do you think we live in? A barn?" And today it was kind of funny because of the rabbit in my lap. The music stopped.

"What's going on?" My tough-yet-admirable sister asked, gazing down at me.

"Barn's on fire," I answered, proud to know something she didn't.

She didn't bother to look out the kitchen window but just ran outside barefoot. My mind swirled with admiration that she could stand the frozen ground on her naked feet. She was tough about everything. When my mother beat her with the broom, she laughed. My hair-twirling-pretty sister and sad-tittering sister came into the kitchen and stood on their tiptoes to look out the window. They didn't ask me any questions, they didn't even seem to notice me, but I was glad I'd eaten the pie and cookie dough when I did.

I'D HEARD MANY TIMES ABOUT ALL THE FIRES IN THE HOUSE before I was born and the fires in the houses my family had lived in before that and the fires up the road on the hill beyond us. I knew my mother had lost her wedding dress, all her school papers, newspaper clippings, marriage and birth records. She'd told me about the one fire that took everything. She didn't know how it had started. The mystery scared me the most. She'd prepared my father's breakfast as usual, driven him to work, and then went to the library with my siblings who I hadn't yet met.

"Your house is on fire and you need to go home," a librarian had told her, as if he were talking to a ladybug.

"We could see the flames and smoke in the distance," my mother had said, her voice sad. "We got to our road, but we couldn't get near the house because of all the fire trucks. I'd smelled something the night before, searched everywhere, but couldn't find anything and went to bed."

I could imagine my mother asking my father before they went upstairs for the night, "Do you smell smoke?" sniffing in all the rooms, wandering through the house, upstairs, downstairs, feeling walls for heat. My father might have said, "You're imagining things, honey. It's nothin'."

My mother worried most at night, often asking my father, "Do you smell smoke?" And he'd always answer, "It's nothin', honey," and drink his coffee as she felt the walls in the kitchen, placing her hands beneath light switches and near outlets as if evaluating them for fever. Then she'd go down to the cellar to sniff and touch the furnace. My father might follow her down the stairs and add, his tone slightly annoyed, "You're working yourself up over nothin'." The cellar was his private place.

At school a fireman gave me a sticker to put on my window so that firefighters would know which room the kid slept in. I went home and stuck mine dead center on the glass. My sisters' classes were visited by firemen, too. My father didn't like the way the stickers made the house look from the outside, so when he repainted he scraped them off with a razor blade. With their removal, I felt a lifeline to safety had been sacrificed for house pride, although my real fear was how the firemen would get to our house in time to save us. I went to bed at night planning for fire, leaving clothes at the end of my bed, wearing socks if it was cold. I watched my mother feel the walls at night, her forehead wrinkled.

After every Happy Birthday song, she sank the candles in a teacup of water and left them overnight. She took used matches and covered them in water at the bottom of the sink. It was like she thought they could reignite on their own. I worried they could.

My BLUSTERY-AND-FAVORED BROTHER UNLOADED A PANTING SIX-month-old lamb to the floor. I was used to lambs in the house; my mother brought them in to warm up at the registers and sometimes to feed them. I loved their loose gray coats and their long tails that wiggled excitedly when I put the black rubber nipple in their mouths.

I set Blackie on the carpet next to Whitie, who my sister-who-holds-grudges-longer-than-God had just brought in. His mouth was slightly open as he panted, wide eyed. Now that Blackie had a friend, I wanted to see the fire. I climbed onto the kitchen sink beside my hair-twirling-pretty sister and stared out into the yard. Sheep and chickens wandered around bleating and clucking. I worried that the sawhorses I rode would get hurt by the fire, and I tried to see them but couldn't. I felt affection for them as if they were real ponies.

"It's mainly in the back where the sheep are," my blustery-and-favored brother said behind me. "It's all smoke out there. The rain's helping." He looked out, too, as if he needed to see from this angle to understand better. His eyes were bloodshot, his clothes dirty. There was sweat on the sides of his hairless face.

"Know-It-All was out there. Probably smoking near the hay. He's such an ass," my sister-who-holds-grudges-longer-than-God said, setting a second panting lamb to the floor. This one scrambled on the slippery linoleum, leaving behind a trail of tiny balls that dropped from beneath his short tail. My tough-yet-admirable sister held a cat. Cats, unlike lambs, were not allowed in the house. If there were any kittens in the hay, they were dead now.

"He's such a bullshit artist," my blustery-and-favored brother agreed. "He was probably smoking in the back of the barn before he left to go hunt. There's an empty coke bottle out there. I just hope the sheep don't get sick."

The bullshit artist was a family-hanger-on, a man I saw as a loud-mouthed, unfair, violent Skipper from *Gilligan's Island* who always drank Coke and chain-smoked. A man who terrified me. I would forever associate Coke with bullshit artists and asses.

The animals looked homeless in the yard as they wandered, trying to graze on the brown grass. Blackie and Whitie and the lambs pushed themselves into corners. No one seemed concerned about missed lunch as they watched down the road for the station wagon that eventually appeared around the bend and came up the hill. My parents ran in through the entry door, and I was surprised they weren't angry that it was open.

"I saw the smoke. Where's the fire?" My mother rushed forward, frantically trying to understand, looking around the kitchen and then out the window. Now that she had arrived, I knew she would take care of everything. My mother could solve any disaster, it seemed. She had a clear plastic rain bonnet on her head that was tied beneath her chin. It was covered with tiny drops of water. "What happened? Thank goodness, it's the barn. Are the animals okay? How'd it start?"

My father only said, "Can't we leave for even a second without all hell breaking loose?" And he shook his head before blowing his nose on a hanky and returning it to his pocket in a lump.

"Know-It-All was smoking out there," my sister-who-holds-grudges-longer-than-God said. She didn't dare say, "ass" in front of our mother. "He was out there before he left to hunt up in the woods."

Without a pause, barely a heartbeat, my mother's face hardened, "I've just been waiting for something like this to happen. I told you," she turned to my father, accenting each word as if it was a sentence, "to tell him not to smoke in the barn." She untied the plastic rain hat that held the shape of her head and placed it on the Formica counter, where it dripped slowly.

"I did, honey, but you know you can't tell him anything," my father defended himself, and to avoid further blame he walked outside to assess the damage, shaking his head and muttering, "Cussed fire," as he went.

My mother stood at the kitchen window, still in her jacket that was damp with rain, and looked from the animals outside to the animals inside. She told my sister-who-holds-grudges-longer-than-God to finish the cookies because the oven was on and she was wasting electricity, my blustery-and-favored brother to go outside and help his father, and my tough-yet-admirable sister to sweep up the trails of poop and mud that littered the white linoleum. Then she went upstairs to change from her downtown clothes to her at-home clothes. When she came back I was again with the rabbits, smoothing their cold ears flat against their warm bodies, and she went into the entry to put on her barn jacket. I was worried about Whitie, who continued to pant, his mouth open.

"I hope Molly is okay," my mother said, more to herself than to us, and before she left to check on her sheep, all of which would need antibiotics, I noticed water on her cheeks that couldn't have been rain. I was suddenly sad that I'd stolen pink pie and cookie dough.

When the bullshit-artist-ass-Skipper returned from the woods, holding my father's rifle over a shoulder, with a cigarette hanging from his mouth, my sister-who-holds-grudges-longer-than-God saw him out the kitchen window and said with a sneer, "What a big shot."

Now that he was here in front of us, everyone kept their real words behind careful expressions. To him they spoke of neighbors down the road starting the fire. Someone mentioned a possible electrical short, then they returned to blaming teenage boys, possibly the same ones who had started the fire at the old house up the road, burning it to the ground. I didn't understand then, their fear, but I learned to respect it. The fire ended, the back of the barn was rebuilt, but the worry never stopped. My mother would forever feel walls and ask, "Do you smell something burning?" What I remember of that one barn fire are the wandering animals, Whitie panting slower, and slower still, before all breath ended and his body turned rigid and cold, the family-hanger-on who was never questioned, and my guilt for stealing cookie dough and a fistful of pink pie.

4

Pigs Can't Swim

ON A CAR TRIP IN THE SUMMER THE WATERGATE SCANDAL BEGAN I listened to my parents talk about Nixon getting his just desserts. I sat on my mother's lap, between her chest and the dashboard, with three sisters and two brothers piled in the back. I was six, musing about taped keyholes on office doors, privacy, getting caught, and ice cream–themed desserts.

We were on our way to my aunt's camp, a bare-bones New England structure on a man-made pond. More shanty than cabin, the camp was where we all longed to be as kids. My sister, the pretty one who twirled her hair into little circles that she put in her mouth, sat in the middle between my father and mother, trying not to bump the steering wheel or kick the half-full ashtray. Each time she moved I could hear her sweaty skin peel off the vinyl like ripping paper.

"It hurts," she said, her throat hanging onto the letters u and r.

"There's nothing we can do about it now, so there's no need to go on and on," my mother answered, an expert on just how long "on and on" was.

I'd once seen a car seat with a blanket on it when I waited in a parking lot. I was a nosy child, peering often into cars that didn't belong to me, on the lookout for a dog, a candy bar, soda, a better life. "Why can't *we* sit on a blanket?" I asked.

"Because that's for fuddy duddies," my father said. "I'm having none of that."

My hair-twirling-pretty sister sat still between us, and I sat still on my mother's knees. Whenever anyone told me not to move, moving was all I could think about, and this is what caused my mother to tell complete strangers, "The surest way to get Helen to do anything is to tell her not to do it."

On this day the car took us away from pulling weeds, shoveling manure, shelling peas, scraping corncobs, and mowing yards and took us toward rowing, floating on inner tubes, and swimming in the lake. But the most important things we left at home were tirades on how hateful and disagreeable we could be, a topic that burned like the eternal flame at John F. Kennedy's gravesite. At my aunt's camp my parents would chatter and laugh, play Spades and Hearts, swim and fish. They wouldn't need Maalox or aspirin for heartburn, indigestion, or headaches. They wouldn't require the heating pad for sore backs, shoulders, and acting-up knees.

My mother would have time to dog paddle with me and my sisters. She'd row with me to a shallow part of the pond my cousins had named Turtle Bay after the many turtles who sunned themselves on logs, and we'd pick blueberries on the small island a few hundred yards from shore. She would ask me questions and wait patiently for my answers. The laughter and pleasant chatter would drift across the water, echoing like the loons' haunting calls. All my escape routes led to this run-down haven until age fourteen, when they all led to Portland, but this camp would forever remain with me, showing itself in my dreams long after the owners of the camp were dead.

WITH WORK, SCHOOL, AND THE COST OF GASOLINE RISING FROM 35 to 50 cents a gallon, we didn't leave home often, and when we did, we didn't travel far. Sometimes in the late afternoon, after a day of weeding row after row of corn and shelling bushel after bushel of beans, we might go to Sabbath Day Lake for an hour of swimming before it closed. The ocean, although only thirty miles away, seemed as distant and unreachable as California, where my Aunt Helen lived. Once a year, if my parents had time, they might take us to Reid State Park, where we swam in the salty yet calm lagoon and I could pretend I was a castaway despite the crowds of people. We weren't allowed to swim in the ocean, but we could stand knee to thigh high at the shore, where the large waves rolled in and smacked us. Although people around us screamed when the cold water hit their mostly naked bodies, we were trained on "there's no need of making all that racket," so we restrained our joy and our voices. If no one was watching, I'd give pieces of my lunch to the gulls whom my family guarded their food against.

When we couldn't leave the farm, I would wade with my sisters in the muddy pasture pond or walk with them down the dirt road to the brook. We would splash to our hips in water that swirled with rotten leaves, frogs, bugs, and blood-seeking leeches, hoping that this day the snarling German shepherd tied to our nearest neighbor's house wouldn't get loose. We might walk farther to the man-made pond where my sisters met boys. On the way to my aunt's camp, four of my five sisters, the hair-twirling-pretty one at my side and the three behind me, were still innocent of penises and all the trouble feeling them could bring. They all giggled as they yelled, "Stop touching me. Get your elbow out of my side. I hate you! Get off my foot!" at two brothers, the blustery one and the one-I-barely-knew, who were always putting some part of their bodies where they didn't belong.

"Knock it off. I can't hear to drive," my father yelled periodically as the tires ate up the miles that separated us from home. His yell signaled my mother into action. Turning her torso in a sharp twist to see her children, forcing my body forward and my head into the windshield, she scolded, "That's enough racket. Just behave and stop annoying your father or we'll never get to camp." If a child's face was close enough to grab, she'd pinch the cheek between her practiced fingers.

When she faced front again we saw a black and white piglet trotting down the road.

"Well, I'll be damned. Look at that, a pig. Let's catch him," my father said, forgetting his annoying offspring at the prospect of free meat. Not one to waste time considering, he pulled over in front of the GE Electric plant on Route 202, and my brothers, eager to out-smart a baby animal, tumbled out beside him.

"I wish you'd stop swearing," protested my mother, her voice ris-ing in frustration because he listened to her even less than her chil-dren did. "And you can't take that pig. Someone owns him. What are we even going to do with a pig until we get back home?"

She asked these questions as if he might obey her, as if he were still in the car.

"I want to get out too," chorused my sisters in the back who hadn't been quick enough to bolt before the doors slammed.

"Just stay put and behave yourselves," my mother commanded, her inability to control or influence my father causing her to speak forcefully to her daughters like a dog who has lost the top spot and lets the one beneath him know he has some power. In fury or gaiety, my mother enunciated her words in bold strokes, whereas my fa-ther's fell into the air.

Those of us left behind in the sun-heated car listened to distant curses of "goddamn pig," "son of a bitch," "you almost had him," and the anguished squeals and oinks of the still-free-but-soon-to-be-damned swine. When my father had parked, the air seemed to stop as if waiting for the start of the engine as a signal to come back to life. I willed myself not to wiggle as I sat in widening puddles of sticky sweat and wished the piglet to run faster but also wanted him caught so I could hold him. Minutes that felt like hours passed be-fore my blustery-and-favored brother pushed into the crowded car, gripping the flailing baby pig who sounded like a screeching bird. I was glad my father hadn't seen a stray calf.

I twisted in my mother's lap to look at the new captive. His eyes bulged even as his pupils darted and rolled, assessing the sudden change between his walk on the road and the steaming interior of the station wagon. His short legs pedaled, and his cloven hooves dug into my brother's stomach as he tried to leap forward. I saw it was over for the pig, that no pigs had a chance anywhere in the world. With a sudden anguished wave of knowing, I understood Wilbur was imaginary and literate spiders were a miracle.

"I'm gonna call him Waterboro," my blustery-and-favored brother announced, "Because we found him in Waterboro." The piglet screamed and kicked furiously at the news.

"He belongs to someone," my mother said, her breath puffing hot against what she called my dirty-blond hair. "You can't just take a pig, even this far from home."

"Oh, no one owns him," my father said, irritated that she refused to accept their good fortune. "You're never happy about anything that's free."

Finally we arrived at the nearly impassable road that ended at the pond we called a lake. My blustery-and-favored brother handed Waterboro to his uncle, "We found him walking on the road," he said, wiping the sweat off his freckled face. "Nobody owned him."

My uncle, his black hair greased into chunks that stuck off his head at angles, his stained teeth appearing suddenly large when he opened his mouth to bellow lustily like a newborn adult, "How about that? A free pig! I'll be damned!" And he threw him into the back of the truck with a black and tan dog and two fully mature geese. Waterboro, unrestrained, zipped in circles away from the prodding canine nose and the flapping birds. When he couldn't find an exit, he scrabbled at the slippery walls of the truck to leap out, risking death over being a part of my family.

My sisters, brothers, cousins, and I climbed into the truck bed, which was so scratched that the floor was a mass of white and black lines flecked with red, the truck's color. I sat in the corner, trying not to get bitten, pecked, or stepped on. Once the truck moved, the smarter ones hung on away from the hissing geese and circling pig while the others fell against the bed's metal sides as the truck bounced downhill over boulders and into ruts. I watched them rub at their bumped knees and shoulders before they fell again, and I listened to their conversation:

"You douchebag."

"No, you're a douchebag."

"Oh yeah, you're a bigger douchebag than I'll ever be."

"No one's a bigger douchebag than you and you know it."

"It takes one to know one, so you ought to know better than anyone."

"What's a douchebag?" I dared to ask.

"She's such a douchebag," my cousin said. His bangs hung in his eyes, and his cheeks and neck shone with the grease of old and new sweat. I remembered a conversation I overheard between him and my aunt about the differences between blackheads and whiteheads, and I shivered at the grossness of it all.

"Just look at him and you'll know. He's the biggest douchebag around," a sister snorted and pointed to her cousin, whose stomach overpowered the waistband of his shorts, pushing them down to show the cleavage of his pale buttocks.

I wondered if a douchebag was anything like a piss-pot, a name my mother frequently called us. Then I got lost in my head thinking about words I'd put in a web to save Waterboro, as I watched him try to climb the pile of sleeping bags. Good, Sweet, Nice, and Young were all I had time to come up with and reject because they all might make the reader of the web think of eating him. Loud was a possibility, and then we reached the pond's edge, where paint-peeled wooden rowboats waited.

Everyone leaped out in a blast of sweaty bodies, noise, and anticipation to unload the dented truck and my parents' car, distributing the supplies into the boats that would float us across the lake to the camps.

I found my denim cloth tote, a birthday gift from my mother, among the sleeping bags and coolers. I loved the raised embroidered initials and the soft decorative flowers on the one front pocket that identified the bag's contents as mine: butcher paper and crayons, a pencil, a worn copy of *The Wind in the Willows*. Carefully, so as to avoid explosive commentary on my intellect if I spattered water or sprinkled pine needles on anyone's bedding or clothes, I stepped into a rowboat that didn't contain the snake-necked hissing geese.

THERE WAS NO SWIMMING UNTIL EVERYONE HAD EATEN A LUNCH of hamburger and hotdogs and then waited an hour. No one wanted to wait longer than they already had. For days my older sisters and brothers had been talking about swimming to the island that sat in the middle of the lake. Considered too little, the three youngest weren't allowed to swim with the others, despite promising to wear life jackets and not slow anyone down.

The previous summer, after what I thought of as the big-island-swim had begun, my aunt had said to my mother, "I hope they stay away from that gas line and don't run into any loons or snakes. I saw a couple of snakes in the water a few days ago. Your girls are fine with snakes, aren't they?"

"Oh, those snakes will go the other way when they hear all that noise and splashing," my mother had said confidently with a shake of her head.

"Well, they weren't afraid of me," my aunt had said. Then she'd sat in an Adirondack chair that creaked and shifted with her weight, and picked up her Harlequin romance as if she didn't care that her kids were out in the deepest part of the lake near confrontational loons, fearless snakes, and a gas line that was posted with KEEP OUT signs.

"Move your fat ass," I'd heard my uncle's voice float over the water, possibly at one of his daughters or my sisters. "I don't have all day!"

"Shut up and just row the boat!" A female voice had snapped, and I'd marveled that she had the courage to speak like that to an adult.

There had been splashing—sounds that made me yearn to swim, to feel the water on all sides of me. Oars had clanked against the oarlocks, and I'd heard my father say, "Hey, let me know if you see any fish, will ya?"

"I think I can feel one nibbling my toes," my blustery-and-favored brother screeched, followed by a raucous laugh.

That summer I decided that the big-island-swim wasn't something I wanted to do even if someone would let me.

DESPITE THE PROTESTS AND BEGGING, MY PARENTS AND AUNT and uncle wouldn't bend on the swim-one-hour-after-eating rule. They let us hang from the sides of a moving truck with wing-pounding geese at our feet, drape our bodies from open car windows, play in a yard filled with snakes, and mow the lawn barefoot, but all of us had to wait exactly sixty minutes following meals even to wade in the pond. Because of their reminders, I continued to worry about the swimming-too-soon-after-you-eat cramps. I couldn't stop myself from thinking that if drowning was such a risk, it might still be a possibility at sixty-one minutes. I feared cramps might be so swift that a person wouldn't be able to swim a few feet to touch the bottom. What exactly had these drowning victims eaten?

"If you'd just tell me," I said, following at my mother's heels into the camp kitchen. "I'd stop asking."

"I don't have time to answer such silly questions when you're too young to understand anyway," she said, setting plates on a plywood counter so high that I couldn't imagine ever growing tall enough to reach it. "Your nagging would drive a saint to drink, I swear," she said, but not with the same impatience I was used to at home, where I often drove her up the wall.

Pigs don't care about the no-swimming-for-an-hour-after-you-eat rule. Waterboro escaped from his barrel prison when I tipped it to see if he'd eaten the hotdog I'd dropped in while I counted the minutes. People jumped up from picnic tables and creaky Adirondack chairs exclaiming, "Get the pig. Get the pig!" when I knew what they really meant was, "Get the pork. Get the pork!" They chased him in circles, leaving no exit but the pond.

"Pigs can't swim. He'll cut his throat with his hooves," my blustery-and-favored brother shouted, frantic because he wanted to fatten the pig and kill it himself.

My sibling's pig trivia appeared to be incorrect, but as soon as he said it, my parents believed each word as if they couldn't see Waterboro swimming from the shore out past the float toward the distant dock on his way home. His little white head and pink nose above the water, his legs paddling like a dog, he didn't look like he suffered from either small or big cramps. The adults, believing that Waterboro couldn't swim and not wanting to miss the opportunity to kill him themselves, got into rowboats. We were guests, so my uncle gave the orders.

"Get behind the float and don't let him pass," he barked to the brother-I-barely-knew. "Hold the boat steady and cover him on the dock side," he commanded my father. "And you head him off from the island," he ordered his son, the one whose pimples were a topic of conversation. This son didn't row his boat toward the island but instead rowed it straight at the swimming pig, sending Waterboro fleeing toward Turtle Bay.

"Can't you do anything right, you knucklehead?" my uncle shouted so that, although I was safely beneath the pine trees, I worried he meant me. "He'll drown if you go at him that way."

The women on shore, lacking rowboats but not opinions, yelled loud and strong across the water to be heard above the clanking oars, honking geese, and barking dog. "Just circle around and push him back to shore. Once he gets his feet under him, he'll get into the woods and you'll never catch him." Taking their distraction as an opportunity, I waded up to my knees, the small rocks hard and slippery beneath my feet, black pine needles bumping pleasantly against my shins.

My father, motivated by the thought of lost meals, put his back into it and rowed in circles around the pig, herding him to where my blustery-and-favored brother leapt from his boat into the shallow water and captured Waterboro a second time.

"Well, that was a close call," my father said, pleased with himself as he pulled his rowboat up onto the roots and tied it loosely to a pine tree.

"See," I said, using the piglet as a reason to walk in up to my waist. "He didn't slit his throat."

"You don't know what you're talking about," my blustery-and-favored brother panted. "Everyone knows pigs can't swim." Then he dropped Waterboro back into the barrel and began to build a small pen out of old wood from the shed that held inner tubes and hundreds of daddy longlegs spiders.

Wanting to do something to show Waterboro he wasn't alone, I threw leftover lunches into the barrel from the picnic table. I could hear him clattering in his prison searching for freedom, sideward, backward, forward, grunt, snuffle, sideward, forward, backward. I sat on the ground, not daring to walk around to the front of the camp where the geese stood guard or around to the back near the outhouse that held complex webs of spider workmanship, piles of rotten leaves, and suspicious wet marks all over the wood. I shivered in my half-wet suit and disliked the grit of the pine needles that had glued themselves to my damp legs. Neither Waterboro nor I had any place to go, but we both had places we wanted to be.

"If you sit and stare at that pig long enough, you just might grow a curly tail," my mother teased as she threw dirty paper plates into the open fireplace. "You should go get the inner tubes out of the shed with your sisters. The geese won't get you again this year."

Last summer they'd attacked from behind, pecking at me with their bills and beating their wings so rapidly that it was like being in a rock storm.

"Are you thinking about all those pork chops?" my father asked on his way to fish off the shore. "I can almost taste those ribs now."

My blustery-and-favored brother, after thirty minutes of hammering, dragged the barrel over the uneven roots, his bare feet white against the pine needles, and dumped the piglet into a board cage, much as a person dumps trash from a smaller can into a larger one. Waterboro tumbled to the ground, his legs working to find his footing, squealing.

"What life did you have before?" I asked him, thinking of Wilbur and knowing it wasn't that. And then, because it's what I said to all animals, "I love you," and let him lick the salt off my palms.

FOR THREE DAYS I SWAM AND MY SIBLINGS SWAM, RIGHT TO THE second before we ate and the sixtieth minute after. No one feared trouble, no one discussed it, and no one got in it.

"Helly Welly, you keep swimming like that and you'll turn into a fish," my mother laughed from the shore.

"Heck Cat, can you go see what snagged my hook?" my father, who didn't know how to swim, asked. I tried to think up things I could do to make him happy enough to call me Heck Cat.

"Helen spends more time underwater than on top of it," my aunt said. "I thought she had that ear problem from the bead she stuck in it copying her sisters play Gilligan."

"She does," I heard my mother say, "but kids don't care about those things. You can't tell Helen anything."

Underwater I dove again, allowing silence to fill my head. My damaged right ear pulsed with pressure and pushed at my throat, bringing me back to the moment of rupture. The memories of that night lived close to the surface, ready to be clicked through, one after another, as if on View-Master paper disks:

Arms and legs secured on a table in the hospital, I could move only my head freely, the one thing they demanded be still. Side to side, back and forth, I exercised my neck muscles. Screaming and bucking my body, I hated them with a hate that I held somewhere in my brain for just such a moment. Bright surgery lamps shined in my face, and I clamped my eyes tight so as not to see the people who stood on each side of me. There was no comforting deep outer space to journey to behind my lids.

"That's enough." The doctor said like a man who had chosen to remain childless. I stopped twisting to bite him.

He turned to a nurse. "How hard is it to hold a four-year-old?"

"If you just lie still, this won't hurt, and it will be over before you know it." His words meant one thing, but the pointy tool and the hand holding it meant another.

"Let me go!" I shrieked, wrestling away with all of my strength. Like a dog who doesn't listen to words but watches body language, I knew they were all liars.

Two green-coated men came into the room and grabbed my head and the middle of my body. Now I could no longer shake and twist, but I could shriek and gag. The doctor poked tweezers into my ear. I heard thumping so loud that I stopped screaming for just a second, then the sound changed to crunching, like boots on snow, followed by a sharp burst of pain in the center of my head and throat. There was a great whooshing that, many years later, I would learn was the sound of my carotid artery, the beginning of my right ear listening inward instead of outward.

"I can't get it. Not under these conditions," the doctor announced. "You'll have to bring her back so she can be put under."

My mother touched my hand as the nurses unstrapped me. His words had jerked me to stillness—I worried about the difference between being put under and being put down.

Above the water, my older sisters and cousins pushed each other off the float and competed in short-distance races, from which my age and size excluded me.

Each time he asked, I untangled my father's hook, the pale worm hanging in tatters, each piece wiggling weakly. Although I liked feeling wanted for my fetching skills, a part of me needed to repair the worm.

I counted the seconds I could hold my breath, experimented with pretend cramps, drowning and saving myself again and again by standing up. I stood on the large rock beneath the water, the one that marked the halfway point between the float and the shore, and pretended I was a scuba diver. I liked how my fingers looked, wrinkled and soft from the water. Although I anticipated the dreaded "It's time to get out," I preferred that over "It's time to leave," both of which were inevitable.

On the return trip Waterboro sat in the back on my blustery-and-favored brother's lap, beside my four other siblings. He didn't squeal. My parents, after a weekend of adult conversation with my aunt and uncle, talked about President Nixon.

"He'll get his just desserts," my mother repeated. "No one can do anything they want and get away with it. Not even the president."

Like strippers and sticky dollar bills, President Nixon's crime made no sense to me at six years old, but what I felt more than confusion was fear. If even the president, the most powerful person in the United States, could get into trouble, then no one, I realized with a panic that traveled from my bowels to my throat, was ever safe from trouble, ever free. No one. I couldn't detect even a sliver of light in a reality that weighed so thick and heavy.

Instead of the happy excitement two days earlier, the voices in the backseat had an edge: "I said, get away from me!" "Stop touching me!" "I'm not doing anything!" "Move your elbow!" "There's no place for my feet!"

"Knock it off! I can't hear to drive," my father roared.

Seconds later, my mother turned around, bouncing me forward into the dashboard as she twisted. "We'll never get home if you don't stop being so disagreeable!"

The voices quieted, knowing that infinite work and potential punishment with switches and bars of soap were less than two hours away. I sat on my mother's lap, feeling the loss of swimming in my muscles, feeling weighed down by trouble and the power of punishers.

When we approached the town of Waterboro, my family began to reminisce, as if it had been years and we all needed reminding, instead of the days it was.

"There's the culvert where we finally caught him," my father said.

"Remember how he ran?" my blustery-and-favored brother added. "He's pretty smart for a pig. Bet he'll taste pretty good too." He laughed at his clever use of the word "pretty," the pig's four legs held tight against his chest.

"It's possible that he lived up a side street and escaped his pen," I said. "Maybe he misses his mother."

"You always say the dumbest things," my father said, his tone gruff, his words aimed at the windshield but meant for me, "As if pigs can miss anything."

The distance between camp and home narrowed with each rotation of the tires.

Years after Waterboro had been slaughtered and eaten—when the story had been repeated many times, my mother suggested that maybe Waterboro had been in the back of a truck and fallen out. His owners might have driven on several miles before noticing his absence and, when they did, decided it was too much work to turn around. They had other pigs.

But maybe they noticed the loss and did go back and continued to go back for several days in the hope of finding their pig. Then, as the months passed into a year and they didn't find him, one of his owners might have said—might still say, as they drive route 202—"Remember, that's where we lost our baby pig. I wonder whatever happened to him."

5

Pecking Order

WHEN I WAS SEVEN MY BLUSTERY-AND-FAVORED BROTHER BOUGHT Donny, a fifteen-hand thoroughbred, from a horse dealer for three hundred dollars, money earned from working on cow and chicken farms.

"Three hundred too much," my father said, shaking his head in disgust, and he shifted his greased hair over his bald spot before putting his cap back on, "I don't want that cussed animal breaking down the barn. Can't even ride the thing or what have you."

My blustery-and-favored brother didn't have any horse experience, had never done anything with animals but capture them, clean their stalls, truck them to slaughter, and eat them. But he worked hard all day every day in and outside the home, as he had been taught. He not only bought what he wanted but gave my mother money to help with clothes for the three youngest kids. The fact that he got a blanket, a saddle, and then himself on the thoroughbred meant he'd successfully trained Donny to go western. A *Happy Days* watcher, I thought of him as the country version of the Fonze, Fonzie, Fonzerelli, although he looked more like Richie Cunningham. He made us all laugh with his comedy routines shouted from inside the bathroom when he took showers. "Oh no, there goes my toe. Now it's my knee, ahhh, it's got . . . " and my mother would laugh the hardest, so proud of her hardworking funny son that he could say a forbidden word and do things the rest of us couldn't.

After Donny arrived without permission and wasn't forced to leave, my sister-who-holds-grudges-longer-than-God brought home an adult Irish setter who jumped on the counters, stole thawing meat, and deposited mounds of soft poop in the entry for my father to discover with his deep-treaded work boots. "Goddamn dogs don't belong in the house. It's not right I can't walk through my own entry without stepping in a pile of shit."

I listened and watched and fantasized about what animals I would own without permission once I was big enough to go get them myself.

Each day I nagged my brother for a ride, and he always gave in, taking Donny out of the pasture and lifting me up onto his back. This brother led the three-year-old stallion and turned him around at the end of our dirt road. This was the brother who had captured Waterboro twice, rescued him half-frozen from the pigpen his first winter, nursed him back to health, and in the spring helped cut him up and put him into the freezer.

Once on the stallion's warm back, I wrapped my seven-year-old arms tightly around his muscled brown neck, my temple resting against his reddish mane, my bare legs and feet hugging his defined ribs. Still wrestling with animals, my blustery-and-favored brother attempted to hold Donny steady, but the thoroughbred fought his teenage strength, rearing away from the hand that gripped the halter beneath his chin. This stallion, with a brain that released testosterone so swiftly he would harm himself to get to a mare, resented anyone who tried to control him. There was no bridle, no rope.

"All set?" my brother asked, his longish thin hair flying in wisps above his tanned, smooth face. Narrow trickles of sweat hovered above his ears. His biceps strained against his skin and his words lacked breath. He used all of his weight to hold Donny down, as if he were ballast to a hot air balloon.

My stomach rose in anticipation. I nodded.

He let go, leaping backward from Donny's bucking hindquarters. At the same time that his feet landed, the horse lunged forward.

Pebbles and gravel shot up from pounding bare hooves, stinging my legs. The world of the half-mile dead end passed in a blur of green and brown. I clung to Donny's leg-pumping body. My arms squeezed the stallion's neck as hard as my legs squeezed his sides. Someday I would learn that my position on Donny was like that of wild cats when they kill horses. I will think of Donny when I read about predator-prey relationships and be deeply sad that this special horse of my youth could have thought I was a predator and was trying to escape me as he raced for the safety of the barn.

The wind whipped my dirty-blonde hair, which was often tangled with grass from reading on my back in the field or from trying to wiggle free away from my tough-yet-admirable sister who tickled me until I thought I couldn't bear another second. "Stop! I hate it!" I would shout, thinking I might die, between deep-bellied laughs.

"Oh, you do not either," she'd say, digging her fingers in harder.

On Donny I was free of all teasing if only for minutes, and it was exhilarating because no one dared approach the stallion when he was galloping. I was untouchable even to the teams of flies and independent square-tails that dive bombed and hovered just outside the vortex of the whooshing air Donny created.

The horse crested the hill to the driveway, turning sharply before angling across the yard under the towering weeping willow trees. He slammed his untrimmed hooves deep into the grass when he saw the barn. Cantering for a few yards before breaking into a trot that tossed my body on his back, Donny aimed for the open door in the low barn, his chest heaving, nostrils blowing. I gripped his sides and neck as tightly as I could. My bare feet slipped against his sweaty ribs. I was thrilled to feel so weightless, so secure. Donny entered the barn, slammed his shoulder into the chicken coop, which caused hens to explode in a series of squawks just as he slid on the plywood floor, knocking over a shovel and a rake with a loud clatter. He swung his rump sharply around the gate into his stall, and my leg scraped roughly against the boards. He threw his nose down and ate the sweet molasses grain, reward for his return. I thought it looked so good that I would steal some to eat before I left the barn.

As soon as Donny stopped I began to anticipate my next ride. I was never satisfied with what everyone said was "enough." Sometimes my tough-yet-admirable sister would lead the horse to the end of the road. She'd walk close to me and tell me what to do: "No matter how fast he goes, don't let go of his neck," she'd command. And it was then when I realized she didn't want me to die.

She repeated this before releasing the stallion. "Are you sure you're holding on? Don't stop holding on, even with your legs."

"I'm sure," I'd say, eager to be on my way, not minding her bossiness. Only to my hair-twirling-pretty sister and my sad-tittering sister would I shout angrily, "I don't have to listen to you. You're not the boss of me."

In the barn I let go of Donny's neck and sat up. The top of my head almost brushed the low exposed ceiling. If the horse were to rear, I would smash into the two-by-fours. "Again," I begged, when my blustery-and-favored brother arrived to remove me.

"Don't nag," he said, breathing hard from his walk, and he carried me in a wide arc around the horse's head and feet to exit the stall. Donny was a fierce biter and kicker, especially around food. I envied his carelessness about causing trouble, his immunity to anger. "Just stand over here, out of the way, and you won't get hurt," my brother added in an attempt to prevent a string of pestering words from exiting my mouth. He placed me on the other side of the gate, and I felt blood roll slowly down my leg to meet the raw bug bites that festooned my shins and calves. I stood in awe of this horse who made me feel as if anything was possible and this brother who showed no fear when Donny whipped his nose around to bite him.

ONE OF THE FIRST I'M-GOING-TO-SHOOT-THAT-GODDAMN-HORSE tirades occurred on an early summer evening, only a month or so after Donny arrived. It was after supper on a night that the man my blustery-and-favored brother called a bullshit artist and my sister-who-holds-grudges-longer-than-God called an ass and that I thought of as the Skipper visited.

Even though this man was larger and older than my brothers, sporting a different arrangement of facial hair every week, he would fistfight over who had the biggest rifle, the better horseshoe throw, or the loudest chainsaw.

On that early summer evening one of my young nephews pointed at the thoroughbred stallion from where he balanced on my hair-twirling-pretty sister's hip. His bare feet and knees were a dark brown from time spent in the dirt; his bottom was raw from soggy diapers. "Horsey," he said, kicking at his young aunt. "Horsey."

My hair-twirling-pretty sister was about nine, and although she didn't like Donny and was afraid of him, she wanted to keep her nephew happy. She walked up to the pasture's wooden gate. The horse stood stomping and nipping at his sides against relentless bug torture. None of us dared to breathe in too strongly for fear of sucking in black flies. My hair-twirling-pretty sister bent and picked some trodden grass and held it out as an offering, careful to keep her hand flat and her thumb tucked out of teeth range.

The toddler, his hair hanging longer than Donny's straggly mane, reached to pat the stallion's nose, "Horsey," he said again, his brown eyes peering through his bangs.

"Cut his girlie hair," my blustery-and-favored brother had yelled during supper earlier that night. "He looks like a fairy. You want him to grow up and be a faggot?"

"Nice horsey," this boy, oblivious to faggot fear, jabbered while he rocked and pushed at my hair-twirling-pretty sister's bottom and thighs with his dirty bare feet.

Donny threw his head high to avoid the intrusive hand and just as quickly lowered it, his teeth long and white below raised lips. When he lifted his head again my hair-twirling-pretty sister's shoulder hung clamped in his mouth. A foot off the ground, she looked frozen like prey, and Donny, more wolf than stallion, shook her up and down, side to side before dropping her. Then he turned with a buck, a series of farts firing from his raised hind end like a machine gun, as he galloped across the pasture.

Blood spread on my hair-twirling-pretty sister's shoulder beneath her tooth-torn shirt, and I wondered if she'd get in trouble for the rip. I don't know when she let go of our nephew, but as she jumped up and down, flapping her arms, he was on the ground looking up at her, quiet against her screams.

My father exited the house and ran across the lawn toward the pasture, my mother behind him, and saw that the noise was coming from his favorite hair-twirling daughter. "I'm going to kill that son of a bitch!" he erupted. He tried to climb the gate in his attempt to rush at Donny with his fists, but by this time the horse grazed on the other side of the pasture, whipping his anorexic tail at relentless nature.

My mother, dishtowel over her shoulder, scooped up my nephew and hugged my hysterical hair-twirling-pretty sister. "What mess did you get yourself into now?" she asked in a soothing, I-can-take-care-of-anything tone. They disappeared into the house, letting out the sister-who-holds-grudges-longer-than-God, the one who had wanted an Irish setter until she got one.

She ran toward the pasture shouting, "You will not either shoot him!" and climbed over the wooden gate to spread her arms wide in an attempt to hide the horse from view. I didn't think, even mad as he was, that my father would fire at family.

My blustery-and-favored brother trotted out of the barn, a shovel in his hand, eyes darting from one screaming person to another, as he tried to figure out what had happened. Including him in his fury, my father punched the air and called for his gun. "There's no need of having that cussed animal in the barn. If you don't get it out, I'm going to shoot it," my father repeated so loudly that I marveled he didn't cough. I hadn't seen him this angry since he'd discovered his kids had been slowly filching the cigarettes he hid from my mother.

Then the Skipper, in full-blown bullshit-artist-ass mode, burst from the house, eager to demonstrate the strength of his character, the screen door slapping the house when it closed. He joined my father at the pasture gate, and together they yelled words in random outbursts—"Jesus," "goddamn," and "son of a bitch"—as they stomped the sparse grass flatter into the dirt.

We had guns and bullets everywhere, but the men of the family rarely got anything for themselves, so they shouted and kicked the fence while they waited for women to appear with what they needed. "No one's gonna shoot anything," my blustery-and-favored brother shouted back and, having learned at his mother's knee the value of laying blame, said, "One of them kids must have stuck his stupid fingers up Donny's nose. How can anyone expect a horse to just let someone stick fingers up its nose?"

"You better find another home for that horse before I do," my father bellowed at his independent-hardworking son, his brown eyes challenging and narrow behind his glasses, "a home six feet unda."

"I'm not too worried about it," my brother muttered as he disappeared into the shadows of the barn. Twenty minutes later, tired of storming back and forth in front of the gate, my father took my hair-twirling-pretty sister to the emergency room, and the bullshit-artist-ass-Skipper retreated to demand a cup of coffee and cigarettes that he left on tables and counters for my siblings to steal.

RIDING ACCIDENTS HAPPENED—SADDLES SLIPPED, REINS BROKE, Donny reared and spun, bucked and took off, or scraped riders from his back against trees and sides of houses. Whatever the reason, the stallion arrived at the barn without a rider more often than with one, and no one minded being dumped so far from home.

The second month after Donny arrived, my blustery-and-favored brother decided at my mother's insistence to geld his stallion, and he got the idea that his freshly neutered horse might stop biting, kicking, rearing, and running away if he had a female pasture companion. This led him to buy an elderly black standardbred mare named Lady. She cost a dollar but should have been free, my mother said, because she lay down whenever anyone sat on her. Her former owner had fed her bread and potatoes, and for years I thought all horses who had u-shaped backs with large hanging bellies ate potatoes, so I am forever suspicious of this root vegetable and what it might do to my stomach.

Frustrated by my begging, my blustery-and-favored brother put me on her back first.

"That'll teach you," he said plopping me on the middle of her sagging spine.

Teach me what? I thought.

I sat on the bony ridge of her bowl-shaped back and leaned forward clucking. She didn't move. I bumped her sides with my bare heels. Slowly, as if deflating, Lady sank to her knees and rolled. I stood up.

"Let me ride her again," I nagged. "Pleeaaase, just one more time."

By ACCIDENT MY BLUSTERY-AND-FAVORED BROTHER LEARNED THAT if Donny walked ahead, Lady would follow, even if ridden. To show her displeasure of being used, she would turn her head swiftly in an attempt to grab her rider's leg or foot with her teeth. I learned to ride with my feet tucked under my bottom. Over the months we owned her Lady honed her skill to a stride-bite rhythm. The horses liked each other so much that my brother decided to stake them out side by side. Several times a day the horses wrapped their ropes tightly around the iron poles and didn't have enough slack to put their heads down, which caused rearing and farting panic. Sometimes they managed to pull the stakes out of the ground and gallop off into the surrounding fields in an attempt to get away from the predator pole that bounced behind them, collecting milkweed seeds and yard-high timothy.

My blustery-and-favored brother thought he could prevent the horses from circling the stake if he gave them longer ropes, but the added length tangled around the horses' feet, hobbling them to the ground like pigs tied to spits.

Several times I ran screaming, "Come quick! Donny's on the ground and he can't get up!" My blustery-and-favored brother would put down his shovel or rake or posthole digger and run with me across the gravel driveway to the field. He'd walk up to that mess of flailing feet and convulsing muscle, and I'd admire him for his daring. No one else would rescue the horses, although my sister-who-holds-grudges-longer-than-God might have tried if she'd been around. During the summer this sister worked as a chambermaid at a motel that she biked to up and down huge hills. When she was home she rode the horses in between completing her chores.

Donny, set to right on all fours, shook his body, his fur plastered flat from stress and effort, before throwing his head to the ground to rip grass in fierce bites from its roots. Lady, who had pranced and whinnied while Donny was down, would settle beside him, and I would wonder what these two horses communicated to each other. My brother, sweaty and out of breath, his eyes a bit wild, would look at me and say, "Thank you," and I'd think he was the nicest and most capable person in the world and understand why he was favored.

INSTEAD OF LADY MAKING DONNY NICE, DONNY MADE LADY mean. Both horses bared their teeth and lunged at anyone who approached. My nine-year-old hair-twirling sister, bitten but still pretty, climbed onto the barn roof when the horses were in the yard, even if someone was leading them. The bullshit-artist-ass-Skipper was too ungainly to climb on the roof but not too ungainly to gesticulate from a distance, curses flowing from a mouth my mother oft compared to a sewer.

A few months after Lady arrived, an older sister decided she wanted to ride Donny. This sister had a reputation for making poor choices. "She made her bed," my mother often commented to dismiss parenting from blame. "Now she has to lay in it." Whenever she said this I worried about the kind of bed I would make.

My sister-of-poor-choices had run away to Delaware to elope when she was seventeen. I always pictured her sprinting along the turnpike, dragging her heart-of-gold fiancé behind her. When my parents drove across five states and into a sixth to scream at her, they brought both runners back to Maine because my sister-of-poor-choices was minus a high school diploma. My blustery-and-favored brother spoke of a shotgun wedding, and this didn't seem unusual to me because we had so many guns.

This sister gave me a candy bar once when I was crying after our mother left for town without me. I was so amazed by the chocolate that I forgot who and what I missed and was silent in rapture. She liked to tell stories of how she was a mother to me when I was a baby. When she began to recount all she did, my real mother's face would harden and she would cut in to tell of how this sister once pinned my cloth diaper to my hip and made me cry. My sister-who-holds-grudges-longer-than-God told me, years later, when we were exercising in the gym, that our sister-of-poor-choices took care of me only to get out of working in the gardens. "She'd do anything not to get her nails dirty," she said, and I was suddenly sad that all those stories my sister-of-poor-choices had told me of how she loved me might have been lies, that I was just an excuse not to work.

"Please," my sister begged our blustery-and-favored brother, sounding like the toddler who had pointed and said, "horsey."

"I don't think you can handle it," he argued. "Donny's fast. He's a racehorse."

"You let everyone else. Why can't I?"

The bullshit-artist-ass-Skipper, our family hanger-on, was hanging on that day in full force. He might have been in the yard emphasizing with stomps of his fancy-booted feet that his car, the one without a muffler so that it thundered into our driveway, was the fastest goddamned car ever made. He might have been telling my father how he made the most money, had the most skill, and was the smartest employee his company had ever seen. He cut off my blustery-and-favored brother's attempt to save his sister's life with a superior grunt of disgust: "Jesus Christ, if you don't saddle that mangy horse, I will," and he lunged toward the barn to illustrate his intent.

Muttering "idiots" and "big shots," my brother decided to use tack, possibly to minimize the chances of his sister falling off. He loaded her onto Donny's back and stopped a quarter-mile down the dirt road instead of the full half, at the brook that washed out the road each spring. Perhaps he thought Donny might not be able to get up as much speed a shorter distance from home. Whatever his reasoning, none of it made any difference. When he released the reins, the thoroughbred leapt forward, his hooves leaving deep marks of energy in the dirt. With Lady whinnying in the pasture and grain in his trough, Donny had double the incentive to get up the hill. It was difficult for him to pump his legs as furiously as he usually did with my sister hanging half off his withers, her hair-sprayed hair flying stiff behind her, her carefully lipsticked mouth screaming, "Help me! Oh God, someone please help me!"

Donny tried to end her agonized pleas by knocking her off under the weeping willow tree in the front yard. My sister didn't see the large branch coming at her. She fell, but she didn't stop wailing, as one of her feet remained in a stirrup. Donny, practiced at dragging poles across fields, didn't let this bother him, and he continued to the barn, his rider trailing close behind him on the hoof-dented yard. I raced from window to window, following my sister's bumpy progress, while the bullshit-artist-ass-Skipper, my heart-of-gold brother-in-law, several other sisters, and my parents watched openmouthed from the yard. Even they hadn't thought they needed to yell, "Duck" when my older sister had reached the tree.

Curious to see if Donny was going to enter the barn, I went outside.

"Jesus! Stop that son of a bitch!" the bullshit-artist-ass-Skipper yelled, losing his fake southern drawl but not his volume in the chaos. None except my blustery-and-favored brother dared to get near the three-year-old freshly ex-stallion on his way to sweet feed and female companionship. Donny chose to stop at the pasture near

Lady, my brother hanging from his bridle, my sister tumbling to stillness but not to silence somewhere behind him.

Love, I concluded, trumped food.

We all ran over to the pasture to see if my sister was broken. Even my sister-who-holds-grudges-longer-than-God ran to check, and this surprised me because she frequently wished this sister would go to hell. Stretched on her side crying, the fallen rider wailed up to us, "I hung on as best I could!"

"If you'd hung on," I said, "then you wouldn't be on the ground."

My father turned to me, furious, "Can't you just be decent for once?"

"Helen," my mother warned, one grandchild on her hip, another hanging onto her leg and pulling at her shirt, "you know better. Just mind your Ps and Qs and get in the house."

"Crocodile tears," my sister-who-holds-grudges-longer-than-God said. The bullshit-artist-ass-Skipper, desirous of controlling the very air we breathed, glared at both of us and stomped in circles, bellowing, "Get me a gun. I'm going to shoot that son-of-a-bitch right now before he kills someone."

My sister-who-holds-grudges-longer-than-God yelled, "No one's going to shoot Donny. Just sit your fat ass down." She helped our blustery-and-favored brother remove the gelding's tack and open the pasture gate to let Donny in without letting Lady out, and the horses raced into the distant pine trees.

"Jesus Christ, you can't talk to me that way. I'll shoot whatever I goddamn well please, and there's not a goddamn thing you can do about it," he roared as he shook his fists like an impotent gorilla before clomping away in his cowboy boots.

My sister lay on the ground waiting for her husband, who, my parents oft repeated when one of us might complain of too much weekend company, had a heart of gold, to give her a hand up.

Her heart-of-gold husband reached out to her, pulling her to wobbly feet and soothing her with the lie: "You did the best you could." He gathered his tumbled and grass-stained wife to him and walked with her toward the house. "You're going to be just fine." He acted as if he'd been injured too, and his voice cracked with emotion.

The bullshit-artist-ass-Skipper watched them go and boomed at my sister who holds grudges longer than God, "I'll shoot him just as soon as I get my hands on a gun, and you need to learn some manners! No child of mine would ever talk to an adult that way!"

Everyone tried to ignore him, as if he were one of the many midges that hovered about us looking for a successful place to land.

Donny and Lady, now deep beneath the pines, didn't lift their heads to see who was making the racket in their yard. Those in charge don't need to pay attention to the small things.

The next day my blustery-and-favored brother would lead the two of us down the road, me hugging Donny's strong warm neck, sharing a position of power and freedom for just a few thrilling minutes before my brother would arrive in the stall, out of breath. He'd set me down and warn, "Just stand over there out of the way and you won't get hurt."

6

Breakdown

WHEN WE RETURNED TO OUR HOME AFTER BEING AWAY, THE AIR in the car seemed to change a few miles from our house. Expressions hardened and tempers shortened. It was as if the hill we lived on pulsed with its own darkness. This is how I remember it and feel it even now when I near the network of tangled roads that would bring me into the world of my childhood if I were to take them.

It is no coincidence that writer Stephen King sometimes used rural Maine as a setting. I recognized a road like mine in one of his more recent novels, set in Florida but eerily reminiscent of my childhood landscape. The dead-end road to my old house looks like what he describes minus the upside-down birds and oversized frogs with "teef" in *Duma Key*. It too terminates after half a mile. Wild branches and vines reach out to scrape anything that tries to pass. I understand the physical distress King describes because my own stomach shifts uncomfortably with memories of the old broken and burnt house past my childhood home and the even older cemetery past that.

My years on that hill are quasi-supernatural. There must have been peaceful times, like, after school, when we watched *Bewitched*, *Star Trek*, *Gilligan's Island*, and, later, *General Hospital*. Christmases were magical. We played: I cut pictures out of Sears catalogues to use as paper dolls and played house with my sisters in the woods. But the special power of darkness is that it makes you believe there was never any light at all.

My mother was determined and desperate to raise good children. However, just like those people who buy sweet baby chimpanzees and are surprised when they grow into adolescents who bite them repeatedly before one day escaping in a flurry of hoots and hollers, my mother lost control. Lacking the teeth and strength of apes, my siblings used cigarettes, alcohol, and sex to rebel.

THERE WAS A NIGHT MY MOTHER FELL TO THE FLOOR, HER ARMS outstretched toward the door that her eighteen-year-old had just slammed. The catch of a car engine followed by the popping crunch of tires in the dirt driveway seemed to say, "gone, gone, gone." My mother collapsed. With each fading tire crunch, she cried as if the children who stayed behind meant nothing.

I watched this standing in a doorway that divided the kitchen from a room that burst at the seams with a sewing machine and pool table, and I didn't believe what my eyes were telling my brain. The Formica table and green vinyl chairs were between us, and my view was interrupted by a forest of metal legs. She lay crumpled with her arms reaching out for a person who was no longer there, offspring whose desire to please her, based solely on fear, had left long before his body did. I looked at her hands clenched into fists and wished she were holding mine now. With her holding your hand, everything would be better soon.

"I can't even stand to look at your hateful face. Get out of my house and don't you dare come back, you piss-pot!" she'd screamed seconds before. But she hadn't expected the eighteen-year-old to take her at her word. We kids were supposed to stand silently, show shame, and then plan to do better when she listed our crimes against her.

Just before supper my mother had found beer cans beneath the seats of her eighteen-year-old's car, which also held an ashtray full of cigarette butts. The eighteen-year-old had neglected to lock his doors against our mother, who made it her business to scan bedrooms and vehicles for evidence of her children turning out bad. She read mail, notes, letters, and diaries with the reasoning that it was her job to keep her children from having secrets that weren't good for them to have.

"You good-for-nothing piss-ant," she'd yelled at her departing child, meaning that he had failed at turning out into something significant.

We feared many things, isolated at the top of our hill, but tirades made us want to "turn out" the quickest we could.

It was black outside our house, which was twenty minutes from anywhere. The windows were dark rectangles that startled nerves with confusing reflections. No street lights or houses were visible through the trees, making night impenetrable without the high-powered flashlights my father kept on the shelf above the stove. Watching my mother through the legs of the table and chairs, fear twisted my gut and trembled in my muscles. Life had fallen apart. How could anything ever return to normal after this?

Minutes before my mother had been in control, her voice vibrating with authority, "Don't think just because you're eighteen that you can smoke and drink with neighborhood riffraff. I won't have it." She'd stood in front of her eighteen-year-old, her finger getting closer and closer to his chest, which I knew she'd jab when she gained a few more inches. Then she'd pinch and yank his cheek, and I felt my own face and chest muscles tense in readiness. "You may think you're pretty hot stuff now that you have a car, but you're nothing but a bum, and you better change your tune right now. No ifs, ands, and buts about it."

"I'm not going to listen to this," the eighteen-year-old sassed. "You can't tell me what to do anymore." His words were tough, but there was a tremble to his voice. He was edging into uncharted territory.

"Don't you dare talk to me that way," my mother screamed. And then she closed in on him with her finger, poking accented beats on his sternum, her face seething inches from his. "You're a good-for-nothing bum, that's what you are, hanging out with those druggies. Okay, Mike!" She contorted her face, acting out her version of being stoned, emphasizing her contempt by lengthening the word into

"Maaa-iiii-ke." Often she called us the name of a different person she disliked in order to shame us, altering the tone of her voice, making faces. Sometimes the person she disliked at the moment could be one of her other children. She played free with our identities as if, without her to give us a name, we were nothing.

"I'll do what I want and you can't stop me!" The eighteen-year-old stared at her with his characteristic smirk, defiant.

"You think you're pretty special, don't you, Mike? Just the cat's pajamas." My mother smacked her teenager on the head with the dish-towel she kept work-ready on her shoulder, then she walked purpose-fully from the kitchen to the next room, angling around me, my hair-twirling-pretty sister, and the pool table to the senior portraits above the black-and-white television that stood on the floor. The screen watched us, blank and silent. In a flash my mother tore down the eighteen-year-old's picture and stomped back to the kitchen, ripped it out of the inexpensive gold-painted frame, crumpled the paper, and, like a maddened basketball player, slammed it into the trashcan.

Everyone was still, seeming to hold breaths collectively, and then the eighteen-year-old decided he'd had enough. He was finished here, and he turned to leave, presenting his back to my mother's rage and her Uncle Sam–like finger.

I was at that age when my mother was always right, and I was her staunch supporter, angry at anyone who caused her sadness or distress, even my father. I loved her so much and believed every word she said that I couldn't understand why my siblings didn't live to please her too. But even amidst this crisis, I wondered at what age it would be okay to smoke and drink and not get in trouble.

"You walk out that door when I'm talking to you, and you best know you're never welcome back," she shrieked and stared, open-mouthed, as the eighteen-year-old continued away from her. She instantly altered her strategy to look like she was still winning, and I admired her and hoped I would grow up to be just as clever: "Go! Get out of my house and don't you dare come back!" Then, as soon as he did, she fell to the floor.

My father came up from the cellar. "What's all this racket?" he asked. "I can't hear myself think."

When he walked into the kitchen he stared down at my mother. Once, when he'd chased her with a crab and she'd fallen, he had continued to tease her, thinking she was laughing when she was actually crying from a broken elbow. Maybe he thought of this mistake now as he calculated her sounds and position, suddenly unsure.

I looked at my hair-twirling-pretty sister beside me. With nervous fingers, she'd worried her hair into a knot, and her mouth, with the only straight teeth of the family, gaped as she stared. Another sister, always quiet if she wasn't tittering, was twelve. She left the room sucking her fingers, a dirty blanket scrap clutched in her hand. A third sister, older by ten years, stood with an exasperated expression on the other side of the table.

I didn't understand why this sister, the one my father said could hold grudges longer than God, just like his mother, didn't move or say anything. She often set things to right. She worked all the time just like my mother; although, unlike my mother, she would sit down in the middle of the day and watch *Somerset*. That's the difference between being told to work as a helper and having to do the work as its owner.

Many years later this sister told me she'd thought our mother was faking to get sympathy. I question if someone can pretend this much anguish and grief.

"Why . . . why is he like this?" my mother cried. "I can't take it. No, I just can't." Her back rose up a few convulsive inches each time she coughed out the words as if vomiting them. Her head rested on the square-and-diamond design of the white linoleum where she'd fallen. Her curls, hard won with prickly plastic rollers, were plastered flat on one side and chaotic on the other, her glasses jammed askew against her head. One of the arms of her glasses hovered above her curls.

"That's enough of that," my father said, trying to pull my mother to her feet while she hung heavy like a toddler who didn't want to be picked up. Her cries changed to gasps. This was the time of day when she would usually push her broom in long sweeps to capture the dirt or wipe down the counters and the cupboards in a series of quick strokes. Even when ill or in pain from a back injury or a sheep-worming accident, my mother never used how she felt as an excuse not to work, to break from her chores. "I can't let a little thing like a broken bone bother me," she'd say, her arm in a cast, as she carried wood and made supper.

"Just stop it now. You're going to make yourself sick." A tone of panic crept into my father's voice.

But his wife had passed the line of reasoning into hysteria and couldn't turn back. Like a dog getting into a fight, she couldn't hear those of us who hadn't walked out the door. She retched and gagged, clutching at her heart as if it were breaking. "I don't know what to do. I can't. I can't. I can't. I can't."

My father pushed past my sister to get to the phone. A short ring burst from the bell when he grabbed the receiver. The horseshoe cradle bobbed erratically, trembling, as if in sympathy with my mother's nerves. "Get off the phone! I need the line!"

I could hear the tiny voice of a neighbor on our party line. For an instant I pictured a quiet family, maybe a mile away, sitting in comfortable chairs, legs crossed, laughing as they discussed school and vacations, the phone connecting their fun with friends across the miles. I imagined them eating Reese's Peanut Butter Cups and sipping Pepsi while they watched *Happy Days* or *Laverne and Shirley*. I fantasized about other people's lives the way teenage boys fantasize about generous girls. "Please, please, please," I'd pray aloud to the ceiling above my bed, my hands clasped, my eyes shut tight to indicate sincerity in case I was being evaluated on form and style. "Make time go faster so I can be an adult and begin my real life."

My father jiggled the hook, making loud clicking noises in his neighbor's ear. He listened for less than a second, tapped aggressively again, waited briefly, and dialed, copying the number from the red emergency sticker taped to the wall. Although he listened to other people's conversations, he talked openly as if no one listened to his.

He spoke in quick broken sentences, then, "Yup, yup, right, bye," and slammed down the phone. I knew someone was coming. He'd said, "Turn onto the dead-end dirt section."

Unless people were visiting us or searching for a quiet place to drink beer or target practice, no one turned on our road, knowing from the change to dirt and the yellow sign warning DEAD END that they might go nowhere, that they might get stuck without any way to go back. I pressed my back against the woodwork of the doorframe, allowing my shoulder blades to roll and drop against the wood yet careful to keep my dirty fingers off the casing. I repeated silently in my mind: You will be in bed tonight like always, promising a familiar end when none was expected.

My father carried my mother from the kitchen through the dining room where we never ate but instead folded laundry, and then into the living room to the scratchy green couch my mother had recently tried to make nicer by sewing a red, flowered slip cover. She could sew anything and did. I followed with my hair-twirling-pretty sister. For a few minutes my mother gained her breath, and it seemed she might stand up, arrange her glasses, smooth her hair and get her broom, but then she slumped, "No, no, no, I don't want to do this anymore. I just can't." The snot ran into her mouth, and she panted.

I was worried she really couldn't, that she'd just stop, and was nearly convinced that this was what an older brother meant when he talked about the Apocalypse. The world would end and Jesus would take only those who were saved. It didn't matter if you were good; it only mattered if you'd been saved, and I was certain I wasn't because I'd told a brother I wouldn't go any place that didn't have animals.

"Animals have no souls," he'd said confidently from his great height. "They're not God's children and cannot be saved."

"They can too. God saved only animals on the Ark," I'd insisted, referring to the only story in which I'd understood God's motives.

By the time the paramedics arrived and pushed past our barking spaniel/pug mix Tippy and went to my mother, I was worried one of them might be Jesus in disguise. She let them lift her and put a mask on her face. My father suddenly seemed small, insignificant beside the tall men. He said something like, "She was fine, and then she started crying. Now she says she can't breathe. I don't know what could have happened. I tried to calm her down."

He didn't tell the paramedics about the eighteen-year-old, about the drinking, the lying, the smoking, or the screaming. He didn't tell the men much of anything, but they weren't looking for a story anyway.

One of them said, "Breathe. Slow down. That's it. Take the air in and let it out. Breathe in. Breathe out. You're doing great. Breathe in. Breathe out." As if acquiring oxygen was a learned skill, as if this is what it meant to be saved. Usually my mother knew everything, took care of all problems, especially sickness. This night she had to be told how to breathe.

Then suddenly they left, including my father. Tires rolling in the dirt driveway—gone, gone, gone—followed by the absence of sound within the house, the sudden silence that accompanies leave taking. The guiding force of do-this-do-that disappeared down the dirt road into the black. Each one of us stood still. I didn't know what to do next. If there could be a next.

"When is she going to come back?" I asked no one in particular, and no one answered. I stood in the kitchen in front of my father's rocking chair, looking out the window, feeling the tears prickle and a lump rise in my throat so that I couldn't swallow. I waited for the taillights to reemerge through the trees when the ambulance rounded the bend in the road. There was no siren.

I tried not to think my mother is gone. But I did, and she was. My hair-twirling-pretty sister stared outside too, into the night that had absorbed all color. She sucked on a circle of hair as her fingers moved. Tears rolled from the eyes that my father complimented so often that he made my mother's mouth tighten and her chin tremble. This is the part of the night my hair-twirling-pretty sister remembers and doesn't want to think about.

Sometimes she says to me, "Isn't it funny how I don't remember hardly anything about my childhood?" I think this is an invitation to remind her, but she shouts, putting her hands up like the traffic cop in "Frosty the Snowman," "No! Don't tell me. I didn't say I wanted to remember." She causes me to wonder what it would be like not to look back and see nothing. And I am envious of her once again.

THE NEXT MORNING WE BOARDED THE SCHOOL BUS, THE FIRST stop on the forty-five- to sixty-minute route over pot hole–covered dirt roads. I sat in the front, one of the four youngest kids in the neighborhood, and opened *Little House on the Prairie* as soon as my bottom touched the green vinyl seat that was patched with duct tape. I leaned against the rectangular window, felt the coolness of the glass, and tried to close myself off.

Teenagers, dressed in jeans with ripped-out knees with Rolling Stones tongues sketched on their thighs, boarded the bus. Students who had sideburns and mustaches along with others who didn't strolled confidently to the backseats, throwing their books ahead of them before they sprawled into a semi-sitting position, part of their bodies in the aisle. I'd tense in the front as these passengers boarded and walked by my seat. Instinct told me to never look into their eyes. This morning they took their seats with the words of my father's demand for the phone exiting their mouths, making fun of the way he spoke when they spoke the same way, "Geroff the phone," one teenager laughed. "What a retard." My siblings laughed with him because that's what they had to do.

Sitting at the front of the bus, I tried to make myself invisible as I pushed my mind into the words of Laura's world on the prairie with her dog, Jack, where Ma and Pa lived simply and no party lines connected people in a web of half-told stories. While I read I was able to prevent hearing what my subconscious tried to tell me— that I needed to learn how to be on my own because my parents couldn't even protect themselves.

7

The Killing House

WE DIDN'T EAT HORSES. OR GOATS. BUT ALL OTHER BARNYARD animals were potential fare. If any food put up too much of a fight and got away, my father would shout, "You dummy," a funny thing to say when the creature outwitting you is a chicken.

"Get it," he might yell to me at hen harvest. I'd race at the birds, shooing them in his direction, and he'd snatch a chicken's leg with a thin, hooked pole and drag the flapping animal into his hands. The chicken kicked and screamed, and my conscience refused to be silent about the betrayal. Oblivious to what the chicken communicated to me in that one blink of its three eyelids, my father saw only white meat, dark meat, chicken wings, and drumsticks: a feast on six toes. "Now get in the house," he'd say, "so I can get this done."

No one allowed me to see what he did to the chickens. I wasn't even supposed to see the stump where he slaughtered them, which stood in a circle of birches and young maples. I could feel its presence looming as if it were alive whenever I walked near the woods.

One morning of a killing day, my hair-twirling-pretty sister and sad-tittering sister wanted to see one of the hens run with its head cut off. They angled their bodies to peer out the windows at the back of the house. My tough-yet-admirable sister was in her tiny bedroom upstairs, listening to the portable transistor radio. Bachman-Tuner Overdrive's "Takin' Care of Business" might have thumped through the ceiling or Poco's "Crazy Love," both of which were easier to listen to than Janis Joplin's "Mercedez Benz" and "Piece of My Heart," songs my blustery-and-favored brother played on his stereo until I thought I wouldn't be able to breathe from the great sadness behind the words that tore from the singer's throat.

"That's not music," my mother would shout, disgusted. "That's caterwauling. Turn it off!"

From inside the house, despite the music, we heard unchicken-like death screams. One by one, each voice ended unfinished in what sounded like a flurry of rebellious feather and muscle. I marveled at all the sounds animals could make and how some sounds are made only once, then silenced forever.

My mother filled large kettles with water and carried them to the stove. Every few minutes she checked out the window, peering up toward the woods. Finally she turned to us and said, "Go outside," then she went to the foot of the stairs and shouted, sounding as though she'd already had to say it more than once, "Shut that racket off and get outside to pluck chickens." Dressed in an old work shirt and worn jeans, she turned and picked up one of the kettles off the stove, staggering a bit under its weight, careful to keep it away from her stomach.

"Bring that box," she said to me over her shoulder.

Now came our part of the killing process. Barefoot and bare handed, we walked the worn grass path across the backyard to the pile of freshly beheaded chickens my father had dropped near the barn, dead bodies tossed so carelessly that it was difficult to tell, by sight, where one began and another ended. We sat in a circle around the pot and chicken pile, holding the birds by their bony legs as we dunked their limp, warm corpses repeatedly into the hot water. Nearby was a small hill blanketed with clover and tireless bees. We could hear bird whistles, crow shouts, occasional bleats of sheep, the lowing of cows, and the clucks of live chickens. The smell of flesh and guts crept into my nose, and feathers stuck like glue to my fingers.

My mother helped me with the tiny resistant pinfeathers in the human-like armpits and, while she worked on my nearly bald chicken, told me to take another from the heap on the ground, teaching me that minutes should not be wasted. I ripped feathers with one hand while holding the chicken in my lap, its wet, headless neck flopping against my bare arm. My three older sisters competed to see who could pluck the fastest, but they couldn't best my father, who cleared the feathers rapidly with his muscular wide fingers. He sat on an over-turned plastic bucket.

"Do you think it's sad for the live chickens to see us plucking the dead ones?" I asked. "Do you think they worry they might be next? It could be like watching a scary movie for them." I had seen *The Wizard of Oz* and *Rudolph the Red-Nosed Reindeer*.

My family pretended not to hear me, as if I were a person asking for donations outside a grocery store. Born with a gift for persistence, I repeated myself, asking louder and louder, "Do you? Do you? Do You?" until finally my father yelled, his eyes never leaving the half-naked chicken in his hands, "For God's sake, stop being such a pest and just pluck the damn bird. This is what they're made for." His bloodstained fingers deposited a fistful of feathers onto the ground. "Chickens don't think none anyways."

I noticed he said don't, not can't. "How do you know?"

"I just do. How does anyone know anything for Christ's sake?"

And because I was the age when I still wanted to please my mother, I watched my mouth and stopped my next words from exiting into the air: "You might not have to ask if you hadn't quit school before the eighth grade."

My mother, whose job it was to protect my father from annoyance, said, "Just pluck the chickens, Helen, and stop talking nonsense."

"Just shut your face," my tough-yet-admirable sister said, bouncing her half-plucked chicken in front of me.

My hair-twirling-pretty sister giggled, which made my sad-tittering sister giggle.

My father hated giggling. "Just stop the racket," he shouted, "and get to work."

After the chickens were defeathered, my sisters ran off into the woods, where it is likely they met up with neighborhood kids and drank dribbles of beer from cans or smoked used cigarettes. My father picked up the box of bare, stiffened yellow bodies and carried it down the spider-filled bulkhead entrance into the dank cellar. There he gutted and cut the chickens into pieces on a large stainless steel table, separating wings, legs, and breasts from unprotesting bodies.

Bones cracked and flesh tore beneath his hands. He gave the parts to me to rinse off in water that was so cold my fingers refused to straighten. Nearby was a meat grinder for what knife and strength couldn't do, and an old cast iron stove sat in the gloom beside the bottom of the stairs. Inspired by the raw meat, moist and smooth in his hands and unable to wait any longer, he flayed a breast and placed it in a frying pan after starting a fire in the stove. The flesh sizzled while he emptied chest cavities and set giblets and shell-less eggs into a bowl for later. Flies buzzed amidst the wet sound of innards sucking away from muscles, tendons, and veins. I swallowed back the bile that rose from my stomach. Stress churned at my insides and sent its fumes up and out. The breath that I exchanged for oxygen smelled so rank that my mother would take me to the doctor.

"Your breath smells like death warmed over," she'd complain, holding her nose away from me. Then she'd ask accusingly, "What'd you eat?" when the real problem was what she'd *tried* to make me eat.

OUR TWO GOATS WERE SAFE AS LONG AS THEY DIDN'T GET ILL. Sick animals, dogs included, were put down with the .22. Vets were expensive; bullets were cheap. Cats were flung into the pond or drowned in buckets of water.

Goats were difficult to fence in, and this left the stake and rope method. One summer afternoon my mother left a son in charge. I chose to go with her instead of staying behind with my siblings, who might try to lock me out of the house because I talked too much.

We returned after an hour or so and saw instantly that something was wrong with the goats. There, on the front lawn beside the driveway, Nikki and her baby lay strangled in each other's ropes, eyes bulging, tongues swollen several sizes too big for their small mouths. I would never see any goat again without picturing these two as they lay in the yard, flies eating their open eyes.

"They were fine a few minutes ago. I just checked on them before watering the sheep," the brother-I-barely-knew said when my mother screamed for him to get his lazy butt outside. His lower lip stuck out like the first in a series of weak chins, and he took on an expression that said, It couldn't be helped. That's life. I would see a similar expression on another brother's face after he tried to castrate a bull by going out to the pasture with wire cutters and slicing into the scrotal sac. Bellowing in fear, pain, and confusion, this bull exploded away from him at a run and then suffered for three days before falling to the ground, belly bloated with urine, his body covered in flies, his urethra severed. When I saw the that's-life expression applied as an inevitability for unnecessary suffering and death, I felt hate take root and bloom in my gut.

DEAD ANIMALS COULD BE ANYWHERE. MY FATHER AND BROTHERS and in-laws target practiced on woodchucks, porcupines, and raccoons. When a furry head appeared above the peas or corn, they raced to see who could get the first shot. Boom! And little heads disappeared. Bam! And deer would crumple. Crack! Birds would fly up from where they roosted on stone walls in a flurry of flight and anger that sounded like thunder. I'd find fur-covered bodies rotting around the gardens until something either dragged them off or ate what it wanted. I learned that dead animals begin to rot instantly. First they're alive and warm; then they're stiff and covered in flies. To even out the odds, I left my bread crusts under the rollable dishwasher and in the registers to feed the mice in the house walls.

Living in Maine, on the outskirts of civilization, people thought they could do what they wanted with guns. Game wardens and policemen rarely made an appearance. Our woods were the perfect set-ting to drink beer, smoke pot, have sex, hoot, and fire guns randomly. Good manners, discreet arguments, and gun and hunting regulations were for other people, not for those who drove the winding miles from town to target practice on the crumbling sheds on our dead-end country road. Maxwell House coffee cans full of bullet holes and smashed Budweiser bottles lay in the long grass.

My family resented anyone they didn't approve with a gun in their territory. Hunting season began and ended as a competition. To keep the advantage and despite my mother's protests, the men drove deer with neighbors on weekends and week nights, scaring them out of the woods toward the waiting guns of their friends and in-laws. Beams of light would disturb the black night, bouncing here and there around the trees like a drunk Tinkerbell when my blustery-and-favored brother attempted to track a deer whom his brother had wounded but not killed. The gun shots that followed would shatter the stillness as they shattered the deer's hearts. My brothers and their friends tagged a few bucks here and there to appease the adult in my life who had a conscience—my mother.

"They have no right to be in the woods after dark. I caught those faggots coming out from the gas line where I drove those bucks just last night. I should call the game warden," a brother would yell in the kitchen, waving his arms and stomping his feet in a noisy display of dominance. "Unbelievable."

"That ain't right. It's probably some cussed Frenchmen," my fa-ther commiserated from his rocking chair. "Those idiots couldn't hit a barn from three feet away, but they'll ruin it for everyone else."

My mother took pictures so no one would forget which brother shot the buck with the magnificent rack. A hand on the deer's shoul-der indicating ownership, a boot up on a rung of the play gym lad-der, where the carcass hung upside-down, a gun cradled in one arm, and a smile on my blustery-and-favored brother's thin face—this picture said, "Be impressed."

Outside, guns blasted in all directions.

"Can't even walk in my own dooryard without thinking I might get shot," my mother complained. "We should put up NO TRESPASS-ING signs."

"Won't do no good, honey," my father said. "Seeing those signs will only make it worse."

I wore my father's orange hunting jacket to walk from the house to the barn, imagining what it'd feel like to die by a bullet. I'd seen the cowboys on *Bonanza* and *Gunsmoke* gasp, heads thrown back in surprise just as they grabbed their chests with both hands and sagged slowly to the ground. I expected to get shot whenever I went outside, so I didn't think I'd look surprised. I hoped to have the kind of look on my face that would make someone say, "I wished I'd given her those candy bars and dogs she wanted so bad."

When I got home from school in the fall I could see the hunters on the edge of the property, pointing their rifles in my direction, sighting me through scopes. Because I had an adult's attention, I performed cartwheels and walkovers in the front yard and penny drops off the play gym in the back. Some days there were so many hunters in so many directions that my mother drove my two sisters and me the half-mile home after the bus dropped us off to prevent my sisters from bumming cigarettes and "God knows what else" from the hunters.

My mother said the men would do their best not to shoot me, but I had to do my part and wear orange. There were bullet holes in our chimney, in our trees. Men in camouflage vests and padded bright jackets smiled as they passed in trucks and on foot. Some had teeth; others had none. The majority had crooked overlapping incisors and canines, as if they were wounded soldiers trying to get up and leave. Few seemed to have combs or soap and water. They asked to use the telephone, but this was forbidden. "Never let anyone into the house," my mother ordered as if she were the mother goat in the story "The Wolf and the Seven Kids." Denied the phone, they wanted information.

"You see any deer? Which way they go?" they'd ask, their cigarettes wavering slowly in the spaces between tan-streaked teeth as they spoke, making smoking of any kind look like a messy business. I would feel powerful because someone wanted something that was only mine to give: answers. I directed men toward stonewalls where I'd seen snakes and to the haunted cemetery up the road. I sent them on elaborate journeys through the woods to where a grumpy old man lived in a rusted-out trailer. I chanted silently to the deer to never be fooled by the salt licks and sweet feed my brothers put in the fields.

"I WILL NOT," I SAID ONE FALL DAY AT SUPPER, STARING DIRECTLY into my mother's hazel eyes that glared at me from behind the lenses of her glasses, "eat any animal ever again." Then I cut up a tiny boiled potato and poured ketchup on the pieces.

My mother laughed.

My father wasn't paying attention.

"She always says the stupidest things," a sister said.

"She'll grow out of it," my mother said, in a rare moment of agreement with a daughter she never tired of threatening to send away to live with opportunistic boys.

I covered tomatoes and lettuce with sugar, poured maple syrup over Rice Krispies, and soaked English muffins with butter. I reveled in the innocence of plain macaroni scooped before my mother could taint it with lamb and stringy tomatoes. I begged for SpaghettiOs and ate them between two slices of white bread.

"You're such a gross pig," my sisters said to me, curling their lips.

"Takes one to know one," I said as stain-causing SpaghettiO sauce dripped on my second-to-only clean shirt.

"She's so disgusting," they complained to my mother—the ones who smoked cigarette butts they picked out of trashcans.

"I don't know what's gotten into her," my mother said. "But I've had just about enough."

A few weeks later she put steak on my plate, thinking I'd come to my senses, and I gagged. First she pretended not to hear me. But her fuse, as my father often pointed out, was shorter than his pinky was wide.

"Stop being so dramatic," she snapped. "This foolishness has gone far enough, and I'm done playing your little games."

I pointedly pushed the steak off my plate onto the table, illustrating my disagreeable nature.

"You're wasting the best part," my father grumbled, leaning over the table in his white undershirt to snatch it before I could feed it to the dog.

THE FOLLOWING SUMMER, AFTER A BRIEF CAMPING TRIP, MY mother went out to the barn to visit her shorthorn heifers, Bonnie and Jessie. She spent valuable work minutes petting their noses and scratching their red and white rumps as if she valued them more than just for their milk. I went into the barn so I could check to see if a cat might have given birth in the old crates my father stored in the tiny attic. There was no ladder. I climbed the door to the chicken coop, my toes clinging to the wire holes as I pulled myself up onto the dusty plywood landing. If our house were attacked by robbers one day, this is the place I pictured myself running to hide—I didn't think any adult could climb the door. Plus my father said it was too damn hot up there. There was a hornet's nest in the vent. Mother cats liked to use the attic to hide their kittens, and it was exciting to find them in pockets of old tarpaulins or in wooden half-filled crates. If I found them first, I was certain I could keep my father and brothers from finding the kittens and drowning them.

That attic must have meant something important all those hours I crawled around in the heat, trying to hear the mews of new life wanting milk, because I see this place repeatedly in my dreams. It's my hiding place if I can just get to it before the thing, usually the bullshit-artist-ass-Skipper, chasing me catches up.

Lost in my search, I hadn't known my mother was in the barn until she screeched, "Where are my heifers?" I heard her clomp across the plywood floor below, the attic shaking a bit with her hasty exit, and then she was out of the barn. Her voice, wobbly and high, floated to me from the yard, where my father was fiddling with his boat's small motor. I scooted across the boards, swung down onto the wire wood-framed door, which strained under my weight, and walked out slowly to listen.

"I sold them," he said and, because he was at the top of the food chain, expected that to be the end of it.

My mother sat on the ground and collapsed in large hiccupping cries.

"What are you making such a big fuss about?" my father asked, genuinely confused. I heard him explain that her blustery-and-favored son had taken care of the delivery while we were away. "They're just cows, and I got a good price." He went back to the motor, tapping his screwdriver in one place and then another as if trying to find a secret compartment.

"How co–coul–could you se–se–sell them?" she wailed. "They were mi–mi–mi–mine. I loved them. How co–coul–could you d–do–do this to me?"

"Oh, quit carrying on about nothing," my father scoffed, but with an edge of worry in his tone, knowing she had the power to carry on for months.

I trotted to my mother and squatted on my haunches nearby to offer company. Bonnie and Jessie had been good friends. I'd often ridden them, squeezing their sides to relieve them of bloat and gas. I understood her pain because my father had killed my pet rabbits. The ending to my story was different, though, because my mother had cooked the animals I loved for supper.

"Why do you eat cows if you love Bonnie and Jessie so much?" I whispered so my father couldn't hear, while I patted her back, thinking now the mystery would be explained.

"I don't love the ones I eat," she wailed.

THERE WAS THE DAY THE CHICKEN FARMER GAVE ME TWO CHICKS, and I swore to them they would live.

"Here's two for you," the farmer had said, smiling at my astonishment, his beard looking as if he decorated it with dust each morning.

I'd been standing in his barn, waiting for my parents to pick out their new laying hens and fryers, feeling a bit lightheaded from the smell.

"Thank you," I gushed, although I wasn't sure if he expected gratitude so much as money.

"That's so generous of you," my mother said. I figured if she chose to pay or not to pay, the potential trouble was now removed from me to her.

I brought the babies home and put them in a cardboard box in the entry. I patted their bony little heads and smoothed their little feathers.

"Helen's so queer," my hair-twirling-pretty sister said to my mother, who was sewing a pair of gauchos for my tough-yet-admirable sister. "Where'd you get her from anyway?"

"I don't know why she is like she is," I heard my mother say in the pause of the machine. "All you kids went through odd phases. She'll get over it."

"Who could love a stupid, filthy chicken?" a sister commented.

"A stupid, filthy Helen," another sister scoffed. They passed me with an air of superiority as they went to hide behind a bush to smoke cigarette butts they'd found in the school parking lot that day.

"Behave yourselves!" I heard my mother shout from her seat behind the sewing machine, but the door had already slammed.

THE CHICKS GREW VERY FAST AND PEEPED IN EXCITEMENT WHEN they saw me. Then one afternoon, a month and a half after the chicken farmer had plopped the two babies in my hands, I arrived home from school and stared at the bare spot on the entry floor.

"Where are my chickens?" I yelled when I found my mother, who was folding laundry in the dining room. I noticed how her thin gold band and small diamond slid loosely beneath her knuckle as she worked. I saw the scar where she'd had a wart burned off and, knowing about fire, wondered how the doctor was able to burn the wart and nothing else. I worried I would get a wart and the doctor would burn off something important.

"Your father put them outside with the others," she said, concentrating on a white undershirt that had brown paint spots all over it from when my father had painted the house. "He was tired of all the mess, and he didn't like the noise."

I raced outside to the coop, not even trying to let the door swing quietly or to keep out flies. All the same color and the same size, my two chickens had disappeared into the flock. I stood in the middle of the pen as they circled me, climbing on top of each other in their haste to get away. "Go, go, go," their squawks communicated, as if I was the predator. Guilt clouded my mind that I couldn't tell which two were my own. I had not only failed on my promise to protect them; I had failed in my ability to know them as individuals.

THE FOLLOWING SPRING, AT CHICKEN HARVEST, THE BODIES LAY in a heap, headless, twitching furiously to complete the last command their brains had given their muscles before the final chop. "Could any of these be mine?" I pestered my father as only a practiced nagger can.

"Do you think you killed mine?" I yelled in the next silence of conversation between my siblings, who spoke of a dance and a football game they would go to at school the next Friday. "Do you? Do you? Do you?" I repeated until finally my father had to say something to stop the racket.

"Goddammit, what's it matter?" He exploded, looking down at a floppy body in his hands. And to prove his point that compassion and affection had no place in the animal world, he yelled, "A chicken's a chicken, and that's all there is to it." He threw the naked bird into a box.

I felt my brain stir into a huff and my lower lip stick out, and I refused to take my place around the pots of water.

"Time's a wasting," my father ordered. "Less talking, more plucking."

I looked at the pile of decapitated bodies and thought of the stump in the woods and the heads around it, the expressions not of surprise but fear, eyes wide open. What was the last thing they'd seen—part of a tree, grass, the axe, the next chicken in line? Did two of them remember their short baby chickhoods where they'd been petted and loved? Did their brains show them pictures of a particular moment, pictures of the past and present? A future? I'd watched dogs, horses, and pigs dream, their legs trotting in their sleep, their eyelids fluttering as they whined or grunted. Did chickens dream too? I looked at the pile of decapitated bodies and knew I would not eat any of them, knew I would never eat any animal again because how could I eat anything who might have dreams of her own?

8

The Tell-Tale Lamb

"STAY IN THE HOUSE AND BEHAVE YOURSELVES," MY MOTHER HAD said before leaving for town one afternoon. She'd said it as if we were already in trouble, emphasizing, "And NO hanky panky!" with a jab of her pointer finger. "Don't let the wood stove go out, and there's lamb in the pressure cooker, and you need . . . " I'd stopped listening, assuming she wasn't talking to me because I was the youngest and not in charge of anything. I was busy planning how I'd steal a few of my father's hard butterscotch candies.

The large silver pressure cooker sat silent on the softly glowing burner during my mother's while-I'm-gone-speech, its dents indicating rough usage. The weighted jiggler on top of the cover was still. I couldn't see even a whiff of the steam that would soon burden the air particles with water. It would begin to hiss and spit, first as a sputter, then faster and faster until as a scream. Even the sight of the two or three jigglers my mother kept on the window sill over the sink usually sent a wave of darkness through my brain when my eye caught them while washing dishes. I'd wrestled with the cooker pot often, pinning it down with my sponge in the lukewarm flat water to scrub off the gray film of boiled flesh, trying not to remember the lamb or the cow as she had been in life, trying not to think of what the slime really was on the rubber seal of the lid.

That day I was happy to go outside and leave the pressure cooker behind, poised on the stove top, its nerve-wrenching performance pending, as I walked upright on skates, which were loose from inadequate shoe strings, across the entry and porch. If my parents had been home, I'd have crawled until I could stand outside, where my blades would dig harmlessly on frozen ground, but there were already so many crisscross lines on the linoleum and gashes in the porch wood that I didn't think anyone would notice if I allowed myself a little convenience. Not for the first time was I glad Tippy couldn't talk.

When I arrived to the pond through the creaky wooden pasture gate, my hair-twirling-pretty sister, my tough-yet-admirable sister, and my sad-tittering sister were already there, two of them smoking by the well. Grateful for winter and the safety it provided from the nests of snakes who lived around the pond and the barn, I walked without hesitation over the hard, snowy ground before wobbling out onto the ice and falling down. Strings of smoke curled slowly away from my sisters' hands and mouths, hanging gently in the air. Although I envied the warmth they might be receiving from the tiny flame and ashes, I worried whenever I saw them smoke. Not for their health or their reputations, but for the stress of consequences.

While they were doing it, they looked content, but after the cigarettes were stubs and they needed to begin to prepare for parents, they panicked: rapidly chewing stolen gum, spraying air freshener and perfume, washing their hands with soap, and brainstorming on how to dispose of the physical evidence. I took the same care with the wrappers of stolen butterscotches—bringing them to school trashcans, the yellow plastic sometimes crinkling alarmingly in my pockets. I worried my mother might stop by the school one day and catch me. I worried a janitor would call her and say, "I thought you'd like to know that Helen put at least twenty yellow candy wrappers in the trash this morning."

I gambled worry every day. Cigarette butts, like used condoms, I would learn a few years later, had a way of coming back when you least expected them. Never flush anything down a toilet that is on a septic tank or is the sole toilet for a dozen people.

Two things we could not do while our mother was away, even if we were innocent, were change our clothes or take a shower. She talked often about missing an opportunity to be a nurse or a secretary, but her true talent was in investigation. I would worry late at night in my bed when I heard the distant television playing *Columbo* or the unmistakable voice of Telly Savalas as Lieutenant Theo Kojak. I'd believe she was learning tips and honing her detective skills. She could locate one drop of water on the tub or the vinyl curtain after a sister had taken a shower to remove traces of smoke or sex or simply to feel clean. This sister would wipe down all the surfaces with a towel that she then put in the dryer because cleanup of any sort creates a trail just as Dr. Seuss illustrates in *The Cat in the Hat*. My mother checked hair for suspicious fluffiness and softness, any strands for dampness. She could remember the clothes we all wore and knew when we changed, inspecting our bedrooms and the hamper for evidence of our wrongdoing. I knew, as if I was born with the knowledge, that hair, clothes, and bedding hold odor. Fortunately, when people who live in the country leave for town, they are gone a long time.

WE WEREN'T SUPPOSED TO ALL BE OUTSIDE THAT AFTERNOON, just as none of us were supposed to be smoking, but as soon as our parents left we attacked our freedom with senseless abandon, which is why none of us wore jackets. The afternoon sun began to cast long shadows and a deep orange glow that lightened something within my chest and made me smile.

Ice dust and snow speckled my jeans and melted in a slow trickle from my exposed knees down to shins that stung with January cold. My hair-twirling-pretty sister's hand-me-downs, which might have originally belonged to my tough-yet-admirable sister, included pants that were ripped out fashionably at the knees from stress pressure. Three sisters skated near me on the pond, shout-laughing each time they succeeded in tripping one another and sliding on all fours across the pond's sometimes smooth, sometimes bumpy surface, their blades balanced between their butts and the frozen water. Each time I slammed to the ice my knees got redder and colder until I could no longer feel the impact.

"You're such a queer," "Pig face," and "I hate you" echoed with friendly vibrations in the below-freezing air of the empty sheep pasture behind the barn.

To brake I skated into the pond's snow border, my arms circling like wild propellers to keep me upright. I wore red knit mittens that strangled my fingers because my grandmother had left the yarn tails to tangle in a web on the inside. My sisters' hands were as bare as their arms and heads because no one looks cool smoking in mittens. I was new to single-bladed skates and had grabbed the smallest pair I could find from the hook in the cellar stairwell, the white leather now stiff and yellow with age like someone's old teeth, the ragged laces knotted to an almost unusable length. They were too big even with the pair of scratchy wool socks I'd taken from my mother, and my ankles trembled with fatigue just as my gut trembled with anxiety each time a sister skidded close to me because I feared running over her hand and cutting off her fingers. I'd seen my hair-twirling-pretty sister come home once with a deep gash in her leg from skating. She'd been so cold that she hadn't even known it was there.

She now shouted, "Watch me skate on one foot, Helen!"

I did as she asked, pleased she wanted me to see. My sad-tittering sister, who could skate better than any of us, twirled in a circle on her long, thin legs, and we all admired her and tried it ourselves, cutting the ice with our blades' teeth and enjoying the sound of our efforts. They were all practicing twirls and skating on one foot while I struggled to glide when we heard a sound that stopped us midbreath— even me, who was half deaf.

The boom echoed into a dramatic silence that was broken by my tough-yet-admirable sister shouting, "Oh my god, the pressure cooker!" before she glided off the ice and ran on her blades toward the house. My hair-twirling-pretty sister sucked in her breath: "We're gonna get it now!" and raced after her sister's muscular legs across the snowy path. I hobbled off the pond last, trying not to turn my ankles in the loose skates. I didn't even dare to look at the house when I was outside and it was empty, for fear I would see a curtain shift and someone or something looking back at me.

When I arrived my three sisters, still in their skates, were standing just inside the kitchen, staring upward, openmouthed and silent. I stared too. Pieces of lamb meat clung to the now-gray ceiling in the shape of a large circle. In the center of the circle, as if the ceiling were a target, was a dent where the weighted jiggler had rocketed off the pressure cooker. Lamb stuck to the cupboards by the power of its own greasiness. Tippy licked at the lower cupboards, grabbing at the meat with her tiny teeth. Even my father wouldn't want to eat it now.

"It wasn't my fault," my tough-yet-admirable sister said. "The pressure cooker must not be working right. It hasn't been that long since I checked. We've only been skating a few minutes."

We would go with that tale, adding embellishments as they occurred to us.

She pulled out a chair from the kitchen table and began to unlace her skates in a rush of noise.

"What are we going to do?" my hair-twirling-pretty sister asked, dropping in one fluid motion to sit on the floor. "We can't clean this before they get home."

I backed up and sat in the entry, my toes beginning to throb with pain as they came to life in the heat. My sad-tittering sister sat beside me. I heard the creak of the wood stove door and the thump and hiss of the logs, the crackle of newspaper, as someone fed the dying fire.

When I returned to the kitchen in my mother's oversized socks, I could feel the heavy grease, which was really the lamb's fat, tugging at my feet before I even reached the places where I could see the meat, which was really chopped-up lamb flesh. The trouble extended beyond what our eyes could show us. My tough-yet-admirable sister was filling the sink with hot soapy water and standing on the counter as she scrubbed the ceiling. My hair-twirling-pretty sister was washing the upper cupboards. Together we all worked; none of us laughed or called each other names. We knew it was only a matter of minutes before we'd hear the car come up the hill and into the driveway, before our mother would open the entry door and begin to sputter anger, until her rage gained strength with her understanding, and no one was safe from blame, not even my father, who wasn't a fan of the pressure cooker either because he wasn't a fan of anything that made noise.

"It's not coming off," my tough-yet-admirable sister said, her voice no longer tough and sure. "It's getting worse."

We gathered around the stove and looked up. She was right. The gray circle of grease was darker and appeared to have grown tentacles. It contrasted vividly against the white of the ceiling, as if the stove had a poorly made halo.

We forgot to listen as the information our eyes sent our brains stopped our ears. Suddenly our other senses burst through the focus barrier, and our hearts pounded and our minds grew heavy with *Here it comes.*

"What's going on here? What are you doing on that counter?" My mother's voice shot into our ears like poison-tipped darts that coated the air particles with her fury. "How many times have I told you not to stand on anything but the floor? It's disgusting. I prepare food on that counter."

That would be impossible to answer.

"Get down from there!" my father yelled, coming into the kitchen behind my mother, both looking larger than usual in their coats. Then he noticed the hole in the ceiling and the ring of grease.

"Dammit, what have you done now?" He stomped to the stove, and we stepped back, away from anything that could be thrown, leaving my tough-yet-admirable sister to jump down by herself.

"It's not my fault," this sister yelled back, curling her lips contemptuously and scrunching her face despite her dread.

"Look at this mess!" my mother wailed. "Just look at it! I can't ever leave you alone for even a second. You're just so selfish and lazy!" She aimed her words directly at my tough-yet-admirable sister but looked at all of us. "All you ever think about is yourself!" she added, as if we didn't know what selfish meant.

As I backed away out of the kitchen I thought that if she truly thought this daughter was selfish, lazy, and couldn't be trusted, why did she leave her in charge of a pressure cooker full of lamb? I continued down the hallway and up the stairs, distancing myself physically from further explosions, although I could still hear the aftermath in my room with the hollow door closed.

MY FATHER SPACKLED AND PRIMED THE SURFACE ABOVE THE stove the next day, let it dry, and then painted the entire ceiling twice. The drop cloths and the smell lingered for three days. My parents' anger slowed but didn't dissipate until evidence of the lamb and grease was gone. It seemed each day someone would find yet another stray piece of meat dried onto a flashlight or the Mecuricome and Merthiolate bottles that my mother kept by the stove. Eventually we stopped looking at the ceiling each time we entered the kitchen as if our eyes were magnetically drawn to the spot. Then one afternoon my blustery-and-favored brother leaned against the counter conversationally on his way out to work and asked, "What's that over the stove?"

My father, who was sitting in his wicker rocking chair where he drank coffee, stopped midrock and slammed to his feet. "God dammit!"

"I thought you said you used primer," my mother said, not questioning but accusing.

"I did, honey. Twice." He peered up at the ceiling, assessing his painting failure. "Tippy could have done a better job watching that cussed pressure cooker!" my father snapped as he yanked open the cellar door and clomped, his feet heavy with weariness, down the stairs to get his roller and paint. "Next time, ask Tippy!" he shouted to those behind him.

My blustery-and-favored brother, appearing sorry he'd asked, continued out the door with a shake of his head. He might have muttered "Unreal" or "Unbelievable" as he so often did when life seemed too much.

I pushed my chair back quietly from the table where I was reading a *Hardy Boys'* mystery and withdrew from range.

In another month the ring of lamb would return. Again. With each additional coat, it took longer to reappear, but it appeared nonetheless. When the stain returned over the years my mother would get angry all over again, targeting the child who remained at home, targeting my father's ability to paint. And if that person were already in trouble for something else when she happened to notice the circle emerge gray against the white like a hidden picture, it could trigger a full-blown event. Like the lamb grease, the effects of her repeated explosions settled within my brain, emerging unexpectedly yet stubbornly, reminding me that evidence of any sort can never be truly covered up or hidden away.

9

Where's Margaret?

OUR ROAD HAD ONCE BEEN A THROUGHWAY CONNECTING TOWNS, rich with vegetable stands and working farms. Those farms failed as farms often do, the people died as people always do, and the town terminated the road at the last house—ours—maintaining it only as far as our mailbox. Over the years the road deteriorated to a narrow path of rocks, gravel, and exposed rusty culverts, with seemingly endless woods to each side. When night came anywhere on the dead-end side, pitch black really did mean black as pitch.

I remember trying to explain "real" night to my second-grade city-living classmates in Mrs. Gray's class, and they nodded, bored, as if they were aware of all kinds of night. The teacher talked about how beautiful the stars must be, but I replied we were so intent on trying to see what made the noises in front and to the sides of us that we didn't consider looking up. When a friend visited, her first response if she held her hands in front of her face and didn't see them was, "Way cool!" But then the coy dogs and coyotes would begin to yip and howl in the distance, and unseen things would crash through the woods, and her second response, the one she kept to tell kids at school, was, "You should see Helen's house. It's haunted."

From inside, black seemed to encase the house and push at the windows.

With an old cemetery just up the road, my father decided that Margaret, a grave occupant, regularly visited us. Slanting tombstones marked the resting spots of men and women who had worked the land that grew wild on each side of the graveyard. These woods and fields hid old foundations, stonewalls, and chimney fragments.

The grave markers, tilting backward and forward as the earth let go around them, told a story about the men, women, and children who lived in the late 1700s to the late 1800s in the Maine wilderness. Margaret died in 1834 at the age of forty-four, but her husband, Charles, died in 1892 and had remarried after each wife died.

When I stood on the uneven topsoil of the cemetery I thought Charles must have been a foul and hard man to have had so many women and to not have mourned the loss of Margaret so deeply that he could never marry again. I felt sorry for Margaret, who appeared to have been easily dismissed once dead, as if Charles only needed a woman to serve him, and he didn't care who filled that role.

When I stood on the uneven topsoil of the cemetery I thought men treated women as if they were nothing but workers, and I hated them because I feared one might expect me to serve him.

When I stood on the uneven topsoil of the cemetery I thought back to the fairground women and wanted to know their secrets for attracting men and their money without marrying into a full-time job, those men who would wait in the October cold without shouting, "Get a move on. I haven't got all day!"

As time dribbled forward and I stood again and again in front of Margaret's grave, with a Stephen King or James Herriot book tucked beneath my arm, it occurred to me that Charles might have had a hand in the deaths of his more than a few wives, and I wondered if when one died, he'd had that look that said, "It couldn't be helped. That's life."

"It's just Margaret," my father would tell us when the stairs groaned and no one appeared or "Margaret just wants to say hi," when the floors creaked. "Hi there, Margaret," he would say to the air, a half-smile on his handsome face. Or at the end of the day, when we ate supper in the kitchen and the wicker rocker moved a bit forward then backward, he'd say, "Margaret gets tired too. Poor old girl works hard." And although the rocker was his chair, the special one we could sit in only if he wasn't around, he'd sit elsewhere. When a door slammed by itself or a picture fell off the wall, he would comment as if it were a fact: "Margaret's mad about something," and then shake his head as if he were really confused: "What'd one of you do now?"

Believing his every word, I would narrow my eyes and focus intently on the air. Sometimes I thought I saw something move just after I'd given up searching, and I'd turn back sharply, my heart filling my chest and ears with a deafening thump at the prospect of meeting a ghost and my possible demise. Other times I'd watch the chair move and hear the cellar stairs groan with weight, but I'd see nothing.

"There's no one there," my practical mother would say firmly. "It's just the wind and your eyes playing tricks on you."

I wished with all my heart to share my mother's confidence.

If anything but vegetables were out of place, Margaret was responsible. The grumbling, wild-haired man who lived in a rusty camper in the woods bordering our gardens was the one to blame for missing carrots, corn, and potatoes.

Margaret was as much a member of our family as any of us except she never got punished for causing trouble and was only noticed when she did. Nine children, one daughter's husband, and two grandkids stuffed in a five-bedroom house with overworked parents who lacked expendable cash, time, and energy meant that unless I made myself a pest, I was invisible too. Margaret and I were connected by invisibility and, I imagined, a dislike of men who thought they were better than us.

My sisters liked to walk up to the cemetery. A ledge jutted out over a large field behind the stonewall that enclosed the tombstones. My mother assumed I would tattle if any sister smoked or met a boy. But I feared crossing my tough-yet-admirable sister who had the daring to pick up snakes and chase me or, worse, throw them at me, their bodies twisting like rope through the air, and even as I ran screaming, I'd be impressed that she had the guts to pick them up.

We all screamed—the kids, the in-laws, the farm animals, and the parents—out of fear, frustration, and fury.

I REMEMBER A SERIES OF SCENES IN THE FIELDS BELOW THE OLD cemetery and ledge. And although one sister insists they never happened, another sister confirms that they did, as does my nervous system any time I am more than a few feet above the ground. I spent many hours in these fields picking wild strawberries and wildflowers, snow-mobiling, and, when older, riding a horse. In this series of scenes it is possibly late summer after haying season. I tagged along behind my sisters to an ancient barn that leaned sideways in the tall grass. With the cemetery not far in the distance, I could feel the presence of the dead people, of Margaret, lying rotten in the ground. The barn's beams, the few that were left, sagged and drooped as if the weight of the crumbling roof were too much to bear. Bales of hay formed stairs for easy climbing to a rickety loft. I watched as my tough-yet-admirable sister pointed at my hair-twirling-pretty sister and my sad-tittering sister, and chanted, "Eeny, meeny, miny, moe. Catch a nigger by the toe. If he hollers, let him go. Eeny, meeny, miny, moe," to decide who would jump first. She did not point at me, and I hated being left out.

My hair-twirling-pretty sister leapt off the second-floor platform to the dried grass pile below, shouting with delight in explosions of timothy, alfalfa, and dust. My sisters looked and sounded like human birds as they landed in the loose hay that covered the wooden floor. I gathered my courage and followed my hair-twirling-pretty sister's slender dirty legs up the square bales. What had looked soft scratched my skin. At the top the hay mountain appeared flat and distant. Dust tickled my nose.

"I want to turn around," I said, my voice trembling. My skin flushed hot with a wave of blood pounding through my veins. "I don't want to jump anymore," and I turned to go back the way I'd come.

"You can't go back," announced my tough-yet-admirable sister. She stood behind me and blocked the exit with arms wide. "I didn't tell you to climb up. Now just go."

I didn't understand why the bales could be climbed up but not climbed down. I was trapped.

"You're just Mamma's little baby. We're all jumping, and no one is crying. We didn't even want you to come, and now you're in our way." Her strong arms waved at me.

I turned to look down again, considering, careful to keep my feet from the edge. "But I don't . . ."

She hit me in the middle of my back, pushing me out of the loft. I didn't feel like a bird, and I landed not into the hay but onto the floor, knees and hands first, before collapsing onto my chest and stomach.

"Ughh . . . ucch . . . " I couldn't breathe or seem to move, but I was flailing.

"Why did you push her?" my hair-twirling-pretty sister screamed from somewhere.

"Get off the floor!" My tough-yet-admirable sister's body stood solid as a boulder, too close to my head. "Built like an ox," my mother always said.

"If you dare tell, I'll make sure you won't tell anything ever again!"

SOMETIMES MY FATHER WOULD SIT BACK WITH HIS COFFEE, lower his voice, and tell stories about Margaret, about how she came down from the cemetery to haunt our house. I'd sit there beside my mother, my stomach jittery, my breath foul from stress, afraid to look behind me, knowing that in another hour I'd be in bed, in the dark.

"A man died in the bedroom upstairs," my father told us one night. "In the room right above this kitchen." He pointed upward to what would be my three brothers' room and, later, mine: "He never woke up. Went to sleep and died. No one ever knew what happened. Something or someone killed him. Maybe it was Margaret, but maybe it was Mr. Cootsy."

Who was Mr. Cootsy?

I went to bed that night with my head full of a second invisible person, wondering how many others there were that I hadn't heard of yet.

Trembling beneath my worn blue bedspread, my stomach churned with the certainty I wouldn't live through the night and that my death would be preceded by unimaginable torture. Even with my hair-twirling-pretty sister sleeping five feet across the room, I went to sleep with the covers pulled tight over my head, thinking anything exposed was fair game for ghosts and monsters.

"Don't let the bedbugs bite," my mother said before I finally got up the courage to explain that I didn't dare stretch out my legs to the foot of the bed, where I knew snakes and bedbugs waited. After that she began to say, "Don't take any wooden nickels," which made me feel guilty because I'd recently taken some of my father's butterscotch candies and gum. All taking without asking was sinful.

Then one night, after she switched off the light:

"Ooohhhh!!!"

A moan cut through the inky-octopus dark.

"What was that?" I screeched from beneath my blankets. I heard the bang of my hair-twirling-pretty sister's bed frame hitting the floor followed by a wail of terror that I can only liken to a rabbit's scream.

Always aware that any moment could be the Apocalypse, I threw the covers off my head and sat up shouting for the real person who could save me: "Mamma! Mamma!"

In the shadowy dark I watched my sister's mattress and box spring begin to rise off the metal frame. I didn't think it could be Margaret. The bed was too heavy with my sister in it for a female ghost, and the voice was too deep. It had to be Mr. Cootsy. Or another male ghost.

My mother thumped up the stairs and burst in, ready to assess damage and assign blame. "What's going on now? There's no reason to make such noise. You girls know better than that!"

That's when my father crawled out from under the bed, laughing. He stood between our beds.

My mother stared at him silent, her eyes speaking volumes.

My hair-twirling-pretty sister sat in the middle of her bed, hugging her trembling body with her arms, her hair wild, her beautiful brown eyes large and confused.

I sat parallel to her in my own bed, my nervous system in sync with hers as we determined what had terrified us in the dark.

"Stop trying to scare the girls!" my mother shouted. "You want them to wet their beds?"

"Oh, they know I'm only joking around," my father defended himself as he walked out of our bedroom. I heard him say in the hallway before he descended the stairs: "They like to be scared. They're always watching that damned *Scooby-Doo*."

ALL OF US KIDS HAD ROUTES OF ESCAPE, EVEN IF IT WAS ONLY to go to the sandpit a quarter-mile beyond the cemetery or onto old logging trails on the other end of our dirt road. My tough-yet-admirable sister favored the cemetery so she could sit on the large mica-speckled ledge and smoke privately amongst the prickly juniper bushes. One morning we crested the rocky hill and saw immediately that something was wrong. Margaret's tombstone stood as usual, but her grave was a rectangular gaping hole. A granite slab leaned against the far rock wall.

"Where's Margaret?" my sister asked, gazing down into the black-filled emptiness.

At the sound of her voice, a sudden rumbling and thundering of wings cut the air as a flock of pheasants flew up from the stonewall. I screamed, my nerves tingling with electricity from head to toe. My heart pounding like a jackhammer, I ran out to the dirt road.

"Ooohhh, the birds! They're gonna get you!" she taunted, pretending to tremble in fear, then she leaned against Margaret's tombstone and lit a cigarette.

With the proof of the empty grave before me, I knew Margaret had escaped. I sprinted home over the rocks, leaping the rusted culvert, ignoring the stones that bruised my bare feet, and raced up the sun-warmed porch boards to tell my mother, who was sitting at the kitchen table shelling peas.

She didn't believe me, "Oh, just stop with the foolishness and stop being so dramatic," she scoffed, because she was forever busy and we were, as she oft repeated, all filthy liars.

"Margaret's really gone," I panted. "Her grave is an empty hole. You have to come see." Something in my face made her drop a half-opened pod into her bowl of peas and stand up.

"If this is a trick because your sister has some snakes up there . . . " she didn't finish the sentence. She didn't need to.

My mother went to the sink, poured water into a green plastic cup, and drank it all down quickly before shooing me out the door ahead of her. We walked up the road in silence, my bare feet silent on the rocks, and her cloth sneakers saying, "whisp, whosp, whisp, whosp" with each step on the gravel. Back at the cemetery I could tell she was surprised that I'd been right. She didn't respond immediately; she stared down into the hole, pondering, until she noticed the smell wafting off my tough-yet-admirable sister.

"That better not be what I think it is," she said, looking around for a stick to whack her with. Then to me and my hair-twirling-pretty sister: "Either kids have been fooling around, or the town dug her up."

I wanted to believe her, but kids robbing Margaret's grave was too much of a coincidence. There were other graves they could have chosen, like Henry's that sat all by itself in the lower right corner of the cemetery, or the ten-foot-high monument on the left that marked the burial site of several family members. A large urn sat on top of that towering stone, and my blustery-and-favored brother had told me a story about that grave I'd never forget.

My brothers had climbed on the monument and lifted the urn. There had been money beneath it, and when they saw it, they were thrilled at their good luck and took it. They replaced the urn and climbed down. Oddly, the urn refused to remain secure without the money. Each time my brothers climbed up to balance the urn so it could not topple, they would leave only to hear it thud heavily to the ground behind them. Terrified that something worse would happen to them if they kept the money, they put it back—and the urn stayed in place.

When I questioned the possibility of the urn needing the money as a shim, my blustery-and-favored brother said, "The top was flat and the urn wasn't tippy. Something else was going on, and I wasn't fool enough to find out what."

As he told the story I remembered how he used to run and save Donny, rushing among the flailing hooves to untangle the rope, and I felt a chill of fear because this blustery-and-favored brother was the bravest person I knew.

MARGARET'S GRAVE REMAINED EMPTY FOR ALMOST A YEAR, AND then one day I followed my tough-yet-admirable sister and her boyfriend up the road, and it was filled again. My parents accepted the refilled grave just as they'd accepted the empty one, making up their own explanations and believing them—city maintenance, kids fooling around, or "these things just happen."

The curious aspect of Margaret's disappearance is that my father no longer talked about her haunting our house as he once did. Mr. Cootsy took the blame for mysteriously odd noises and things out of place.

Having been part of my world for so long, Margaret stayed with me. There were moments I thought I saw her out of the corner of my eye, but when I turned straight on, nothing and no one was there. The shape of a woman moving rapidly to the side of me had been so real that my stomach had leaped and my heart had accelerated in speed and increased in volume. "Oh piffle wiffle. It's just your overactive imagination," my mother said when I told her I'd seen the ghost.

It occurred to me that my imagination seemed to work overly hard just to show me ghosts and monsters. Why would it do that when what I really wanted to see was horses?

One night the need to pee too badly to wait until dawn drew me from the safety of my bed. Heart beating in my ears, stomach trembling with fear, I raced through the darkness down the stairs, turning the light on when I got to the kitchen. Even the bright fluorescent did nothing to ease my something's-gonna-get-me terror.

The house always felt alive, shifting and sighing as it settled, but tonight the air felt charged. I dared to peek at the wicker rocking chair in front of the window, and just as I did, it creaked. Terrified of what invisible thing was in it, I sprinted to the bathroom. When I finished and stepped into the dining room to get back to the kitchen hallway that led to the stairs, peripherally I saw a shadow move to my left and heard the heavy sigh of a person who had decided to let the air out of her lungs. I yelped, startled, and leapt backward, pressing myself against the wall next to the table. It is true that fear can paralyze a person. My legs refused to move forward but instead allowed my body to sink to the floor, my knees pressed against my chest. Then I heard, close to my ear, "Shhhh," the h's dragged out slowly as if the speaker had a slow leak.

My brain decided the best thing to do would be to scream for help in the form of my savior. Over and over, louder and louder, my throat raw: "Mamma!"

After what felt like an eternity, I heard her feet thump on the stairs. "What?" her voice answered, slightly hardened from the annoyance of being wakened. I would be blamed if she were unable to get to sleep again, that unreachable place if interrupted even once. She narrowed her far-sighted eyes at me, "What's all this noise?" I never liked to see her without her glasses.

"Someone said, 'shhhh'," I answered, my stomach now sick as if I might need the bathroom again. My mouth was dry.

"Well, do you blame them?" she asked, turning on the outside light with a sharp click of the switch and looking around. "You're making enough noise to raise the dead." Then, after peering out and circling the four downstairs rooms, she said, "I don't see anyone and the dogs didn't bark, so there's no one here. Go back to bed."

With my mother moving briskly around and the lights on, I felt brave enough to run in front of her up the stairs, but I never got back to sleep that night. I lay under the covers urging the sun to rise.

The shhhh memory is as strong as the Margaret's-empty-grave memory. If there are such things as ghosts or spirits, they would have known the importance of us kids being quiet at night. They would have heard the yelling and the punishments for getting out of bed, so I should have accepted the "shhhh" for the friendly warning it was. I question what it was about me, then, that believed ghosts were bad.

YEARS LATER I DROVE UP THE DEAD-END ROAD TO PHOTOGRAPH Margaret's tombstone and those of her family. From a distance I could see the house, no longer brown but blue, sitting on the hill. There was no car in the driveway, although some other family lived there now. Slowly, I drove past the house that stared at me with its face-like windows. The skin tingled, and the hair rose on my arms and neck. I could feel it behind me, a presence, and I didn't dare turn my head to see if someone or something stood at a window.

I parked and hiked up the crumbling path to the cemetery, sorry to leave the security of my car. The sight of the graveyard surrounded by a low stonewall gave me the familiar quiver of fear. Margaret's tombstone stood tipping a little back, just as I'd last seen it twenty years before, moss and uneven topsoil finding its way around the granite. My family had accused her of so much, but in truth she'd probably worked land, had a family, and died, probably hoping for the same things we all do. I realized that I had warm memories of Margaret, more as if she'd been a fellow sufferer of getting in trouble than as an adversary. That night of the "Shhh" edged into my consciousness, and I regretted screaming for my mother. What might have happened if I'd obeyed and remained silent? I suddenly felt as if I might have disappointed Margaret, and without planning to, I placed my hand on her gravestone and said, "I'm sorry." My voice was loud, like it didn't belong to me. I traced the letters of her name and the dates of her lifespan and thought what I always did when I considered Margaret. *Where did you go that year? How did you manage to get out? Did you really rock all those times in the wicker chair in front of the lookout window? Did you make our pictures crooked, and did you wander up and down our cellar stairs? Did you shush me? Why?* Then I heard my mother's admonishment speak from my subconscious: "Do you always have to ask so many questions? I swear you'd nag God Himself," and here I was nagging a ghost.

10

Left and Leaving

THE FIRST TIME WAS JUST AFTER MY NINTH BIRTHDAY, IN JANUARY, seconds after my mother smacked me over the head with a yardstick. She could have caught me stealing lumps of brown sugar or handfuls of chocolate chips, but more likely it was because I complained about everything. Each time I saw a way to make life better I let my mother know. I gave her ideas on how all my waiting for her might be avoided if she would be honest about how long a minute was, how she might be able to buy me books and a pair of boots if she bought macaroni instead of more meat. Or how she might yell less if she just gave my sisters the things they took without asking. She wasn't receptive to advice. The words "just leave" came to me as the wood caught the knuckles that were protecting my head.

I wasn't the first to run away. It's the lot of the youngest child to see all the older siblings leave ahead of her, to see them exit amidst a flurry of hard words, tears, and slamming doors.

I grabbed my jacket and stomped outside in my cloth sneakers to get Daisy, my black setter-lab mix, and headed down the driveway. The horses had been sold the previous winter for a snowmobile that took my slew of sisters and blustery-and-favored brother more reliably from home than Donny ever could.

I hoped my mother was watching from inside the house, could see me disappear, and feel loss or at least worry because it was so cold and I wasn't wearing snow pants or boots. Maybe she would come after me and apologize for losing her temper.

My sisters had run down this road often.

"Get off this property before I get you off," a parent would scream. "I don't want to ever see you again!"

"I hate you," the daughter would shout back as she walked down the dirt driveway, her bare feet silent. "I never wanted to live here anyway."

"You can go to hell!" The screams would grow shriller, voices breaking and cracking with volume and force as Janis Joplin's did in "Cry Baby."

"I hate all of you!" the daughter might scream, holding so much hate that sometimes she would laugh at the strength of it, and after she disappeared around the trees the silence would ring with the echo of her words. She might be gone for hours, a day, or, the last time, she'd return only to get her stuff.

SCARED THAT THE TIED, SNARLING GERMAN SHEPHERD DOWN the road would break free to hurt Daisy, I veered into the woods to avoid her, feeling sorry for myself. I used to do anything to get inside the house, and now I would do anything to get out. I shivered from the cold and wished for mittens and a hat that I hadn't dared to get myself since that day I'd pulled the storage cabinet on my head. I no longer tugged on any handle without flashing back to the scene three years before. I could almost hear the glass in the doors shatter onto me and over the game of Monopoly my sisters had been playing at the table:

"Um vah," my hair-twirling-pretty sister had said, dragging out the nonsense syllables her school friends used to indicate trouble. "Look what you did. You're gonna get it now."

Certain she was right, I stayed put beneath the wooden cabinet that pressed on my back. My mouth dry, my ears pounding, I evaluated myself for damage as sweat trickled beneath my wool snow pants.

"What's going on now?" I heard my mother come in from outdoors and yell from afar. She sounded exhausted, like she might be at her wit's end again.

The heavy steps of my father's boots got louder and louder, "Goddammit! Now I have to replace more glass," he shouted. "Why is Helen always breaking the cussed glass?"

In my family, if someone did a thing even once, they earned "always." Hearing that weighty word while stuck under the china cabinet that doubled as a mitten cupboard made me try to yell, "I do not always break glass," but it came out "I–I–I," because I could never get my tongue to work properly in those early years.

"How'd you get way under there?" my mother asked. The lenses of her glasses shimmered like I imagined Mrs. Who's did in *A Wrinkle in Time*, as she knelt to peer in at me.

Focused on the injustice and my need to pee, it was too exhausting to explain.

ABOUT A MONTH BEFORE, I'D BROKEN THE CELLAR WINDOW TO get in the house, the reason behind the "always." There were nine kids and only one house key other than the spare my parents wouldn't tell me where they hid.

I'd arrived home from kindergarten at my usual half-day time and found no one to let me in. The snow was deep, I had to pee, and my sneakers were soaked from recess, and when the wind blew and Tippy barked at me from inside the entry, I thought of witches stealing small dogs. That thought led my brain to conjure up images of flying monkeys. Before I knew it I could feel an entire flock behind me, wanting nothing more than to grip the back of my purple snorkel jacket with their monkey claws and carry me off. We weren't allowed to use the outdoors as a bathroom. My only choice was to break a window.

"How'd you get in?" my mother had asked when she got home. "Did I forget to lock the door?"

Before I could form words into a sentence, my father, who had gone straight to the cellar without seeing me sitting in his rocking chair, entered the kitchen.

"She broke the damn window, that's how," he huffed, taking off his cap to throw it on top of the refrigerator.

He looked at me sternly. "There's no need for breaking windows," he said.

"There's no need of being destructive, that's for sure," my mother added redundantly, poking her finger at me. "Next time, just wait."

That's when I knew I was old enough to stay home alone.

"Something might get me outside," I said, my heart sending hot blood from my face to my toes as I said the words that proved I was a chicken. "Like flying monkeys," I added, scooting my feet underneath my bottom to keep all parts safe, even in the kitchen. Snakes could be anywhere.

"There are no flying monkeys around here, only coy dogs, and maybe a bear or two and what have you," my father said, taking a ratty blue sponge from the sink to remove fingerprints from the white woodwork opposite the fridge. "Why do the damn kids have to touch the walls?" he muttered grumpily. "How hard can it be to walk down the hall and not touch anything?"

"Well, there's also the riffraff and potheads who go up the road to sit in their cars smoking and drinking all the time," my mother noted knowledgeably, turning on the burner as she placed a pot of water on the stove for macaroni and then a cast iron pan on a burner for my father's steak, "and the bum who lives in the woods."

"That funny fella ain't gonna hurt nobody," my father said, now scrubbing at the white cupboards below the sink. "He's harmless."

My mother took out a jar of bacon fat and scooped several tablespoons into the black frying pan. "He might be harmless, but he's a nuisance," my mother said. "And his camper is an eyesore."

"What about painting these cupboards yellow so the dirt shows less?" my father asked. "What do you think, honey?"

WHEN I ARRIVED HOME A FEW DAYS LATER, AGAIN TO AN EMPTY driveway, a locked door, and a window I wasn't supposed to smash with a rock, I decided to get in the mailman's car when he drove up the road.

Mr. Simon's kids were grown, and once he brought me a naked doll with a missing eyelid that he didn't need anymore and a few old stuffed animals. My hair-twirling-pretty sister took the stuffed dog. When he saw me outside alone, he drove closer.

"Where are your parents?"

"I don't know."

"When are they coming back?"

"I don't know." I had to pee so bad my teeth chattered.

"You shouldn't be out here all alone."

I didn't think so either. I wondered if he was thinking of the homeless bum who lived in the woods, but then I realized the homeless probably didn't get mail, so he wouldn't know about him.

He studied me, not speaking, then said, "Get in the car and I'll take you on my route."

I didn't hesitate.

Mr. Simon backed down the driveway without looking behind him. Then he drove with his wheels skimming the snow-covered ditches to one mailbox after another, while reading the addresses in his lap. Each start and stop jostled my bladder so that I tensed my muscles and gritted my teeth in an effort to hold everything in. I had been taught never to discuss pee and poop with strangers and to work hard despite pain, so I helped Mr. Simon, handing him elastic-bound stacks of envelopes when he stretched out his hand. At the sixth or seventh house I peed on his seat.

The pee turned cold against my legs and stiffened my hand-sewn denims. Mr. Simon didn't let on if he noticed the spreading dark puddle beneath me. He drove in a big loop back to my house. My parents still weren't there, so he sat in the car, the motor idling.

"Are you hungry?"

"A little," I answered, but it was a lie. Each day I was becoming a better liar, especially to strangers. I hadn't eaten anything but the marshmallows out of my Boo Berry that morning. Ghosts were everywhere.

He opened his black lunchbox and gave me half his tuna fish sandwich. I felt guilty for eating his lunch after I'd peed in his car.

The sandwich gone, my parents turned into the driveway. "Big mail day?" my father asked, walking over to the window Mr. Simon rolled down.

I slipped out and ran before anyone could remark on the large, dark pee circle I'd been hiding as if sitting on a nest. My mother, in one expert evidence-seeking-glance, saw I'd wet myself. I hoped she wouldn't hang my dirty underpants around my neck like I'd seen her do to a sister and make me wear them for the rest of the day. I worried I'd have no clean pants for school.

"Next time just wait and use the bathroom," she said brusquely and turned to make tea. As I ran to change, relieved I'd escaped punishment, the word "wait" sent my muscles flexing with restlessness.

"Just wait," everyone said at the slaughter house for things to bleed or smoke, at the car repair place for the car to come down off the lift, in the grocery store parking lot for my mother, for my underpants to go through the wash, for the book I wanted at the library, for my father to wake up and eat his breakfast on Christmas morning. Wait to eat, to drink, to pee. People ordered me to waste my time as if they didn't care about my allotted life minutes at all. My sisters were the worst: "Wait there and watch out for Mamma." If not for books and animals, I'd die from boredom.

EVEN AS I RAN AWAY FROM HOME, I WAS WAITING. WAITING TO see if anyone would come after me. Alternating my stiff, aching hands from my jacket pocket to pushing branches out of my face and grabbing trees for balance, I fought to stay upright. Daisy bounded though the deep snow beside me, more on her hind legs than her front, and I struggled to keep up, with anger and self-pity giving me the energy to plow through snow that reached to my thighs. Before I could make it out of the woods to the road, dusk settled into the naked trees. I'd left the flying monkeys and witches behind me years ago, but ghosts, particularly Margaret and Mr. Cootsy, could be anywhere.

Tree arms reached out to poke me in the eyes and snow melted into my sneakers, and when my next step didn't touch firm ground but instead broke through ice before sinking into water, I realized with the same helplessness I'd experienced under the cabinet and before I got into Mr. Simon's car that I had to go back. I had more time to wait before real life could begin. Someday I would wonder if my mother had experienced the same helplessness when she'd turned back and walked up the hill after my father had yelled at her. When I was smaller I'd stood with her and held her hand as she'd cried, and I'd chased her down the road along with Tippy, who, like me, refused to be left behind.

I pulled myself out of the snow and sat down on a large stump set on a hillock out of the snow. I began to shiver from cold.

Daisy lay beside me, chewing on snowballs that stuck to the hair between her toes, whining softly. I could feel the tug of the air molecules yanking me in the opposite direction of home. Somewhere out there ahead of me, peace and silence beckoned like the Reese's Peanut Butter Cups on the candy racks beside the store registers. I could feel the call, but I had no way to answer. I wanted to go forward so much that it hurt to get up and walk back through the snow to the house on the hill, knowing my eighteen-year sentence still stretched long into the future. I was halfway there with no hope of time speeding up. Time had sputtered to a halting gait just like when I used to stutter.

My pants stiffened to shell-like hardness and my toes throbbed inside my sneakers to the beat of my heart. I walked up the hill like a child of Herman Munster's, trying not to bend my knees or feet. When I got to the front door I took a deep breath and entered the house-of-waiting with Daisy at my side, a house no one had noticed I'd left.

11

The Youngest Child

IN THE FOURTH GRADE MRS. BURGESS ASKED ALL THE STUDENTS to bring in photographs of their mothers for a bulletin-board display about Mother's Day. A construction-paper banner, green with scalloped edges, held the photos. I stared at them with my best friend Michelle Sirois at my side and wondered what each home was like in the background behind the mothers' smiling faces. Was there screaming and stomping of feet, hooting and hollering? Was there a bullshit-artist-ass-Skipper in the family tree who didn't hit people with his hat but his fists? Did those mothers chase teenage children who smelled of beer, sex, and cigarettes with bars of soap or branches from the weeping willow tree, the broom, or the yardstick? Was there daily bemoaning over the high cost of white bread, whole milk, and gasoline? Did cups, potatoes, and corn cobs get thrown at people during supper? Were there Clark bars and Kit-Kats?

Michelle, instead of focusing on which mother might offer chocolate, thought it was more fun to choose whose mother was the prettiest. In each picture the mothers showed off long, unbound hairstyles. Except mine. Where other mothers leaned in doorways or sat on couches, most with smiles, some with laughter aimed at a person invisible to us, my mother held a newborn lamb. Her cheek bones were high and touched her glasses slightly, her mouth was open in a half-smile, possibly at the thought of a future lamb chop. She wore my father's old postal jacket over a clean but stained work shirt. Wisps of short gray hair stuck out from two barrettes holding bangs from her face. Her rubber boot tops stopped just beneath manure-stained knees.

Michelle announced that although my mother was pretty, she wasn't as pretty as Mark Poulin's mother, who wore a miniskirt and had flowing blonde Barbie hair.

"Well, I think she's prettier, and everyone says my father's very handsome. He's Greek," I said, truly shocked by her words.

"Plus," she said, as if not even listening. "Your mother's old."

I gasped in disbelief and loyalty to my sheep-eating mother. Old? I studied the photos intently, turning slightly from Michelle because she'd hurt my feelings. I scrutinized the faces for wrinkles and the hair for streaks of white. Suddenly I recognized in a swoop of truth that all my friends' mothers looked the age of my oldest sister. Standing in front of that montage of youthful motherhood, I realized that mine had lived a long life before me.

Instantly, in that moment of discovery, my mind was hit with dozens of questions and a gripping sense of left-out-ness. Had my mother known there would be one more child after my sister? Had she thought about me, felt an emptiness in her life that she couldn't explain? Where were people before they were born? Had I been out there somewhere without a body, waiting? What if a different me had arrived? Would I know it? Would she know it?

With nine children passing through the school system, my mother's picture must have hung on school bulletin boards before, and at one time she must have matched the ages of the other mothers. For one year the oldest and the youngest child had been the same person.

WHEN I BEGAN SCHOOL, FIFTEEN YEARS AFTER MY FIRST SIBLING, the reaction to my last name on the first day of class could be anything from a roll of the eyes, an exhausted sigh, to a slit-eyed stare. My stutter in kindergarten elicited sympathy from fresh-out-of-college and pregnant Mrs. LeRoux. But my first grade teacher, withered Mrs. Burns, assumed it was a strategy to waste her time.

"Just say it," she yelled class after class. "You think we have all day?" I had held my breath in answer, knowing from observation that any word other than "no" wasn't acceptable. Instead I counted silently until the need to cry passed. More shrew than teacher, this woman taught me that regardless of how I behaved, I could be judged by the behavior of people related to me—guilty by association, my mother would say when she told my sisters to stay away from the neighborhood tramps and riffraff. That's before she found out the neighborhood considered *us* the tramps and riffraff.

School made me realize that other people already knew what I suspected about my bloodlines after watching an uncle with no teeth eat an ear of corn:

They weren't the best.

"Half-baked," I overheard the principal say about the brother-I-barely-knew to my second-grade teacher. They had stared at me, as if assessing my doneness. I wondered if half-baked meant the same as going off half-cocked, which my father said the bullshit-artist-ass-Skipper always did.

Appreciative of a place to stick their nine children, my parents had mixed feelings about school. "Helen used to be so sweet," my mother told my aunt, the one who shouted all her sentences as if she hated everyone. "Then she started school and it ruined her. She's so disagreeable now. It's too bad."

While I sat at the kitchen table drawing a cardinal from a library book I heard her tell my father: "I don't know what happened or how it happened, but it's like Helen's a completely different person, no longer lovable."

My father didn't say anything. He was staring into the bowl of his pipe trying to light it.

I noticed, however, that despite thinking school damaged me, they continued to send me there every morning.

I tried hard to be good, but as puberty approached in fifth grade and arrived in sixth, it was too much work and not worth it. My half-hearted attempt at good-daughter behavior brought on laborious speeches about independent streaks and hateful natures—rotten to the core—and I suspect my mother decided her love would be better spent on her grandchildren, the two who often lived with us because their mother hadn't given the idea of being good any attention at all. Sometimes I wished my niece and nephew would start school too and lose what made them lovable, wishes that proved I was indeed hateful.

My mother blamed school, specifically the middle grades, as the reason behind anything I did or said that aggravated her. "I didn't send you to school so that you could come home and tell me some teacher told you that Jell-O is made of horse parts and you won't eat it. I've had just about enough of your crazy ideas about food and animals."

"It's not just the Jell-O," I argued, which confirmed my disagreeableness. "It's the marshmallows too."

"You will not tell me what you will or won't eat. You will eat what I give you. Put that in your pipe and smoke it." She moved close, leaning her body to yell down on my face and prove she had more authority than my teachers. I was relieved when she left without pinching my cheeks. I had enough problems with kids calling me chipmunk face at school.

My hair-twirling-pretty sister, a freshman, didn't like horses and didn't care about what lay hidden in her food, so she continued to eat Jell-O and marshmallows, smashing a pile of fake whipped cream on top. She often told me things she learned at school, things I thought I should listen to because she was several grades higher than I was.

"A girl at school says that if a person has hair on her knuckles, she's retarded."

I wondered if this was the same girl who'd told her a few months earlier that a boy's thumb indicated the size of his dinky. I instantly examined my hands. "I don't have any hair on my knuckles," I said, relieved.

"Yes, you do. Your knuckles are covered with hair like the hairy ape you are."

"Where?" I twisted and turned my fingers, squinting, my earlier relief replaced by anxiety that I bore physical proof of a mental disability.

"There," she rapped my hand. "You wouldn't know a knuckle hair if it bit you in the face."

Worried, I went to my mother, "Do I have hair on my knuckles?" and held up my hands for her to examine.

"It wouldn't surprise me," she said without looking up from the rump roast she was basting. "You *are* pretty hairy. Now go find something better to do than stare at your knuckles."

I went back to my hair-twirling-pretty sister, the one I loved and admired and who had obviously shaved her hands. "What does hair on knuckles have to do with the brain?" I asked, eager to learn.

"That's for me to know and you to find out," she said. Then she kicked me because she was talking on the phone to her best friend from down the road, and I made it hard for her to hear.

I BEGAN TO STUDY EVERYONE'S KNUCKLES, JUST AS BEFORE I'D studied all boys' thumbs, from teachers to the mailman, to see if my hair-twirling-pretty sister's theory held. Hair covered my father's knuckles, which is why, when I grumbled over the difficulty of keeping arm hair neat, my mother said, "Talk to your father about your extra hair, not me." Then she smiled as only the hairless can and said with a superior flair, "You didn't get any of those embarrassing problems from my side."

But it was obvious to me that my father could do nothing about excess hair. He was covered in the stuff.

"Your legs and arms are so much like an ape's that no one's ever going to love you," my hair-twirling-pretty sister teased one afternoon while I watched *Bewitched*. She gave me an Indian sunburn as she passed on her way to dance with my sad-tittering sister in front of the living room mirror to Bad Company's "Can't Get Enough." Bad Company, Foreigner, Aerosmith, and AC/DC were their current favorite bands. I preferred Lorne Greene's album, *The Man*. I figured Lorne Greene was a good person to admire because he was on television showing America how he loved what I assumed were his hounds in the Alpo commercial, and he obviously loved horses from what I'd seen on *Bonanza*. I had no idea what a band like AC/DC thought about animals, but I didn't think animals, especially dogs, would appreciate them. Their screaming hurt even my ears.

"Your arms are just as hairy as mine," I yelled over Brian Howe singing, "Well, I take whatever I want." Their music interfered with my enjoyment of Samantha evading the lecherous apothecary, and I thought about getting up to kick them.

"But you smell and we don't," my hair-twirling-pretty sister said as she jumped beside my other sister, who was swinging her jean-cut-off-encased hips below a stretchy yellow tube top while she stared at herself in the mirror.

My second popular nickname at school had over the years been Helen Smellin', but I'd thought that was just a rhyming coincidence. I was known in my family for my bad breath, but I solved this problem at school by keeping a wide circle of personal space. My mother entered rooms with nostrils flared and nose pointed to the ceiling, ready to attack if she smelled cigarettes, pot, sex, or alcohol. Wouldn't she have told me if I smelled really bad?

That sixth-grade spring, as I was swinging rung to rung on the monkey bars at school, arms above my head in a sleeveless shirt, I was surprised to hear, "Look! Helen's a monkey with hair in her pits. And she smells like one too!" accompanied by hoots, jungle noises, and hurtful pointer fingers. I would have preferred they call me a chimpanzee. Most upset that my sisters were right when I liked to think of them as wrong, I kept my arms jammed to my sides like a penguin for the rest of the school day. I told my mother immediately when I got home, hoping she could save me from further embarrassment.

"Oh, those kids are just jealous," she said, clamping the sewing machine foot in place over part of a pantsuit.

"Just let me shave and use deodorant," I pleaded. "All my friends use deodorant," I said, assuming they must.

"Do you have to do everything your friends do?"

"Isn't that obvious?" I wanted to say, but I watched my mouth instead. My mother, it seemed, was no longer going to save me from anything.

She looked me up and down and declared, "You're too young, and once you begin shaving you'll always have to shave."

That night my hair-twirling-pretty sister sneaked me an orange plastic disposable razor and a used deodorant, probably because when I ran out of clothes, I wore hers.

"Don't you dare tell Mamma."

"As if," I said, because I thought it sounded cool. Then my sister hugged me quickly and left saying, "You're so queer."

FOR TWO AND HALF YEARS MY HAIR-TWIRLING-PRETTY SISTER had been the youngest child. I took that away from her. But the youngest child spot was not the best place to be. Why would anyone want her mother to call her the baby of the family? I think my mother thought she was being sweet. But would she have liked it if I told everyone she was the old mother of the family?

Everyone used my age against me except when it came to work. I was never too young to stack wood, mow the yard, or do the dishes. But if I cried when an animal such as Rocky the dog died because a coyote had attacked him and made his neck rot, my father said, "Stop acting like a baby. He's right up there," and he pointed to the kitchen ceiling. Until fourth grade I thought Rocky's body was decomposing in the plaster above my head and wondered how my father got him in there without making a mess.

Even after I figured out that my father had meant heaven, not the plaster above our heads, I still thought of Rocky whenever I looked up or the fluorescent kitchen light flickered, especially after I began reading Stephen King novels. And my father, by pointing up, was saying animals went to heaven with the saved people, but that contradicted what my older brother had told me. So I asked my mother when my brother, who thought he knew everything about heaven, was present. "Of course animals go to heaven," she said. "What kind of heaven would it be without animals?"

"No, they don't," he contradicted with a superior tone. "Animals don't have souls."

I left them to their argument. Obviously, what was in heaven was a matter of personal opinion.

I had hundreds of questions about heaven and hell, but these were overshadowed by the development of breasts. My mother told me to stop sticking my chest out, and because I was afraid of acting like a floozie, I slouched, curving my torso like the letter C so she'd think I was good and lovable. There was no way I was going to tell her when I found blood in my underpants. From watching my sisters, I knew what to do. I put them deep in the outdoor trash and stole pads from the bathroom cabinet to bring to my bedroom.

"Where are you going with that?" my mother demanded once at the end of my twenty-eight-day cycle, accosting me as I tried to sneak through the living room to the stairs.

I said the first thing that came into my head, "Nowhere."

"Do you think money grows on trees? Pads are expensive. Don't use any unless you absolutely have to," she looked me up and down, narrowing her eyes suspiciously at what she perceived was my bad intent, "Do you have to?"

"Maybe a little," I answered, my whole body flushing with heat.

"Are you gaining weight?"

I said what I say still when anyone asks me that question, "Not that I know of."

After that I asked my schoolteacher for pads. Tampons were not an option for any of us. My sister-who-holds-grudges-longer-than-God crafted her own pads out of bread bags and paper towels when she lived at home. She told me that our mother kept a Tampon supply in her bedroom closet and counted them to make sure no one used any. Connecting Tampons with sexual shenanigans, my mother hid them to save her girls from turning out bad.

Sex, masturbation, stealing, and lies were all bad. Very bad. Even the thought of them promised my brothers and sisters—promised me—reserved seating in hell. I worried about dying and going to hell before I began to worry about anything, including smelling bad. I would stare up at the clouds shaping and reshaping themselves and wonder if the entrance to heaven was when they magically aligned. Would I be able to get there in time or miss the perfect alignment of water vapor by a minute and have to go to hell as a punishment for tardiness? If I had learned anything from watching *Land of the Lost*, it was that you had to be in the right place at the right time if you didn't want anything bad to happen.

I could die any second. I had seen the animals on the farm be alive before I went to bed and be dead when I got up.

"Beats me," my father would say when I asked why something died.

"That's the way the cookie crumbles," my mother would say.

"Probably Margaret killed it," a sister might add.

"Cancer," my sixth-grade science teacher lectured one afternoon, "can occur if a person repeatedly irritates or injures the same area of his body."

When Mr. Hackett announced this, I felt the tiny lumps on the inside of my cheek with my tongue and knew with heart-thumping, ear-pounding certainty that I'd given myself cancer from gnawing on my cheek when I was nervous, which was constant. Fear of death wiggled its dark fingers into my consciousness.

When I read Stephen King's *The Dead Zone* I realized that I could have a tumor in my brain and not even feel it. A mass in my head, I thought, would explain why I felt as if I lived in the wrong family, why I never understood my parents' answers to any of my questions, why I thought animals were meant for loving, not eating. I went to bed, placing the library book on top of the King-authored stack of novels on my nightstand beside an equally thick stack of James Herriot paperbacks. Waves of heat flushed through my limbs, tingling, as I considered my symptoms and anticipated death. Reading from the James Herriot series, books my best friend Mindy Parker loaned me, did nothing to soothe my fear that I might die any minute because the vet barely got any sleep. Animals almost-died every day all over Yorkshire, England. But his stories did soothe my worry about animals in heaven if I made it there someday. Herriot, when asked by an elderly woman if she would see her beloved pets in heaven, answered, "I do believe it. With all my heart I believe it."

I wished I knew what Stephen King believed.

Convinced of my imminent demise and considering all the hardened brown sugar lumps and chocolate chips I'd stolen when alone in the kitchen, I asked my mother: "If I'm going to hell anyway, why does it matter if I steal?"

"I swear you look for ways to be difficult," she answered, slamming the cupboard door on the baking chocolate.

From the direction of the finger pointing me to my final destination during punishments, I knew that heaven was somewhere up and hell was somewhere down, but this baffled me because heat rises.

"If we sleep downstairs when it's too hot upstairs in the summer," I said to my mother, "why is heaven up?"

She grabbed my shoulders in her two work-calloused hands to stare me square in the face, her eyes bloodshot from the strain of rarely answering, and said, "Stop asking so many ridiculous questions!"

"Why does Helen have to talk so much?" my siblings complained, unanimous in their disapproval and annoyance. "She's such a dumb-face. I wish she'd just shut up."

"I know," my mother agreed in a rare moment of commiseration with her daughters. "Eventually she'll get tired of it."

But the questions only came faster as I grew, irritating my family and frustrating me. Did they think I was having fun asking questions no one answered?

"What does it sound like in the rooms when no one is home?"

"What do animals think? Do they know they're going to die when they see the axe? Do they feel sorry for themselves?"

"If we need to sleep to be healthy, why do you keep waking us up?"

"Why do the coyotes howl at night?"

"Do you think there's another planet like Earth somewhere?"

"Does Margaret *have* to haunt our house? Why didn't she go to heaven or hell instead?

"What color is God? What color were Adam and Eve?"

"If Eve's punishment is women suffering through childbirth and if God is so merciful, how come he hasn't relented by now?"

"If hell is below us, why don't people say you can dig to hell instead of China? Do you have to go through hell to get to China?"

WHEN MICHELLE AND I LOOKED AT THE PHOTOGRAPHS OF mothers on Mrs. Burgess's bulletin board, while she wondered who was the prettiest, I wondered which mothers yelled into the night. All the mothers looked happy when the camera was pointed at them, even mine. Holding that lamb, my mother looked like a person who loved everything. She didn't look at all like a woman who would cut up a cute wooly lamb for the dinner table.

In later years, studyig pictures of my mother, I realized I had pestered her with innumerable questions, and it must have been very frustrating that even when she did answer, I wasn't satisfied. By asking again, I poked at her insecurity of not continuing her education. She wanted her kids to know she was smart about things other than how to shear a sheep and plant gardens. Why else would she repeat so often that she'd been salutatorian of her class? Each time I asked a question she was reminded of what she did and did not know and, perhaps also, of what she'd wanted to know and do before she died.

I had asked in fourth grade: "Did you wonder where I was when you had only eight children?" and she'd answered, "No." In sixth grade, because she was always so angry with me and my teenage sisters, I'd asked why she'd had so many children, and she'd told me—told all of us many times—that birth control methods had failed, had failed all nine times. But the question I really wanted to ask but never did was: "Were you sad when you found out there was going to be yet another child?" I didn't ask because I didn't want to hear the answer.

12

The American Eagle

My father worked at the post office full time for a quarter of a century, and later, in my teenage years, my mother worked there as a casual. Proud to be on the inside of the mail system, my father wore his postal jacket at home as well as to his job. He was employed, as he liked to remind us and anyone else who would listen, "by the government." The jacket was blue and boasted a patch bearing the American bald eagle exactly where a hand would be placed for the Pledge of Allegiance. If it wasn't for the gold letters "United States Postal Service" above nine gold stars that curved beneath talons clutching the words "U.S. Mail," somebody could have thought my father worked for the zoo. This eagle, fierce and unwaveringly severe, jutted his beak in profile as if to say, "I'm better than any other bird."

"The post office animal wasn't always an eagle," I told my father when I learned about mail carriers at school. I was in fourth grade.

"Is that right," he said, not as a question but as three words indicating he didn't care. Impervious to hints of disinterest, I told him what I'd learned from Mr. Lowder, the teacher who'd taught me that Benjamin Franklin was the first postmaster general in 1775. Franklin had decided a horse and rider racing across the newly stolen land of America suited the postal service's mission of delivery and speed. Postmaster General Amos Kendal approved the horse and rider concept but felt he needed to do something because men like to add their mark, so he placed circles around the duo in 1837. Then in 1970 President Nixon, a man remembered for his unwise decisions, changed the em-

blem from a horse and rider to the centerpiece of the nation's Great
Seal, the American bald eagle.

"Who has ever ridden an eagle to deliver mail?" I asked Mr. Lowder.

He smiled down at me from his great straight-backed height, his
rust-colored lips like the skin of an earthworm, and said in a voice
indicating that he was saying what he was supposed to say: "President Nixon chose the American eagle because it symbolizes unlimited freedom and courage."

While he spoke I wondered if Mrs. Lowder got spattered with
spit when he kissed her, and I was so intent on the images of her
ducking and swerving to avoid his angling mouth that I didn't hear
the reasons why the eagle represented freedom and courage. However, it seemed to me back then as well as now that a galloping horse
meant those things too, and President Nixon was foolhardy to
change what made sense in favor of what didn't.

I demonstrated my disagreement when Mr. Lowder gave the
assignment of designing emblems of our own. I drew a black horse,
mane diagonal above the neck, and tail horizontal from the wind
created by its swiftly moving body. The delivery person rode low
like a jockey, in my snorkel jacket with hair that matched my own
blowing around the hood. My horse's pounding feet were hidden
by snow because I couldn't draw hocks and hooves. I added zigzag
lines to indicate speed and attention to detail.

My mother, who wore my father's spare postal jacket around the
yard, hung my picture on the fridge. She wore the thickly lined jackets everywhere except in public. I'd overheard there might be trouble
if she got caught wearing a jacket that indicated she was a government employee when she was really a housewife. As a child, I got all
of my information through eavesdropping, as I grew up in a time
when nontelevision parents didn't include their kids in conversations.
Information was gained through piecing together stolen words, and
stealing of any kind meant trouble.

Trouble baffled me in my attempts to elude it. You could be
nothing but it, and you could have a lot of it, but what it was exactly

seemed to be different every day. You got in it although you did your best to avoid it, and you were always reminded to stay out of it. Trouble loomed ominously, and I'm on the lookout still, playing out my actions and the consequences in my mind before I proceed, like a chess player who loses to anyone who knows the real moves by name.

MY FATHER SAID THE IRS WAS TROUBLE AND WE HAD TO WATCH out for it. I asked my hair-twirling-pretty sister what the IRS was, and she said if I didn't know, I was too stupid to understand even if she told me. All I could surmise was that the IRS had to do with taxes, which had to do with money, which had to do with yelling, but then most everything did at my house.

Living in the country, deep in the woods, money, I was told again and again, might be able to burn a hole in your pocket but could not grow on trees. My mother did not have enough to roll in or any extra to throw down the toilet, even if I acted like she did.

"What class are we then?" I asked, hoping we weren't lower because that sounded like failure.

"We're middle class, of course," she said, placing a cow tongue into the boiling water.

This answer, particularly when I used to wear bread bags on my feet for snow boots, led to much pondering, because my friend Cindy was middle class, and she had a twelve-room house with a pool, her very own horse, and several pairs of boots, including the nonfunctioning fashion kind that my mother insisted were a huge waste of money.

When I asked my father what middle class meant, he said, "The IRS doesn't know how to mind its business."

Class, the IRS, trouble, and money, I realized, were connected, and because my father often said the same thing about the men at the USPS, I assumed that the IRS and the USPS were also related. UPS, the milk chocolate–colored van that rolled into my driveway with parts for the Rototiller, sent my mind on fantastical trips of possibility involving unlimited candy bars that would fill my mouth with sweetness and my body with happiness. Almost like a card from Candy Land illustrating a truck full of chocolate, I didn't think it could have anything to do with either the IRS or the USPS, despite how my mother scoffed that UPS was out to steal business from the USPS and caused more trouble than it was worth.

"Everyone always wants something," my father complained, stomping across the kitchen linoleum to the cellar door, leaving rectangular clumps of dirt behind from boot treads just as Hansel left bread crumbs. "If it's not the IRS or the postmaster, it's Uncle Sam."

I didn't know who Uncle Sam was until I saw a poster of him in Mr. Murphy's class claiming he wanted me. I knew as little about him as I did about the IRS. He looked like just another crazily bearded adult who accused you of crime, yet still expected you to do something for him. He reminded me of the bullshit-artist-ass-Skipper, and for that reason alone I didn't trust him. I didn't know what he wanted from me, but his position behind the teacher's desk, combined with his constant pointing, made me feel like I was in trouble.

My father, when he wasn't speaking of ghosts, often spoke on the power of the mail and the office from which it came. Everyone, in the city or the country, stopped what he or she was doing when the mail arrived. My mother kept time by the mailman, as if he were a traveling sundial. Often she would ask, "Is it that late already?" before ordering one of the kids outside to fetch the envelopes and flyers. I would race to the box expectantly, although I never received anything and was leery of the earwigs who lived in there.

Although my father was an expert on the post office and the mail, he was not a mailman. As a child I knew this from the many times he said how monotonous it would be to drive slowly through the same neighborhood, day after day, stopping every few minutes to stick an arm out the window. He was lucky, it seemed, not to be a mailman. Never hearing what he actually did, I pictured him behind the scenes—sorting, stamping, and bagging packages like one of

Santa's elves. From him I learned it was illegal to touch anyone else's mail. Even a flyer addressed to someone else couldn't be thrown away but had to be put back with "not here" written on the label. There were fines and jail sentences associated with mail tampering—potential trouble dropped into your mailbox.

I learned to blame the mailman for almost everything that went wrong at the end of the driveway. What the mailman didn't do, the snowplow driver did. My father wanted them to come, kept asking where they were, questioned if we'd seen them or heard them as he searched down the road from the kitchen or dining room windows every fifteen minutes for their approach or proof that they might think he wasn't as important as the neighbors. But if the mailman left tire tracks in the yard, got my father's newspaper wet, or gave him someone else's mail, or if the plow operator left snow at the end of the driveway or, worse, left snow right after the kids shoveled or my mother snow blowed, trouble came to all of us in the form of shouting and stomping and orders to get outside immediately and remedy the problem.

There was that one time the plow pushed the mailbox under the weeping willow tree and another time when the mailman didn't put the flag down after removing the outgoing letters. The mailbox empty, none of us knew for sure if we were supposed to receive mail that day or if something mysterious had happened to it. My father taught me, indirectly, that snowplows and mailmen are the harbingers of trouble.

Sometimes, when my mother needed the one family car for errands, I would beg to go inside the post office when she dropped off my father, but no civilians were allowed behind the counter in the presence of mail. Civilians—people like me—had to take exams before they could touch letters and packages. It fascinated me that people had to take tests before they could touch flyers that looked like litter, but they didn't have to know anything to get a hunting license and shoot holes in our chimney.

"Was the test hard?" I asked my father one day as he passed through the kitchen on his way to the cellar.

"I didn't take it, but it can't be too hard," he said, blowing his nose loudly on a hankie before returning it to his back pocket. "Joe Moody is dumb as a post." He wiped at his black hair that he greased with Vaseline and placed his cap firmly on his head. "It's just questions about driving and what have you." He left me sitting at the table with my Nancy Drew mystery, and I concluded that my father must have been very important not to take the test and yet still be trusted in such a high-security building.

It was his importance, I surmised as a child, that gave him the ability to control the time we ate and what we ate. Never considering her own cravings, my mother served him first and asked if he wanted anything else before she allowed any of the kids to eat the last leg, wing, or rib. He got the only rocking chair, the choice of television channels, unquestioned access to the bathroom, whole milk—never did he have to drink the powdered kind—the last slice of bread, special desserts, and the only apples, and he had a personal supply of sardines, Moxie, butterscotch candies, and gum that his kids were forbidden to touch.

He was never told to wait. In fact, my mother told us all firmly: "Do not make your father wait."

My father was special, and I wasn't clear if the reason for his specialness lay in the fact that he worked at the post office and could be a postmaster, if he wanted the job, that he'd fought in the Korean War, or if the reason was that he was strong and extraordinarily loud even when he sneezed. He loved his country and took pride in his ability to fold the American flag into the official triangle, although he couldn't fold what he bellowed was the goddamn map into any shape at all.

I learned by listening to him talk about the Korean War that people of Asian descent were Japs and Chinks. He placed the emphasis on Japs so that spit flew out of his mouth.

My hair-twirling-pretty sister copied how my father said Jap, and she liked to chant a short song that included pinching the outside corners of her eyes to create slits, "Chinese, Japanese, dirty knees, look at these," lifting her shirt in a big finish. My cheeks, through most of my childhood, were significant, possibly a result of my mother pulling and pinching them when I gave her my opinions. When I smiled, my eyes nearly disappeared.

"Get my drift?" she asked against my glare.

"DID YOU KILL A PERSON WHEN YOU WERE IN THE ARMY?" I questioned my father while sitting in the kitchen sorting nails into baby food jars at his request.

"They aren't people like you know people," he said, getting ready to spit. "They'd sooner kill you than look at you. Japs don't have the sense of Tippy."

I was only in elementary school, which meant I'd learned Christopher Columbus discovered America, Vikings were pirates, Indians taught the Pilgrims how to survive and welcomed them to their land, Pocahontas loved a white man, and Andrew Jackson was a hero. I knew I couldn't believe everything I learned at home just as I'd learned people at home didn't believe everything I'd learned at school, specifically when I heard my father say to my mother, "Why in God's name does Helen think we're related to chimpanzees?"

I loved his Army tattoos. One was a large American bald eagle shaded in red, white, and blue. I wanted to draw on my arms too and thought about what animal I'd put there. That night, as I was falling asleep, I realized my father hadn't answered my question. Had he ever killed a person? I decided a cardinal would be perfect for my arm.

I told my friend Michelle Sirois, while comparing stats, that my father had a better job than hers, who drove a school bus.

"But he drives a Blue Bird," she said. "Not a regular bus."

We were playing Four Squares and she bounced the ball back to me. The Blue Bird was a bus I secretly wished I could take to school rather than the small one I did, but it seemed to me that the United States Post Office, with the logo of an eagle, trumped a school bus named after a blue bird.

"Is he a mailman?" she asked.

"No." I spiked the school's rust-colored ball back at her.

"Does he sell stamps?"

"No, but he brings them home in his lunchbox sometimes."

"What else is there to do, then?" She bounced the ball high to an outside corner.

My fingers barely touched the ball's rough underside to send it back to her. "I don't know, but it's more important than driving a bus."

After school I asked my mother.

"Don't you have something better to do than pester me?" she asked, basting the hindquarters of a cow with boiled blood and muscle juice she sucked up from the pan. "Your father does whatever needs to be done."

"What exactly?"

"Why don't you ask him when he gets home?" She closed the oven door with a firm thud, leaving me to wonder why she couldn't just tell me herself.

Working second shift, my father wasn't up before I left for school and was gone before I came home. I saw him only on weekends, and then only at meals or when he walked through the kitchen on his way to the cellar or from the cellar to the outdoors.

One Saturday afternoon I followed him down the unpainted wooden stairs. There were no risers, and I was careful to keep my heels as close to the fronts of the boards as possible to avoid sneaky creatures grabbing my ankles from behind.

"What do you do at the post office?" I didn't look at him but concentrated on centering my bare feet in the middle of the planks over the cold dirt floor. They rocked as I balanced on them, whapping against the hard ground in a way that reminded me of a ruler hitting my bottom. With only a few bulbs hanging between the exposed beams above us, there was no color in the basement. Black reached out at my feet from under the workbenches. Reconsidering the possibilities for attack, I placed one foot on the top of the other to minimize the parts that could be gotten.

My father didn't answer but instead wiped some glue off the corner of the stand he was building. It seemed like he thought that if he ignored me long enough, I'd go away.

"What do you do?" I was an excellent repeater.

Behind me stood handmade wooden workbenches covered with tools as well as hundreds of jars filled with screws, washers, nuts, bolts, and nails of every imaginable size. My father had decorated his work area with old license plates and rusty saws that leaned against grimy canning jars. Traditionally posed American eagles made by my brothers, rested on a shelf. Cobwebs stretched, connecting everything in a community of black and white that reminded me of the Munsters' or the Adams Family's houses.

"Anything that needs to be done," he said as if this was the job description in the USPS handbook, and then he turned the handle of the vice grip to secure his freshly glued corner.

"Like what?"

He blew out his breath, heavy. I could feel the edges of it. The vice's lever squeaked and slid back into place with a metallic clang. "Fixing this and that and what have you."

"What are you called?"

"Maintenance technician," his voice was quick, his eyes on the wood as he searched for white drips along the seam he'd just created. "Go see what Mamma wants. I hear her calling you."

My mother calling was the ploy he always used to get rid of me. As I retraced my careful steps up and out of the cellar, I decided that a maintenance technician must be a person who kept the machines working for the mail to go through. Without a maintenance technician, the mail system would collapse.

LISTENING TO CONVERSATIONS DURING MEALS, MY BRAIN RACED TO understand. The bullshit-artist-ass-Skipper described hunting coons.

"Why would you want to hunt raccoons?" I asked, risking the idiot label and wishing my heart-of-gold brother-in-law was eating dinner with us instead.

"Not raccoons," he said, guffawing at my ignorance, with grease shining on his lips from the sparerib he held in ring-cluttered fingers. "There's nothing wrong with them!" He said "them" like it was a big joke. "Why, honey, they're downright human compared to the coons I'm talking about." He stomped his feet under the table in energetic amusement.

Many of the bullshit-artist-ass-Skipper's stories, like my father's Margaret and Army stories, were told over meals. From my chair I could see the painted ceramic eagle that hung on a red wallpaper, featuring thousands of tiny American eagles. I assumed, because of my failed attempts at drawing horses' legs, that artists drew eagles in profile because it was too hard to draw them front on.

IN APRIL OF 1979 MY PARENTS DECIDED TO TAKE THE WEEK OF school's spring vacation to drive from Maine to Florida. Only the four youngest of the nine filled the station wagon, all girls, eleven to fifteen.

At the ages when it is necessary not to like anything, my sisters alternated between a teenage glower and teenage drama in the backseat. I sat in the way-back with the coolers and totes of clothes, my wrist adorned with the Cat in the Hat watch I'd gotten for my January birthday, the friendly cat's large, white-gloved fingers pointing out the time to me, my 126 camera looped over the other wrist in case I saw anything worthy of photographing.

I'd chosen Stephen King's *The Stand* for the long trip, thinking I'd travel like the characters in the book. My mother disliked Stephen King's books like she disliked Janis Joplin's songs. I didn't understand why it was okay for her to read Harlequin romances about heaving bosoms with rose-tipped nipples or men's swollen members but not okay for me to read about vampires and ghosts in off-season hotels. We could read her romances, but we were bad to consider having passionate romances ourselves. When I asked, she said, "That's enough of that, miss high and mighty."

My parents' voices drifted incoherently back to me until after we left New England, when the volume rose. "Unbelievable," my father said, "Chryslers and Buicks in the front yards of shacks. Houses falling down around their ears, and they spend their money on fancy cars. Damn blackies don't have any sense."

"What do you expect?" my mother's voice floated through the air with that hard edge I had learned signaled harping, "They just hang out on their porches as if they have nothing better to do. I can't understand such laziness."

"Damn coons don't know any better. Maybe they think they can live in their cars when the roofs of their huts cave in."

"What I don't get is how they can afford those cars in the first place," my mother fumed. "And look at those big fancy radios they all have. Something doesn't add up."

I caught the word "coon" in my ears and struggled to recall what the bullshit-artist-ass-Skipper had said about hunting them. Living in Maine, I'd never seen a person who was black. Virginia, I saw immediately from my spot in the way-back, was very different. The idea of hunting people churned through my mind as I looked out the window at the unpainted sagging houses with the large cars parked next to the leaning steps.

WE STOPPED DRIVING EARLIER THAN USUAL ONE DAY SO WE could do laundry. My parents had marked out their trip using AAA and had arrived at the approved KOA campground after only a few wrong turns. My mother knew her daughters would forage for cigarette butts in trashcans the second she left, and not wanting her last chance at a good daughter spoiled by example, took me with her. She left my father to explore the campground. "Wanderlust" she called his desire to roam, to travel, as if it were a disease she'd diagnosed and didn't share.

For several days my mother had been in a perpetual fury at my tough-yet-admirable sister, who refused to wear shoes even at the Arlington National Cemetery. After a security official in full uniform, his back straight, shoulders square even in the heat, had asked this sister to leave, she'd stolen flowers from a grave, and my mother had erupted like a can of frozen soda. I'd stood and watched the armed sentinel walk back and forth in an official pattern of clicks and salutes in front of the Unknown Soldier's resting place and concluded that weeding the garden would be preferable to mandatory pacing in hundred-degree temperatures with high humidity. I wondered if he itched.

I felt the remnants of my mother's rage at my tough-yet-admirable sister as we walked up the street searching for a laundromat, breathing the damp oxygen into our overworked Maine lungs. Her anger gnawed at the edge of my consciousness, and I didn't dare tell her I needed to pee.

We entered the first laundromat we came to, eager to stop walking in temperatures that were strange to us after the snow and mud left behind four days earlier. My mother opened the door and held it for me to enter. I stepped into abrupt stillness. Along the rows of washers and dryers, my focus slid from women who sat on washers to women who lounged against walls beside dryers or who folded laundry. Black faces, one after another, black, black, black—no white face as far into the room as I could see. Skin so black I felt ghostly and insubstantial. Standing there inside the door, I felt as if we'd interrupted a private party and were wearing all the wrong clothes, saying all the wrong things. It was as if life had frozen, like when Samantha Stephens paused time in order to solve witchly problems on *Bewitched*.

I felt a pull to move forward into this group of strangers, perhaps to mix in, and to inquire if there was a restroom. The world's sounds hushed for this staring contest, and I thought for a second how maybe this was a game like Quaker's Meeting that I sometimes played with my farm-girl friend, Julie, on the half-day Wednesday bus ride home. Then I realized they stared not at me but at my mother, who was just as silent, just as still. There must have been laughter and conversation before we opened the door.

I took a step forward, uncertain but needing to set down the laundry bag, heavy with *The Stand*, pressed against my abdomen.

My mother saw me begin to move and jerked me around so fast that I stumbled back through the door, down the one step, and outside to the sidewalk. She pulled me away, my feet frantic to catch up even as my head turned to see the door close slowly between all those black faces and me.

Sound returned. I could hear traffic, honks of horns, shouts, and laughter. What were the women in the laundromat saying now?

"It isn't right they hang out in groups like that, making normal people uncomfortable. I'm not going to put up with it, looking at me like they're better," my mother said. She twisted my hand, pinching the skin against my bones in her distress, stopping abruptly to cross at a corner. My Cat in the Hat watch felt suffocatingly tight on my wrist, constricting itself around my skin like the snakes I feared. I seemed to be swelling from humidity and an intense need to pee—and to escape this situation.

Yanking me across the intersection, so fast that my sweaty hand slipped out of hers, the laundry bag damp and heavy in my cramped arm, my mother pounded her sandaled heels into the tar, planting fury with each step.

"One or two of them is fine," she seethed, "but when they're in a group like that, they act all high and mighty. Did you see the way those women looked at me, like I'm the one who shouldn't be there?"

"Maybe they were just surprised," I dared, because I had been. "Maybe if we'd been friendly . . . "

"Don't start with me," my mother turned suddenly to glare at me. "You are getting way too big for your britches. You just better watch it if you know what's good for you."

Her anger pulled me in a rush until we reached a second laundromat that held white faces behind the plate-glass windows. I could feel my mother's hate and was relieved it wasn't aimed at me. I dropped the laundry on the floor beside her and raced to the restroom in the back. When I returned, breathless and relieved, I sat in a plastic chair, my thighs sticking tight to the seat, and I read from my library book. But my mind kept wandering back to the laundromat with the black women even as another part of my mind was pulled along by a different black female, Mother Abigail, a 108-year-old woman immune to the plague of the super flu. She is patient and kind and magical. After my trip to the laundromat, I was confused as to why she wanted to help so many white people. I worried she didn't know what she was getting herself into, and I feared for her well-being and her life.

THE BLACK WOMEN SENT MY MIND TO THE IDEA OF SLAVERY. I understood these women weren't slaves, but their great-grandparents or grandparents might have been. What must that feel like? Being the youngest of nine, I knew what it felt like to have people look at you like you were less than human, but what if everyone did that to you, every day? What if people did that, and you knew that your mother or father had been actual property?

I'd just learned about slavery in my sixth-grade history lesson. Mr. Hackett's explanation of Jim Crow laws included an experiment based on eye color: brown-eyed students were black, and blue-eyed students were white. All white faces stared up at him expectantly that day without understanding. When he got to me he said, "Brown eyes," and handed me a sheet of paper. "Go sit in the back."

I always sat in the front because I couldn't hear out of my chronically infected ear, and not wanting glasses, I hid the fact I couldn't see well. Fearing trouble, I didn't argue but instead sat in the seat he pointed to and studied the paper. Heat swept over my body, making my scalp tingle. "Brown eyes mean you're full of shit," my blue-eyed blustery-and-favored brother liked to say when my mother wasn't in listening range. I read the rules:

You will sit in the back of the room and not raise your hand.
You will not go to lunch until the blue-eyed students exit.
You will not be allowed in the hallway with the blue-eyed
    students.
You will not speak to the teacher unless spoken to.

You will not exit the classroom to get on the bus until the
blue-eyed students exit.

You will not touch or speak to blue-eyed students unless they
speak to you first.

You will not, you will not, you will not. This couldn't
mean me. For clarification, I walked up to Mr. Hackett's desk and
showed him the paper, pointing at the restrictions. My friendly
teacher, the one I could count on for praise and special privileges,
wouldn't look me in the eye. I desperately wanted him to because I
needed to see the color of his eyes. Why had I never noticed?

Staring down at his desk, he said, "Go to your seat."

"But it says when the bell rings I can't go to lunch." Hunger ate
at my insides.

"Your place," he said, in a tone that cut me with its unanticipated
edge, "is in the back of the room with the others, and I don't want
to see or hear you again unless I speak to you. Understood?"

I looked at Mr. Hackett's balding head and the arm of his black
glasses that hugged gray sideburns. Everything about him suddenly
seemed abhorrent. How did one person have the power to change
my world like this? I turned and gazed at the brown-eyed others
who seemed just as confused as I was.

I said nothing, although my muscles tensed and the words filled
my mouth. I did as I was told because the words of this new Mr. Hackett scared me, and the dread of trouble sat heavy in my mind.

When I entered the history classroom the next day, head down,
afraid to touch anything, uncertain, Mr. Hackett announced that
all the brown-eyed kids of yesterday would be blue-eyed kids today,
and all the blue-eyed kids would be brown-eyed. The emotional
weariness that had been mine for twenty-four hours evaporated. I
was so relieved to be considered normal again that I didn't think
how the new un-normal kids must feel. I didn't look back at them
when I rushed out of the classroom to lunch. I might have brown
eyes for real, but I was free.

THE NEXT MORNING WE STOPPED AT A MCDONALD'S TO USE the restrooms and get my father coffee and a cinnamon sweet roll. The last few hours I'd ridden in the way-back on the lookout for snakes, lizards, and gators that my tough-yet-admirable sister said lived in the tall grass alongside the road. I tried to spot reptilian movement from within the car, my feet curled safely under my bottom, my hands beneath *The Stand*, which was open in my lap.

All morning the conversation had bounced in small snippets from arguments about which route we were on, which route we should be on, and the Negro problem. Hundreds of miles devoted to complaining about people they had never met and knew nothing about. My mother repeated through the hours how several black women had blocked her from a place of business she had more right to be at than they.

"Who do they think they are?" she'd said as she'd slammed her small cooking pots on the camper stove and banged spoons and plates onto the foldout table between the cushioned benches when we'd returned with our clean clothes. "There's no reason why there should be a whole laundromat full of them. It's not right, thinking they're better than me. It wouldn't have happened if they hadn't been in a group. They wouldn't have dared. There's just no need of it."

Finally, desiring quiet while he drank his coffee, my father said, "Will you just stop harping, honey? It's over now. The laundry's clean, for Christ's sake."

I WAITED IN THE MCDONALD'S HALLWAY FOR MY MOTHER TO finish buying coffee, and a man asked me to move so that he could get his mop bucket past. As I stepped aside and looked up into his black face, I noticed his gold tooth and wondered how the dentist had gotten it to stick in his mouth. I read his name tag. Below his name was the title "maintenance technician." He smiled at me, his tooth dazzling, then dipped his mop and slapped it along the tiles, his back bent, his hands rhythmic.

My stomach, minutes earlier fantasizing about unobtainable fries and apple pastries, felt as if the peanut butter sandwich I'd eaten for lunch wanted to experience the ride in reverse. Years of picturing my father handling packages and running letters through postal meters morphed into a slideshow of my father sweeping and mopping floors and emptying trashcans. "Whatever needs to be done," he'd said. My father was suddenly someone else.

My mother motioned she was finished, and I ran out to the car, crawling into my spot between the coolers away from the others and rehearsed silently the question that begged to be asked. I wanted to hear my father say he was a janitor and ask again what he did: Did he repair postal meters? Did he raise and lower the flag? Did he paint mailboxes? Was he the savior of the conveyor belt if it ground to a halt? He couldn't only mop and cleanup. But the tension inside the Ford station wagon didn't allow room for my voice. My mother had gotten the wrong sugar packets for my father's coffee. They were both angry at my tough-yet-admirable sister, who had embarrassed them by walking into McDonald's barefoot, while my two other sisters, the pretty one and the sad one, wouldn't stop arguing about who had more room for their feet.

"How hard is it to pick up two white packets of sugar?" my father yelled, pulling out into traffic and then braking aggressively to avoid cars that wouldn't let him in. "The fake sugar is pink, for Christ's sake!"

My mother began to cry. "There were Negroes all over the place." She slumped in her seat, her shoulders shaking. "It's not right."

I couldn't see from my place in the back, but I knew her hands clutched a map, ready to solve any directional question. I realized in a whoosh of understanding, seeing my mother's neatly brushed brown curls sink lower than the top of the seat, that she must have been afraid to step among the black customers to get the correct sugar. Her dedication to my father's demands was unparalleled.

"If you wanted it so badly, why didn't you get it yourself?" my tough-yet-admirable sister said with a sneer. She was so brave.

"Um va," my hair-twirling-pretty sister gasped.

My mother turned rapid-fire. "Don't you dare speak to your father in that tone of voice! You're an embarrassment to the family—stealing flowers from graves, going barefoot all the time. I can't take you anywhere."

"You wouldn't have to worry about it if I'd stayed home like I wanted."

"Those soldiers fought for our country," my father said. "They deserve respect. I could be buried there."

"Some honor," my sister smirked. "You never even left New Jersey."

The tattoos, the shrapnel scar, the Army stories ran together in my mind with images of my father stuffing mailbags. Questions accumulated like trouble. I sat in the way-back of the station wagon, separated from my family by coolers and the partition of the backseat. Thoughts of the USPS, IRS, black people, bread bags for boots, and class tangled themselves in my mind as I found my place in *The Stand*, closing myself off from the audible confusion inside the car and the silent confusion inside my mind. I opened the book, comforted by its feel and weight, and returned to the Trashcan man and a giant glowing hand, a hand I suspected and, as I read on, concluded must be the hand of God.

MR. LOWDER, MY FOURTH-GRADE TEACHER, HAD TOLD THE CLASS that Benjamin Franklin had suggested other animals over the bald eagle for the nation's Great Seal, such as the wild turkey, which is brave and industrious. In 1775 Franklin published a letter in a magazine recommending the rattlesnake as an animal better suited to illustrate "the temper and conduct of America." I wondered if Nixon would have changed the USPS emblem from a horse and rider to a proud reptile in profile. The eagle, Franklin argued, was really a coward and a thief, heroic only in how it stole so successfully from those who did their best to survive.

I'd wondered why Nixon and Congress had decided that a speeding horse and rider wasn't an adequate emblem to illustrate mailmen. I'd also been confused as to why they'd chosen a severe-powerful bird with a striking white head who stole from others to symbolize the United States Postal Service instead of the good-natured, hard-working black-capped chickadee. Logic propelled my mind to conclude in a rush of clarity how my parents had called President Nixon a crook on that long-ago trip to my aunt's camp, how my father spoke of the IRS as if they were thieves, how Uncle Sam threatened with his pointer finger that he would take us if he had the chance. Then I remembered a conversation I'd had with Mr. Lowder one November day while we waited after school for my bus to be announced. Often I was left alone with teachers because my bus was the first to arrive in the morning but the last to arrive in the afternoon. I saw this one-on-one as open season on questions. I'd asked how Columbus could discover a land that was already home to so many. He'd studied me, seeming to gather his words carefully, before answering in a tone that hadn't matched his kind expression. "Columbus didn't discover land or a new world. He claimed land because he didn't consider the natives who were here part of the human race. In his opinion the land was unsettled and his to discover."

I wondered why Mr. Lowder hadn't explained it that way in class, but before I could ask further, the secretary's voice crackled over the intercom, breaking into our conversation, and I'd had to gather my books to board the bus. What was it about Columbus that had made him think he was better than the natives, so much better that he could just take their homeland openly as if that was how it was meant to be? It would be years before I understood that Mr. Lowder, whose skin was a light tan, whose lips were wide and full, and whose hair was black and tight to his head, might have been trying to tell me that Columbus hadn't actually discovered anything but had stolen everything. Columbus had begun a new world on the same premise as Congress who had chosen the eagle for the nation's Great Seal, that it is not what you act like but what you look like that is important.

13

What the Chimpanzee Taught Me

ONE LATE DECEMBER MY FATHER BOUGHT A CHIMPANZEE calendar instead of the usual Maine landscapes of stonewalls and fall woods. Instantly I knew this animal could offer something dogs, horses, goats, lambs, and rabbits couldn't. My father, he must have felt the same way about these intelligent and funny primates, because as far as I knew he'd never eaten a chimp.

The calendar's glossy pages informed me that chimpanzees ate candy bars, wore denim overalls, cute hats, and played checkers. My father hung the calendar on the cellar door, the entrance to his private room within the jungle that was our home. Opening the cellar door, he might chuckle and shake his head, and my mother might say, "Daddy sure gets a kick out of those chimps," and I would wonder if my father liked apes because the sight of them smoking pipes and cigars made him feel relief, "Well, if even chimps do it . . . "

When other little girls fed their dolls pretend bottles of milk, I had offered my vinyl Baby Tender Love bits of banana.

At birthdays I asked my mother: "Can I have a chimp?"

"I don't want one of those filthy monkeys in my house."

Year after year she said this, as if I'd pulled her string.

I would push the outdated calendar in her face, over the teacup and Harlequin romance she held close as she sat at the kitchen table: "They're very clean actually. Look at this one in a tub of bubbles scrubbing his chest," I'd persist.

"I said no," my mother repeated firmly, shoving the intrusive calendar away. "Now behave yourself and stop pestering me."

I asked my father.

"Sure," he said, swigging Maalox from the bottle he kept in the high cupboard by the sink. "If you can find one, you can have it." Heartburn was my father's constant complaint, indigestion my mother's, the consequence of eating pets, I would think.

There were times my father wouldn't let me pass in the kitchen, chuckling as he sidestepped left then right, pretending he didn't know which way I was going. He'd grin and push out his dentures with his teeth, making faces. After supper he'd cover my small hand with his wide calloused one, the black hair curling over his knuckles, and not let me go. He laughed in bursts at his own jokes and stomped his feet when he sneezed. He paced the house in circles, looking for his hat, which he kept on the fridge. He teased us with a telling, mischievous smile.

He rarely sat down. "I've got too much work to do," he said, "plus I've got crazy legs."

"Like a cricket," my mother complained. "He kicks me all night. I'm lucky I'm not one big bruise."

"Does he sleep through his crazy legs?" I asked, hoping they weren't genetic.

"Oh, he can sleep through anything. It's me who's the light sleeper."

My father was always on the move, but there were moments he'd stop and watch *Bewitched* with me and my hair-twirling-pretty sister before wandering off to hammer or paint something.

"What'd Darrin do now?" my father asked when Endora turned her son-in-law into a pony. "Cussed witches."

MY FANTASY CHIMP WAS MALE. IN MY IMAGINATION EVERYTHING would work smoothly until I considered food. With so many people living in our house, we were always running out of milk, cereal, bread, and fruit. My father got paid only twice a month, so the last four days of every two-week interval we were down to end-slices and Carnation powdered milk. We learned from experience that it was best to leave my mother half a banana for her breakfast cereal. I didn't know if my chimp would respect this rule, and I cringed to think of the consequences. When our animals began to out-eat their value, they weren't worth keeping any longer, and animals left our house on the hill only one way.

I envisioned playing on the swing set, hanging from the monkey bars, and going for walks through the long grass that rose to my hips with my chimp's warm leathery hand in mine. I fantasized about him sleeping with me so that I wouldn't be afraid of Margaret, Mr. Cootsy, bedbugs, or the bogeyman.

"If I had a chimp, I wouldn't complain about not getting what I want anymore, and I wouldn't bug you to do things with me," I tried to barter with my mother as she licked her thumb and turned pages in a magazine.

"You don't need a chimp for company. A dog would do just fine."

My heartbeat quickened. I'd been begging for a dog of my own for months, leaving notes and pictures on my father's pillow and in his lunchbox. In another year she'd cave and get me one for Christmas. "You mean I can have a dog?"

"Of course you can't have a dog. We already have one." She didn't look at me but at her fingers.

"Can Tippy sleep in my room then?" I jumped up and down in anticipation.

"Tippy can't sleep upstairs. She'd keep me awake all night with her jangly tags."

"I could remove her collar before I went to sleep," I argued.

"Helen, you'd wear the patience of a saint thin, I swear."

STARING INTO THE TWINKLING EYES OF THE YOUTHFUL PINUP chimps over the years, it didn't bother my spiritual side at all when, in sixth-grade science, I learned that humans had descended from apes. What did bother me was that no one in my family had told me, which made me suspect they might not know. The first person I wanted to tell was the brother who thought he knew everything about the first man and woman.

Home from Christian college, he liked to lecture all of us girls, including my mother, on the Bible story of man's beginnings when it looked like we'd forgotten our secondary status to men like himself. My mother referred to him as thinking he was holier than thou.

"You shouldn't be reading that trash. I'm going to speak to Mamma about your choice of books," he said to me when he saw me reading in the living room one afternoon.

I held a Stephen King book in my hand, proof of my penchant for evil and contrariness. "I'll read what I want."

"It's not good for you."

"I'll be bad then," I said as if I didn't worry about being bad every day of my life.

Then he gave a speech which began with words and phrases like "millenium" and "Our Lord, Jesus Christ" and ended with "temptation" and "weakness."

"Not too weak," I said, letting my smart mouth say what it would as I put my bookmark in *Carrie*. "Eve dared to talk to a snake and eat an apple." I took an odd pleasure in arguing with this brother who felt he could tell me what to do and what to read, who seemed to think he had creation and death figured out.

"It takes more strength to withstand temptation."

"Adam let Eve take the blame for what he did, and that's the weakest. Adam's a baby."

I believed the creation story showed both God and Adam in a poor light. Taking the apple was Eve's first and only mistake in a brand-new world. She'd been tricked by a talking snake. As I saw it, the real fault here belonged to God, who hadn't warned Eve about a serpent in the garden. The Bible story was full of holes, whereas evolution was airtight.

"You're too young to understand."

"What kind of paradise even has a dangerous talking snake?" I shot back, annoyed that he, like everyone else, used my age against me. "Plus, we descended from apes!"

"You don't know what you're talking about," my brother's voice rose. Then he walked into the kitchen to complain to my mother that I was turning out bad.

I heard her say, exasperated but not yet pushed to her wit's end, "You can't tell Helen anything."

I was disappointed that she didn't seem as excited about our ape heritage as I was and that a discussion on evolution versus creationism was not forthcoming.

"So tell me this," I shouted from the green vinyl rocking chair in the living room, remembering last spring's trip to Florida. "If we didn't evolve, then how come there are so many differently colored people in the world? Were Adam and Eve black?"

"Adam and Eve were white," my brother replied, and I could hear he was disgusted with me. "They were made in God's image."

"If they were white," I argued, always on the search for loopholes, "how did the other races get here?"

He repeated things like "Adam and Eve are made in God's image" with a bunch of words I really didn't understand in the middle, and he ended with the importance of accepting Jesus as a savior and the promise that the faithful shall be rewarded.

Rewarded with what? I thought. A heaven without animals? That was as senseless as a paradise that had snakes. I went to the library and checked out Charles Darwin's *The Descent of Man*, searching for proof that my schoolteachers were right and the Baptists were wrong. Darwin writes, "Monkeys are born in almost as helpless a condition as our own infants." I'd already noticed, over the years, the incredible neediness of my nieces and nephews. They couldn't even pour their own juice or get a cup from the cupboard without whining for help. And we were, without a doubt, an extremely hairy family.

THE NEXT SPRING WE WENT A SECOND TIME TO VISIT MY GRAND-parents in Florida. I was twelve, and like the year before, I begged to stop at all the zoos and animal parks along the way. Each billboard of gorillas and baboons promised an introduction into the great ape jungle, but lack of money prevented us from going anywhere that had admittance fees. Smithsonian's National Zoo in Washington, DC, was free, however, and my mother said we could stop there because she wanted to see the new panda bear exhibit. I was so excited and so happy I could barely sit still, this time in the backseat with my hair-twirling-pretty sister and sad-tittering sister. By Maryland I sat and read with intensity, attempting to bury my mind in King's *The Shining* so I wouldn't hear my mother sobbing and my father cursing God, Jesus, and sons of bitches who wouldn't let him into the correct lane.

But even reading about Danny's fear of the woman in room 217's bathtub couldn't shut out the chaos in the car. Again and again we circled the Baltimore rotary, sometimes with but more often against traffic, amidst screams and blaring truck horns. The first time my mother shouted, "Watch out!" we all ducked, the semi blowing past us in a tumult of honks and wind. I don't know why we chose ducking as a form of protection, but by the fifth and sixth rotations—consistently passing the correct exit despite my mother screaming, "Get off here!" and my father screaming, "Where?!" we stopped ducking. Instead, we held on to anything solid, knuckles white, praying to whatever deity, saint, or hairy ancestor who we had faith would get us out alive.

Once we arrived at the Smithsonian Zoo, my legs and stomach shaky, the words from the *The Shining* that played through my consciousness were not "Redrum, Redrum" like I heard kids chant at school but the black hotel chef saying to Danny: "If there is trouble . . . you give a shout." At this point I'd read enough King books to fear trouble for black characters.

I tugged at my mother's hand. Her eyes were red and her face was pale. "Please, can we go see the chimps and the gorillas? Please?"

And that's how it happened that hundreds of miles away from my collection of calendars I saw my first member of the great ape family in the flesh. I raced to the primate exhibit, my heart beating staccato in anticipation. I pressed my face to the fence, barely breathing, and saw a whole group of black furry human-like bodies. None were like the frolicking, accomplished pinup chimps in my calendars. These sat on the ground, shoulders hunched, staring off into the distance, looking like they needed some books, pipes, and a few tricycles.

"There they are," my mother announced, in a voice hoarse from shouting, "get off here" so many times. "Now are you happy? Is this what you wanted to see so badly?"

I knew from her tone that this was another of those times when the sentences were spoken as questions but were really judgments on my character.

My father made faces, threw pieces of denture-friendly gum between the bars, and gestured with his muscular arms to get the apes' attention. To my astonishment, a large male—his genitals visible between his spread legs—turned and looked at my father, seeming to study him. He ignored the Freedent and stared hard at my father, as if peering into his soul. Then he squatted. Grunting, he stuck his hand beneath his butt and wiped what he found there up and down the bars of the cage.

Mouth open, not breathing, I stared. This was not at all what I'd expected. The chimp slowly licked his fingers.

"Well, there's no need of that," my father said.

"Disgusting things," my mother snapped, her brow wrinkling in disapproval, her mouth thinly horizontal as if she were about to take a broom to the ape.

The chimpanzee looked straight at me and rolled his lips back, showing his teeth in a huge grin. Realizing my mouth was still open, I closed it, my lips feeling dry as they connected. My parents turned and walked away, but I couldn't stop staring into the chimp's brown intelligent eyes. I heard my mother gloat in triumph to my father, her voice floating to me: "See, I told you they're filthy animals. I don't know why they're allowed to do that in front of people."

I stared at the male primate for a few seconds longer, risking my mother's temper. At the zoo entrance she'd said, making me think she didn't know this was my April vacation too, "Stay where I can always see you, or you'll wait in the car."

The chimp held my gaze as if, like our ancestral lines, we shared a joke. Maybe we did if he was thinking, "And I bet you thought I was going to ride a tricycle and blow a party horn." Then he suddenly got up, walked like a short old man who was losing his pants, and sat down to stare at the corner of his cage, again slouched and quiet, reminding me of when I hunkered down to wait out my mother's speeches on my lack of good behavior and lovableness. The ape's thick black fur reminded me of the dog my mother had given me as my Christmas present several years before. The moment of her coming home in the late December afternoon, a small, wiggling, long-haired puppy in her arms is a moment I would treasure as one of the most exciting of my life.

"Here you go," she'd said as I bounded up from the floor where I'd been watching *Star Trek* with my sisters, a show I found scary, bewildering, and comforting all at the same time. I wished, like I wished for the twitch-of-a-nose skill to make things happen, for the ability to disappear from one place and reappear in another.

She pushed the tiny puppy into my arms and said, "Now, don't forget: this is your Christmas present."

I never did.

Daisy was tied at home in the backyard on our trip to Florida. For eight days she would move only six feet if she didn't tangle her chain around the doghouse she shared with earwigs. What did Daisy and this chimpanzee think as they waited for escape? Did they fear their waiting would never end until death? Ever. They couldn't repeat a line of promised relief in their heads like I did when the waiting and discomfort got to be too much. "You will be in bed tonight," was a beacon blinking at the end of each day when nothing more was expected of me. For the chimpanzee and Daisy, the promise of bed meant nothing. What beacon did they have?

I'd been fooled by the calendars, just as I was sometimes fooled by the surface world at home. I'd believed what I'd seen in chimpanzee calendars even though I knew primates were wild animals. I needed to think harder and read even more if I was to understand anything about the world I lived in.

I left the ape exhibit with a new goal that would make me even more annoying to my family. I ran after my mother in the humid heat of Washington, DC, the musty odor of caged apes seeking my nose, eager to research wild chimpanzees. I couldn't help but wonder if my father was as amazed as I was that chimpanzees, staring at us with eyes that left no question of their intelligence and self-awareness, didn't appear to worry about getting into trouble.

14

The Lookout

I WAS THE LOOKOUT, BORN INTO THE JOB. WANTING TO PLEASE, I compensated for my poor hearing with sharp eyes. I was told to wait, watch, and warn. Set on a hill, my house's front windows were a prime vantage point to sight a parent on the dirt road. In those days the view waved and rolled into the distance, distorted by ancient glass panes. My siblings—and, later, I—had a full minute to get rid of boyfriends or to stomp out cigarettes and be in front of the sink doing dishes or sweeping the floor before enemy forces entered the house.

A minute is a long time. Teenage boys can get aroused, ejaculate, and zip their pants in the time it takes a car to navigate a half-mile. Dr. Seuss knew the value of a minute: when Dick and Sally are the lookouts, the Cat in the Hat puts the house in order, even though the clean-up doesn't begin until the children spot their mother on the sidewalk only seconds from the door. When I read those picture books as a child, my muscles would tighten in response to impending trouble. I was scared for Dick and Sally. Waiting in doorways and at windows, I vowed that once my duties to my siblings were fulfilled I would never wait and never again do as I was told.

BY AGE ELEVEN MY LOOKOUT SKILLS WAVERED IN A TUG OF WAR between my need to keep my sisters happy and my need to discover what happened next in whatever book I was reading. Posted in the wicker rocking chair in front of the kitchen window, I waited. The dead-end road in front of our house narrowed into a rocky path that opened about a mile after the cemetery into a large field belonging to the next town over. No cars passed except those of "good-for-nothing yahoos," my mother said, as if some yahoos—those who stayed home—were good for something.

I observed, day after day, year after year, how drinking and smoking can't mean anything but trouble. Sometimes I sat on the sewing room floor looking out the window, pretending I couldn't hear sisters have sex with boyfriends who were the muscled men-like teens I'd seen on the bus, displaying biceps even when it was achingly cold.

My siblings could have sex anywhere just as I could read anywhere. There are no building or comfort requirements for either activity. Both can be done standing. Both can take a person out of the moment and send them off to a private reality. I read *Heidi* on the logging road that had a secret trail leading to an abandoned hunter's shack. Amidst broken glass and torn magazines, there was an old stained mattress on the floor. I wished I could be like Heidi, free to wander with the goats, a stomach comfortably full of cheese and bread, or like the Bobbsey Twins, who had adventures at the seashore. I wanted Flossie's and Freddie's sweetness that charmed adults, and I wanted Nancy Drew's I-can-do-anything attitude and her convertible and her money. I always felt sorry for Bessie, who was described as overweight and often hungry. I wanted their knack for finding secret rooms, hidden passages, and loose floorboards that revealed treasure. I wanted their skill for unraveling mysteries, and I wanted the chocolate bars they ate on breaks from sleuthing. Most of all I wanted their lives because they seemed to be driven by their own desires. Carson Drew, lawyer and widower, never grounded Nancy, called her a piss-pot, or pinched her cheeks.

I sat at a window or stood in a doorway, escaping into the farms of Yorkshire, England, going on calls with James Herriot. My best friend Mindy Parker from school lent me books from her bookshelves. She read as much as I did, and she was the first person I knew who chose to disappear for hours in a world different from her own. When her father was relocated and they moved, I thought I'd lost the only person in my life who was real.

While my sisters did what they did on the stained mattress with men I didn't know, I left my body and went on engrossing adventures with well-fed, well-balanced, well-heeled families and, later, unlucky and often unbalanced Stephen King characters. My sisters tuned a radio to WBLM, where Led Zeppelin, Aerosmith, Black Sabbath, AC/DC, and Queen screamed out their own pain, and I would tune out the music and the laughter as they fell back beneath men or kneeled in front of them.

BEING THE LOOKOUT REQUIRED SKILL. SOMETIMES I SAT AND watched down the road, my book open in my lap so that I could read paragraphs between checking for the enemy car. I was a master of disappearing and appearing from between the pages. I had learned how to reassemble myself magically just as if I were a *Star Trek* character.

Without the library and Mindy, I'd have been stuck with only Harlequin romances to read until the day I caught the attention of an uncle. With his hair greased flat like a *Happy Days'* character, my uncle saw me reading one of my mother's books when we visited his house because there was nothing else. "Don't read those," he said gruffly. "They're not good for you."

He used the "good for me" line, as if he cared about my well-being. But why, I wondered, my teeth grinding tight, did people keep worrying about what I put into my body with my eyes when they tried to put dead animals in the early stages of rot into my mouth?

Then he went to his wall of built-in bookcases and gave me Madeline L'Engle's *A Wrinkle in Time* and C. S. Lewis's *The Lion, the Witch and the Wardrobe*. From that moment I would always connect the two series in my mind.

Even to say normal things like, "Check out these books" or "Want to see the new lambs?" my uncle bellowed in the small space of his house like a giant. My insides contracted in fear and my blood pounded extra warm and loud when he spoke. Afraid of his anger if I bent a page by accident, I thought I should read the books only while I was there, but when it was time to go they were tight in the crook of my arm against my chest.

Before I left, my uncle pulled me back with his large hand on my forearm, his fingernails dirty black from shearing sheep and painting landscapes. I suddenly thought I'd misunderstood his words and was stealing his books. "You don't read any of that Harlequin foolishness," he whisper-shouted into my ear, "and you can take as many novels as you want from my shelves."

Despite the fear, I felt like I might explode from gratitude.

Those were pre–Stephen King years. Once I found *Salem's Lot* at the library, there was no stopping me. Driven by the need to grow up, the library's children's room was now a place I avoided.

ONE FALL NIGHT I WAS READING ABOUT VAMPIRES AS MY FATHER worked second shift at the post office and my mother was learning secretarial skills at a business college. She wanted a job, her first since marrying my father thirty years ago. Her class finished at nine, and I'd been enlisted to begin watching the road for headlights exactly then, even though she took at least fifteen minutes to drive home.

My hair-twirling-pretty sister and sad-tittering sister were upstairs with neighborhood boys, and I sat with my feet curled underneath me in the cushioned wicker chair, with Tippy beside me. Daisy was tied outside by herself because she wasn't allowed into the entry until just before my mother went to bed at eleven. The black window at my back kept me on edge, and I didn't want to turn and look out just in case there was a vampire looking in. The muffled giggles and thumps above AC/DC screaming, "T.N.T. I'm Dynamite," floated down through the ceiling. I wondered how the lead singer could scream so loud and for so long without taking a breath or coughing.

I had never considered vampires a possible threat before, but now that they were alive in *Salem's Lot*, in the state of Maine, threatening Father Callahan and his parishioners, there was suddenly a potential for them to be hanging out in my yard. Our only cross was a

Popsicle-stick creation that my holier-than-thou brother had made and hung by the door for his own reasons.

I was eager to know how Father Callahan protected himself against the vampires. Would the priest's holiness save him from Mr. Barlow and Mr. Straker? I disappeared so deeply into *Salem's Lot* that I didn't hear the car coming up the road.

The repetitive yet rhythmic growl of "Dirty Deeds Done Dirt Cheap" vibrated in my head as the crunch of tires on gravel brought me back to the world inside my house. I looked at the clock and was confused. It was only quarter to nine. I panicked and shouted to my sisters. I knew I was in trouble, and fear settled itself with its familiar heavy grip in my gut, flipping my stomach like a Tilt-a-Whirl at the Fairgrounds. My job—my one responsibility—was to watch for the car.

The male visitors had less than twenty seconds to escape out the back door before my mother came in the front. Naked flesh flopped freely as the boys, clothes in hand, hurtled down the stairs and threw themselves out of the house and into the darkness. Even as they leapt onto the back porch they shouted, "You're so stupid! How hard is it to watch for a car?"

I did feel stupid, yet they were the ones without clothes.

"I'm gonna kill you, you spoiled little brat!" my sister, the hair-twirling-pretty one, her fists probably clenched, yelled halfway down the stairs. "You just wait until we're alone!"

She ran back up to my sad-tittering sister who remained in the bedrooms—turning off the stereo, dumping beer out the window, and making beds. I could hear their frantic feet on the floor above my head. Then my mother opened the first door into the entry, then the second into the kitchen. In a year my teenage boyfriend would liken my house's entrance to a submarine, and I would wonder why I didn't think of the analogy myself.

"What's going on?" my mother asked, instantly furious, forever suspicious.

"Nothing," I said, my voice shaking, the wicker chair beneath me creaking as I shifted my weight and closed my book, holding my place with my index finger. She stood at the counter, Tippy leaning against her legs. Never could I remember her yelling at Tippy. Even when the small dog bit the UPS man's ankle, she didn't get angry at Tippy but at the UPS man for expecting a dog not to bite him when he carried a clipboard, an obvious signal to all dogs that he was up to no good.

"Where are your sisters?" she demanded, placing her schoolbooks and purse on the kitchen table and staring at me as if I were the sole thing in her way of complete understanding.

"Upstairs."

"What are they doing up there?"

"I don't know." I couldn't get my voice to come out solid. If a cartoonist had tried to set it to paper, the lines would be squiggly and broken.

She turned away disgusted, digging her heels into the linoleum as she took off to go upstairs. I remained below, hoping to distance myself from blame.

I heard my hair-twirling-pretty sister say defiantly, "What? I was just going to bed." And I hoped she wasn't thinking about how she would make me pay.

"What went on here tonight?" My mother's voice was hard and thin, as the air carried her restrained fury to me as reliably as if it were her servant. Although my actual eyes saw the wood stove and refrigerator and the archway of the dining room beyond that, in my mind I saw only my mother's hazel eyes narrowed and her day-old hair-sprayed curls flat against her lined forehead.

I knew the real question was, "Were you having sex?" I knew "slut" was only a few sentences away.

"Nothing," my hair-twirling-pretty sister said. Her voice was softer, lower.

"I know you were doing something! What went on?"

"Nothing," my sister repeated, this time belligerently, sounding exactly like my tough-yet-admirable sister.

"What was all that racket when I came in?"

"How should I know?"

"What's that mark on your neck?"

My stomach tightened. I didn't understand why anyone would want a hickey, but I did understand why the receiver should hide them. I'd heard many excuses for hickeys over the years: bug bites; necklace irritation; accidentally rubbed, smacked, or pinched oneself; ran into a doorway, the shovel, the broom, a branch, the locker, the bedpost; mean kid on the bus . . .

"Nothing," my sister said, her voice rising in volume.

My mother knew this brown-eyed, straight-toothed daughter was lying, knew it was a hickey, not an injury. I heard her fury escalate because she'd found nothing. I imagined her teeth clenched, her mouth a line of visible stress. I heard her cross the hallway to my sad-tittering sister who had stayed in her own room, probably wearing a housecoat, possibly in bed. The same words were aimed at her. I couldn't hear the answers but suspected they did not please the questioner because now I could hear her stomp down the upstairs hallway, her feet heavy with parenting, slamming with disappointment and frustration into each carpeted stair as she descended.

"Were there boys here?" she snapped at me when she entered the kitchen.

"I was reading. I don't know what they were doing." I held the book up as evidence. My voice trembled.

She expected me to reveal what she couldn't prove. I struggled to control my voice, my fear. I was getting to be a good liar, but I still wasn't as skilled as my siblings.

"What were they doing?" my mother asked slowly, punching out each word. "Were there boys here? Were they stripping for boys?" She stared directly into my eyes, waiting for me to break. Lately she treated me as if I wasn't shaping up to be the person she expected.

"I was reading down here."

Vampires getting me didn't seem the worst that could happen now. My mother glanced at the book, and I sensed the shift, her new target.

"Why are you still reading that trash? It's a waste and it's going to give you nightmares." She was probably right about the nightmares. "I don't want to see you with this filth again. Do you understand?"

It was smartest to just nod and look down. With restrained aggression, she took the book from between my fingers. Even in fury, she respected library property. I felt a loss, as if the book pulled at my soul when she placed it on top of the refrigerator. I suddenly felt like I was going to cry even though I knew my mother would stop being angry later and give it back.

Defeated, I went into the bathroom and brushed my teeth before disappearing as fast as I could into my bedroom. Crammed with a small bureau, a twin bed, a tiny stand that was overwhelmed with library books because I worried about running out before the next trip to town, this tiny sleeping area held everything I owned except for my dog, who had never even seen the room.

I lay there in the dark, not daring to turn on the lamp to begin another book. Somehow, even though books were inanimate, I felt disloyal to be involved with two simultaneously.

I could just make out the shadowed lines of my Shaun Cassidy poster at the foot of my bed. I listened to my mother clomp outside and circle the house, continuing her search for evidence of my sisters' lies. I admired her daring to be out in the dark alone. It's like she had no idea of all that could get her. Doors slammed, then there was the sound of her rapid feet on the stairs, and I heard her yell at the entrance to my hair-twirling-pretty sister's room. Possibly she had smelled the beer in the grass. To smell was her superpower. I worried that she'd come to my room and demand again I tell her everything.

"I know what you did. Don't you think for a second I don't," she yelled at my hair-twirling-pretty sister, whose door was right beside mine. "You can't be trusted. Just as soon as my back's turned you run around the neighborhood with hooligans like hussies." She paused, and I knew the next complaint would be about her ruined life. "I can't do anything I want," she screamed. None of you care anything about me at all." Then I heard her charge to my sad-tittering sister's door and open it.

I rolled over onto my good ear so that my damaged right ear could no longer hear her tirade. Instead, I heard the beating and whooshing of my heart that rang with guilt, worry, and fear of what tomorrow would bring when my pretty sister got me alone.

My mother would leave in less than an hour to pick up my father. Then there would be silence for thirty minutes. When my father returned with her, he would say something like, "Just simmer down, honey. It's time for bed." And I would marvel, as I always did, how he could, in the face of it all, call her "honey."

On school days we were out of bed at six, seven-thirty on weekends. The bus arrived between 6:30 and 6:45. Bladders full, bowels strained, we had to wait in turn at the bathroom door. There was no getting up at night. No noise of any kind. My brother told me he secretly peed out windows, and my sisters used jars or their tin wastebaskets. I held my urine to the point of dizziness.

That morning fatigue clung to me like a sickness. I put on the clothes at the foot of the bed, the same from the day before, and went downstairs to use the bathroom. The hollow wooden door was closed. I squirmed and bounced on the chair outside, waiting increasingly agonizing minutes. I knocked.

"What?" the sharp-edged reply was my hair-twirling-pretty sister's.

"I need to pee. Are you almost done?"

"No, I'm buuu-ssy," she drawled. I heard her body lean against the door.

My sad-tittering sister arrived. "It's me," she said and opened the door easily, demonstrating whose side she was on. I heard them giggle and whisper.

On television, when a person holds the secrets of another, she is treated with respect so that all remains hidden. Even Samantha Stephens fulfilled blackmailers' wishes just so they wouldn't blab she was a witch. When I didn't think I could wait any longer, my mother, in a voice loaded with leftover anger, ordered my two sisters to eat their breakfast. They threw open the door and kicked at me as they passed, snickering.

I didn't brush my teeth or wash my face, but even with skipped hygiene there was no time to eat anything to settle my stressed stomach. I rushed into the kitchen, asked if I could have my book, which my mother gave me with a shortened version of the trash speech, and I left to walk down the road.

With *Salem's Lot* pressed between my chest and the paper-covered schoolbooks I held in my arms, I hugged the stack to my blue windbreaker, partly to protect myself against the cold but partly to feel the books' solid presence. Wisps of breath floated out of my mouth looking like tiny spirits.

I was anxious to board the bus, where I'd be safe from my sisters. I always sat in the front seat behind the driver. It was a fifteen-minute trip to school in a car, but the bus had to pick up kids on the outskirts of Stephen King land. I slid into my usual seat, disappearing into the Cumberland County of vampires and frightened humans that, in the daylight, seemed so much safer than my own reality.

The bus arrived at my school before I was ready to stick in my scrap paper bookmark, but in comparison the day felt too short because I didn't want to go home. My mother would be gone for thirty minutes to drop off my father at the post office. I would be alone with my sisters. If home, my sad-tittering sister stayed in her room, oblivious to me or my mother's screams about her laziness. In another month she would be pregnant.

I got off the bus and walked slowly up the road. My hair-twirling-pretty sister was already there. By my calculation, my mother had been gone ten minutes. I climbed the steps and went in as quietly as I could, but Tippy was happy to see me and danced around my knees, dribbling urine at my feet. I walked through the kitchen to the hall-way, not stopping to wipe up pee I hoped would disappear on its own. That's when she grabbed me from behind.

"You little pigget. Don't think you can get away!" and she pushed me to the floor, straddling my stomach with her strong, thin legs. Her hands went to my neck, and she shook me. "You were supposed to watch, you retard. You never do anything right. How hard is it to look down the road? I swear to God, if you tell, I'll kill you!"

I felt her spit land on my face, and from somewhere outside of myself I noticed that her eyes, usually so big and brown, were sud-denly small and black. I didn't shout like I usually did. I didn't even struggle. I felt her press on my windpipe and was suddenly too tired to defend myself. Past my hair-twirling-pretty sister, above her head, rows of pictures lined the walls—nieces and nephews, grandparents, all staring straight ahead, as if avoiding what was beneath them.

I'd never seen my sister so angry, so determined to shut me up. The picture of her snarling above my face, her hair wild, is captured in a moving image not unlike the wizarding world pictures in the Harry Potter series. My sister is not frozen in time as in a normal photograph but rather shaking me over and over again. The words "I'm going to kill you" play in a loop.

In about six months from this moment in the hallway I will have to make the decision to tell an adult that this teenage boy who my hair-twirling-pretty sister sneaks into the house hurts her. I will have to risk this sister's wrath to save her from being chased by a person who wants to beat her with a fence post. I will hear her cry and tell this boy to stop hitting her. I will not go to my mother but instead to my holier-than-thou brother with the hope that he can help my sister, that there will be less fallout this way. I will betray my hair-twirling-pretty sister's trust, and she will say again that she hates me and will call me a tattle-tale, but this time she will not try to strangle me. She does nothing.

"RETARD!" SHE SCREAMED, HER SPIT SPRAYING MY FACE, THEN she shoved off me suddenly and left, slamming the back door to go outside and smoke before our mother returned to further harangue her.

I picked up the books that had fallen when she'd pushed me down and raced up the stairs to my bedroom, closing the door firmly behind me. I couldn't lock it against her or anyone because my mother was not going to be barred from entering a room in her own house.

I sat on my bed, tears tightening my throat. *Seven more years*, I thought at Shaun Cassidy, who smiled at me from his place on the wall. He was so cute, so perfect, so happy. Not even one trouble in his world, his clothes store-bought and crisp. My friend Cindy had told me he'd stuffed a roll of quarters in his jeans pocket to look as if he was larger in that area than he really was. I didn't believe her. Shaun wouldn't try to fool people. I had considered the size of his thumbs many times. I imagined his life to be easy and fun and full of laughter because I was certain that anyone who had money was absolved of all hardship. Maybe Shaun would one day wander by accident onto my dead-end road and we'd meet me and he'd fall in love with me. Then my family wouldn't yell and stomp around because they wouldn't want Shaun to know they were loud people. It was a comfort to have Shaun hanging there, looking out for me in my room.

I had failed my hair-twirling-pretty sister, and I vowed to try harder. She was the one sister I knew for sure who loved me, the one who would come in my room and put her arm around my shoulders if I was throwing up and help me to the bathroom. She was the prettiest, but she didn't have it the easiest. Once, not long before, when I walked into the barn and saw my tough-yet-admirable sister crying, I had discovered that tough people don't always have it easy either.

I propped up my one pillow against the headboard, hugged my limp stuffed Snoopy, and picked up *Salem's Lot*, sitting back to learn that Father Callahan was forced to throw away his cross and drink blood from Barlow's neck. He cannot bear what he has become, the life that the vampires have forced upon him.

15

Bus Number Two

LIVING AS WE DID IN RURAL MAINE AT THE END OF A DIRT ROAD, my family was the first to board the school bus each morning, 5 days a week, 180 days a year. Even though I'd had a year of mornings with my mother all to myself, I'd been anxious and excited to leave the house with my siblings, ride off to adventures and friends. My mother had played games–Casper the Ghost or Animal Rummy– with me as she cleaned up after those who'd left for school, but I still felt left out. I resented being the last to do anything when I wanted to be the first to do everything. I wanted to grow up.

The bus stopped for us outside the house that was guarded 365 days a year by the neighbor's German shepherd. The scuffed dirt and flattened grass opposite her driveway indicated the movement of many feet waiting as far away as possible from the snarling lunges of this magnificently neglected dog. Eventually we'd hear the rumble of the bus in the distance and ready ourselves into a line, and Leo, our bus driver of that school year, would open the doors that clunked on their hydraulic mechanism, inviting us in, a cigarette hanging from between his lips.

Trying to avoid what instinct told me was trouble, I slid my bottom across the first green vinyl seat to the bumpy metal wall; rips that weren't covered with industrial tape pulled at my pants with their sharp edges. When I wasn't reading the open book in my lap, in older years Stephen King or James Herriot, I found hidden pictures in the frost patterns on the window: icy trees and fields, the world of a friendly chimpanzee, a small dog, a white pony, and a *Gilligan's Island*–like hut that held a hammock, one trunk of books and another of candy bars, every kind imaginable except ones with coconut or almonds. I never considered what would happen once the chocolate was gone or if the tropical air melted my trunk full of treasure before I could eat it all.

Around me, occasionally cutting into my frosty pretend world, were fights punctuated by mean laughter: "You're such a retard," or "What a faggot," or "You wish, ass-wipe," or "That's my seat, you douche bag, you queer," drawled in tones they might have thought sounded cool but sounded desperate. An assortment of teenage boys threw spitballs, unwanted fruit, and crumpled homework that wasn't theirs to throw. Schoolbooks in paper bag covers doodled with winged Aerosmith logos, Boston's spaceship, jagged Kiss letters, and crude Rolling Stone tongues skidded at angles beneath seats, kicked by steel-toed boots encasing the feet of males who thrived on demonstrating disregard for school property and human emotion. There were high school students sticking feet out to trip elementary school children, laughing when the kids fell, dropped books, or cried. There were people who chose sex partners just for the ride: hands up shirts and down pants, concealing themselves like the smokers who hunkered low behind the seats where the bus driver's large overhead mirror couldn't reflect them.

Sometimes when the noise got too loud or a child wailed for interference, Leo would suddenly pull over to the side of the road in a hiss of brakes and popping gravel, put out his cigarette, and stomp down the ridged metal aisle. That slow placement of his feet, with his large hands resting on the tops of the seats as he passed, silenced the bus to quiet snickers. Leo, although he looked to be in his fifties, was strong. He'd wrap his thick hand in the collar of a jean jacket or T-shirt and say, "I'll boot your sorry ass off this bus, you punk. Don't think I won't." And I would feel what might have been love for this Batman of buses.

But I wished he would tell the girl who sat beside me to stop picking her nose and eating it. I wished that eating your own body fluids was a crime that could get you removed from the bus and the classroom. Penny always sat with me although I never spoke to her. She wove into the front seat from the ground outside the door like an unloved, unwashed blond rabbit, sitting down without looking at me. Her nostrils were crusty with dried snot, and I'd rest my face against the cold of the window glass to keep from gagging.

I attracted the nose pickers. It wasn't smart of me to keep half of my seat clear, an open invitation for the weakest, neediest children to sit and finger their noses obsessively. I was incapable of piling obstacles on the seat beyond my schoolbooks stacked neatly beside me or sticking out an arm and saying, "I'm saving this spot for a friend." I wished I could. My heart would pound at a quickened tempo at the possibility of defending my space, but I couldn't make myself say the words.

Every day for two hours—sometimes more if the bus skidded off the road or stalled—I sat on the bus as it wound its way through the rural neighborhoods to and from school. Some of the houses were unpainted shacks that lacked stairs to the front door. The people, if there were any, yelled and swatted their children off to school. The houses' roofs sagged in the center, as if the weight of the sky were too much. Untied dogs with small eyes and raised neck ruffs walked in a low stance, legs stiff toward the bus. Tied dogs ran in a fury at the ends of their chains that swiped back and forth over mud or flattened snow, like canine windshield wipers.

Other houses were unfinished, as if many years ago a person had put down his tools to take a break and never returned. Old cars, mattresses, rusted barrels, and piles of tires colored the front yards. I'd lean my head against the window and think of the snakes that must live beneath all that trash but still would envy the parents and their children for never having to mow, garden, or put things away.

Our house was better than all of these houses. We lived on a hill separate from the people my parents called riffraff and lazy bums, the dregs of humanity.

"It's one thing not to have money," my mother would say in judgment on the way to town. "It's another to be dirty."

"They could clean that garbage. You can't tell me they're too poor to get out some soap and water, plant a few flowers and grass. I don't know about some people," my father would say, shaking his head in a mark of disapproval as we passed neighbors who lived in shacks that struggled to remain vertical. "There's no need of living like that."

What is "need"? I'd think.

We had small front porches and a larger back porch, we had multiple flower and vegetable gardens; pastures of sheep; several cows, ducks, and chickens; freshly painted shingles; and a wooden trash receptacle out by the barn. My father got angry if any kid left a jacket, paper, jump ropes, or balls outside. Everything had a place. He spent time each summer day with the fly swatter, killing house flies and hornets on the outside wall of the house. Then he hunted them in the kitchen, swatter or rolled newspaper raised high. Neither parent ever interacted with the neighbors, but they knew who each one was, where each one lived, and how each one lived.

My parents could walk outside and feel pride.

Inside, my father, coming up from working on projects in the cellar, would quickly wash down the cupboards, the woodwork, and the kitchen table. He fought against fingerprints, smudges, and stickiness, exasperated with our inability to keep signs of our presence out of his house and yard. "How hard is it" he would ask repeatedly, "to keep your hands to yourselves?"

That's what all the bus drivers asked too, except for Sheila. Sometimes they didn't ask, but ordered. "Keep your hands to yourselves!" the voice would boom. Everyone's hands would jerk back into their laps, even those that were innocent. But if you kept your hands too much to yourself, no matter how young, you were teased. "Look at him play with himself. What a queer," someone might say to one of the neighborhood boys, or "Enjoying yourself, Lezbo?" if a girl.

THE WINTER OF SIXTH GRADE, AFTER I'D READ HUNDREDS OF books aboard bus number two, George slid into the seat beside me before the nose-picking girl could. He was tall and thin and had brown eyes that reminded me of the mud hole I used to swim in behind a neighbor's house—too deep and too dark to see the bottom. I recognized him as one of the boys my sisters had sneaked into the house. A lookout remembers faces.

"I have something to ask you," he said. His voice wavered, and I noticed how one front tooth overlapped the other. George was sixteen, a high school student.

"What?" I was suspicious. I closed *The Dead Zone*, using my finger as a bookmark, not ready to give up the idea of more reading, a sign to the questioner that I wasn't committing to a conversation. So far in my life that "something to ask you" meant nothing good, usually some kind of work followed by trouble.

George put his arm along the top of the bus seat, his long, narrow fingers brushed my shoulder, and he canted his head at an angle like a curious puppy, adjusting his torso to look me in the eye. Twelve years old, short, with hair that was more dirty than blond, with clothes he'd probably seen before on one of my sisters, I tried to remember if I'd washed my face before or after I ate my buttery English muffin.

The noise of all the other passengers, the rumble of the bus's engine, faded into the background to one sheet of sound. George's voice hitched once as he worked out a bit of phlegm and then began in earnest with a wobble: "I'd like to go out with you. It's nice how you always read. I like how quiet you are."

My family complained that I never stopped talking, that they couldn't hear the television for all my yapping. I wondered if he'd think the same way after a few weeks of knowing me, wondered why he would want to go out with me when I'd seen him with my sad-tittering sister. Plus, he was good friends with my hair-twirling-pretty sister. I knew I wasn't pleasant to be around. I was annoying even to myself.

The fact that he noticed me and asked me this question made my stomach do a little flip of excitement. I pictured his home, a faded ranch-style house sagging beneath the trees, and tried not to feel the superiority I was raised to feel, tried not to think "riffraff," tried not to think I could and should do better. Stacked flower pots, weathered window boxes, and an old wishing well in the front yard indicated that someone knew what was needed to separate from the stigma of poor, lazy, and dirty.

"I've noticed you draw." George pushed at a piece of dark bang that hung near his eye. It obeyed gravity, not him, and slid back. His knuckles were cut, bruised. In another month, sitting on the porch outside my house, he would tell me he fought with a stepfather he hated. He would cry, and I would offer comfort. When I rubbed his back I suddenly felt that his future would always be one of sadness and frustration, as if I were a character in a Stephen King book and could just know things by touch and nearness. I tried to distract George from his evident pain like I'd seen my adult sisters do with their toddlers.

"Want a no-bake chocolate cookie?" If anyone refused sweet food, unless they were actively vomiting, I understood there was nothing I could do for them. I wasn't allowed to use the oven because it cost too much money to heat up just for cookies. Refrigerator food was all I had to offer. In a few more months I would learn boys sought more than just cookies from girls, that cookies were rarely the item they had in mind.

THAT FIRST MORNING, THE DAY I HAD BEEN OUT OF BED FOR only forty-five minutes, George said quietly, carefully, as if waiting for me to reject him, "I draw too. Want to see?"

I nodded with an encouraging smile, exactly the answer, I discovered, boys and men hope to get. The yes came naturally to me. I didn't even have to consider—proof that I wasn't as disagreeable as my mother claimed.

George opened his notebook and hovered it over my lap, not touching me or *The Dead Zone*, which now lacked my finger placeholder, the page number in my memory. Schoolbooks between us on the seat prevented his thighs from touching me; I noticed mine appeared wider than his because his legs were long and there was air beneath his hamstrings and the seat, whereas mine pressed against the vinyl. Sketches of motorcycles and pieces of cars flipped before my eyes. I tried not to judge for the lack of animal drawings.

"Nice," I said, because he looked so hopeful and sad. Sad people like nose pickers always seemed to find me. He wore a T-shirt with a word I didn't recognize printed across the front.

"What's Adidas mean?" I asked, having never owned any clothes or sneakers other than the no-label variety from K-Mart.

He smiled a little. "It stands for 'All Day I Dream About Sex'."

I could feel trouble loom in the distance, threatening to attach itself to me.

"You attract these type of people because you're a good listener," explained my mother, who was also the first to say I never stopped talking. "Same reason dogs always like you." Which didn't make any sense at all that I could figure.

I wondered if one of the reasons George wasn't happy had to do with his brother, Michael. An epileptic who had blond hair, pale skin, and freckles, Michael wasn't as thin or as tall as his brother, and he sometimes fell out of his seat into the aisle and writhed on the floor in a fit that seemed to freeze time. The driver would pull over or stop in the middle of the road at the same time that George would leap out from the crowded bus seats to kneel beside his brother and press a leather strap or a spoon over the tongue in the foaming mouth. The other passengers stood and pushed each other to see the boy on the floor.

I couldn't watch. Seeing the spit spill from Michael's mouth into a puddle that I doubted anyone could clean up thoroughly, seeing his eyes roll without focus, and hearing the guttural unintelligible sounds in the deep silence of the bus made me feel ill, made me want to get away from what I could only understand as raw pain. I couldn't bear to see Michael have a seizure, and I thought George was a hero because he could. But he didn't like people staring.

"Get away!" he shouted, as if protecting his brother from predators. "This is none of your business. Go sit down."

I WONDER NOW IF GEORGE THOUGHT I WAS A BETTER PERSON than I really was simply because I'd not watched his brother's fits. I wasn't exercising maturity or a generosity toward his family. The black hole of reality, the loss of control, repulsed me.

George's empathy for his brother was as foreign as seat belts on bus number two. Something depicted on sitcoms by such hyperbolized characters of goodness as the six kids on the *The Brady Bunch*, not at all like the characters in the *The Dead Zone*, fictional but with the ring of real. Johnny saves lives, but he couldn't do it if he hadn't suffered neurological trauma, abnormal brain function leading to one abnormal day after another, and the reader begins to realize the truth: there is no such thing as normal.

How many times did George tell me he didn't know what to do? Years later I would hear his questioning voice, seeking answers from me as if I were the clairvoyant I longed to be. I would see glimpses of his worried kind face flashing through my brain, but I could never catch and hold any of them because they were all overshadowed by the one of him committing suicide in a field, alone, three weeks after he turned thirty.

I know where he did it, with the woods in the distance, and my mind recreates the incident from what my sister and the newspaper told me. I hope George's death was quick, that he didn't convulse or writhe like his brother in an epileptic seizure, that his eyes saw nothing, and if he made sounds in the deep silence that follows a gunshot, I hope he wasn't able to hear them.

One of the last things he said to me before he got his license and stopped riding the bus was, "You are the first person who's ever listened to me. I mean really listened."

We were outside, and I was sitting on a fence, reading. He put his thin arms around me, bent his body low to bury his face in the hair that rested on my shoulder, and said, "I wish you'd grow up so I could marry you."

I remember thinking that, for once, I was glad I was still young. I would never have been able to marry into his unfathomable distress that seemed to go way beyond a frustration over parents and the need to keep animals safe and eat chocolate. When he looked at me with his eyes full of need and dread I felt my insides hurt in response and knew I couldn't be with this person for long. I was saved from saying no.

I WANTED TO BE OLD ENOUGH TO RIDE THE BUS LIKE MY SIBLINGS. Then I wanted to be old enough to leave home, running away unsuccessfully again and again. But with George there were moments I was grateful to be young, thinking youth could protect me like it forever protects Pebbles and Bam-Bam, animated characters who never grow up.

When George would go home I would strain against time again, urging myself elsewhere, like when I pressed myself against the window of the bus to avoid the nose-picking girl. Now I find myself wanting to go back, to run reverse into the years and tell George not to pull the trigger of the gun he held in his mouth. He told his brother: "You're alright" when he was never all right himself.

I didn't see George again after I graduated. The last time we spoke he had his own world envisioned, and I was part of it. Grief combined with guilt floods my brain for never thinking of him until my sister called to tell me of his death. I struggle to recall if the day George killed himself was rainy and cold or beginning to lose the harshness of spring. I can't remember because, for me, the day passed like any other.

There are moments when I can almost feel the coolness of bus number two's frosted glass window against my temple and the taped vinyl cushion beneath my bottom. I can feel, through shards of memory, my eagerness to ride the bus, as if being on it meant I was on my way to adulthood, and I can sense the musty rural school bus smell of unwashed bodies, flatulence, and dried mucous. If I allow myself to sink into the memories, I imagine that I can feel the weight of George settling into the seat, his arm sliding around my shoulders. I see his face, the bangs falling into his eyes, his wide smile, the one that never quite reaches his eyes. Then regret clouds my mind, and I hear again George's voice saying, "You're the first person to ever really listen to me," and I hope with all the mind strength that nonfiction humans have that I wasn't the last.

16

Dakota

THE SUMMER I WAS TWELVE I MADE PHONE CALLS IN SECRET, with the *Lewiston Daily Sun* spread flat on the kitchen table. I waited until my father was in the barn and my mother was in the distant vegetable garden where she couldn't hear or see if a boy sneaked in the house. My mother had said my sisters were probably out chasing "anything with pants on" before she'd closed the door with a sigh and left. After I finished the lunch dishes I was supposed to help her weed.

I scanned the classifieds quickly, my elbows smudged black, then I held the phone number in my mind, walked to the wall phone in the hallway, and dialed it with my pencil the way I'd seen patriarch Stephen Douglas on *My Three Sons* do on television. My mind urged the dial to go around faster. Always the stress of being caught sat heavy in my mind and muscles. After the rhythmic beats changed to distant rings, I sprinted down the narrow hall where my hair-twirling-pretty sister had once tried to strangle me, to be the farthest away from the garden I could get and still be on the phone. My heart beating scared beneath my ribs, I sat on the carpeted stairs around the corner and stretched the cord so that none of its loops remained, risking a static-filled connection. With no air conditioning anywhere except for my parents' bedroom and with only one fan for the entire house, the air stood stubbornly still and rested clammy against my skin.

Sometimes a woman answered my call and I'd relax. But more often a man picked up, and I would tense at the sound of the deep voice, knowing men had better things to do than talk on the phone. I could hear the impatience edging the rough "Hello," held back as if by tight reins.

I tried to sound older, attempting confidence I didn't own. "I'm calling," I said, "about the horse you have for sale."

I rarely knew the breed. The classifieds cost by the word, and the backyard horse owners of Maine, if the trash in the woods was any indication, reserved their pennies for beer, cigarettes, tires, and ammunition.

The response was usually nothing more than a grunt, forcing me to talk on center stage, trembling in both muscle and voice. I chose the least expensive horses and didn't ask why they were for sale or what kind of rider was required—beginner, intermediate, advanced, English, or western—or even if the horses were healthy, sound, or above kicking and biting. My second question was always the same: "Would you be willing to take payments?" I paid my mother each week for grain to feed my four rabbits, which meant I hadn't seen my fifty-cent allowance in months, but I had a baby-sitting plan that would bring in extra money for a horse. "10 yo gelding $350 or BO" would send my heart pumping blood wildly to my ears.

"What kind of payments?" I would be asked, suspicion wrapped around each syllable.

Then I'd take a big breath to steady my voice and list my future assets quickly before being dismissed. "I could give you seven dollars a month and a down payment of ten, maybe a little more," I answered, although I didn't have the ten.

"My horse is fond of his oats, honey. What money are you going to have left to feed my horse?" one man asked.

"I have grass and water," I said, my voice tottering like a little girl trying on her mother's heels. "I'll have hay."

"Give me a call when you're earning more," then there was the sound of the dial tone, flat and dull, as if all life had been sucked from the line.

After the fourth week of sneaking phone calls, a woman said, "Do you have a pasture?"

"Yes." I held my breath, waiting.

"I don't want to sell my mare, understand? I'm just looking for someone who would like to ride my horse in exchange for putting her up for the winter," she said. "I'm going through a divorce, but I don't want to give up everything. I still want to ride. Where do you live?"

My directions included the breeds of tied dogs in front of houses she'd pass as well as the size of the hills. "It's the dead-end side of the old through-road," I finished.

Silence, then, "I'll bring her over tomorrow morning."

I pressed the receiver tight against my ear thinking I'd heard wrong, that my mind might have wandered off for a minute and that what this woman was bringing over was not a horse. "Can't you ever listen?" my mother had asked many times. "Take the wool out of your ears and pay attention."

My eyes, ears, and mind refused to behave. They couldn't be made to do anything on command. If I sat in church, my attention would go on long, wandering rambles while my body suffered the discomfort of the unforgiving pew. Churchgoers would get up to leave, and I'd have to yank my mind back from wherever I'd been, not fearing hell as I should be but having a good time. When people ordered me to pay attention, I'd start to think about what paying attention meant, and I'd be so absorbed in the idea of paying attention that I'd not hear the person speaking to me. If someone said, "Listen," I'd try as hard as I could, but my thoughts might get lost in how the person's eyes were uneven, and I'd be studying the blinks to see if they were uneven too. Or I might stare at her nose and bet myself that if I tried 100 times I'd draw it perfectly, so not 100 but 101 times, and then I'd be reminded of Dalmation puppies and how I enjoyed shading their spots with my pencil, and possibly I'd own one someday, one with a black patch over an eye; maybe I'd name him Snoopy or maybe a better name would be Woof, and I'd imagine teaching him to bark after the question, "What's your name?" And the person who had told me to listen might finish with, "Got it?" and I'd nod with an "Uh-huh" when I hadn't gotten anything at all.

If I was trying to fall asleep and I'd order, make your mind go blank and concentrate on the black behind your lids, I'd see one evil face after another appear out of the darkness where shooting stars used to be. Each face would snarl at me, and sometimes they would be so real that I wouldn't dare to close my eyes at all.

With a horse in my life all those scary, sometimes rotting faces might turn back into shooting stars.

Sweat settled more deeply in the crook of my elbow and spewed from my palms. My hair-twirling-pretty sister's cotton T-shirt glued itself to my back, and I could feel my scalp tingle beneath the long hair tangles. I'd promised myself a few weeks before that I'd brush my hair a hundred strokes a day like Marcia Brady did, but I'd lost interest somewhere around stroke forty and couldn't make myself try again. Now I shoved my hair impatiently out of the way. All my breath was gone and my knees quivered. My brain still wasn't sure it understood.

"Is that an okay time?" the woman repeated. "Will you be there?"

"Yes," I managed to say, my voice higher and smaller than usual.

She said, "Bye," and I gripped the receiver in both hands, unable to let go.

The mirror that I liked to watch myself in as I talked still hung at the bottom of the stairs, the pile of magazines and ripped picture books still sat in the basket beside the stand beneath that mirror, and the large potted cactus on the stand was there as always, but nothing seemed real. Was it possible that tomorrow I would have a horse to ride, a horse all for me? Then panic flipped through my center. The horse would arrive in the morning, and I hadn't asked yet if I could have one.

I went outside to find my father, who listened to requests as the gatekeeper to my mother. Not looking up from the jumble of Roto-tiller parts on the barn floor around his kneeling knees, he said, "Go ask Mamma."

All afternoon my unstoppable "Pleeeeaaase," harassed my mother like a cloud of Maine's hardiest black flies as we weeded.

"I'll do whatever you want. Just let me have her please, please, please. This will be the last thing I ever ask for." I pleaded, begged, and whined.

"You don't even clean up the dog messes. How are you going to manage a horse?" She too was kneeling, except she was in the dirt of the garden in a row of beans. "Do you have any idea how much work an animal of this size is? How are you going to control her by yourself? Don't you remember Donny?"

Her hair hung in small brown tufts around her face, limp and plastered to her scalp and neck in the humidity. Of course I remembered Donny. That's why I wanted a horse so badly.

My mother knocked dirt off the weeds' roots before throwing them in the wheelbarrow, always careful to preserve each nugget of garden soil. I threw mine in a bucket. My handful of weeds, stretched toward the ground in their eagerness to reroot, dangling with their own yearning as she stared at me. When it didn't look like I was taking the potential heavy burden of work seriously she warned, "There won't be any more sitting around reading books. I can tell you that."

Confident that I could always read at school and on the bus, I insisted with all the strength a twelve-year-old nag can muster: "I can do it. Honest." And I pledged all future babysitter wages for a horse I hadn't yet met, punctuating each new vow with a *please* that stretched as long in sound as it did my mother's patience. "I'll even bring in the wood all winter without you ever having to remind me."

Plea upon plea tumbled out in my desperation to convince her that a horse would benefit more than just me. I forgot how the barn scared me at night. I forgot about the howling coyotes and the death screams of small prey. I forgot how I disliked being cold and wet. I forgot about the black night in and outside the barn. I stood there that bright, overly warm August afternoon and promised and promised, without considering the below-zero dark mornings and evenings by myself before and after school. I didn't see myself pushing a wheelbarrow full of manure, hay, and shavings through the deep snow, wind blowing against me, and I didn't see myself outside, wild animals loose and noisy in the heavy black that was night. All I saw was a slide show of feeding, grooming, leading, and riding events.

"Don't think I have time to go out and clean stalls," my mother's voice rose as she slapped dirt off her gloves. "You don't do what you're supposed to and that horse will go right back where it came from." Even though she pointed her gloved finger at me in warning and pressed her lips into a tight line, anticipating my failure, I realized with a rush of happiness that impacted my chest with a foreign wallop that tomorrow a horse would be mine. I raced from the garden back to the barn to prepare a stall, no longer caring about the stifling air, no longer noticing. Heat thunder rolled softly in the distance.

A WOMAN IN HER LATISH TWENTIES, HAIR UNBRUSHED, LANK with oil, eyes darting here and there as if unable to settle, rode a chestnut Standardbred mare into the yard, trailed by a Doberman. I was raking up messes around the doghouse to prove my earnestness. My parents were somewhere in the midst of their unending work.

The woman jumped down off the horse's back and handed me the reins. A roll of flesh hung above her dirty jeans that struggled to contain her wide hips. "Are you the girl who called me about Dakota?" she said, looking around as if I couldn't possibly be the girl. "Heidi is it?"

I stood barefoot in the short grass, my dirty toes digging into the earth, and the fact she couldn't remember my name made me feel insignificant. "Yes, but my name's Helen," feeling a darkness wash through my brain as I voiced my identity.

"Sorry, you look like a Heidi. I'm Paula."

What does a Heidi look like? I thought. *What does a Helen?*

"You babysit my son once or twice a week and you can keep Dakota through the fall and winter," she explained, her hands resting on her fleshy handles. "I'll come by and ride here and there." Her Doberman raised his leg and peed on the lowest rung of my orange play gym before heading toward Daisy, who was barking in such rapid succession that her spit frothed and all her barks were cut off, unfinished.

"Sultan, get over here," Paula yelled sharply, making me jump. He held his ground and snarled at Daisy. I wondered, even while hoping the noise wouldn't draw my parents from wherever they were to add their own shouts of dominance, why Dobermans always seemed to be named Sultan, Duke, or Baron.

"My little boy is two," the woman spoke loudly above the racket. "His dad and me are split, but he's a good kid and shouldn't give you any trouble."

I questioned silently why she gave me information about her son when I wanted information about her horse.

"I live three miles through the woods that way," she said, turning to point to the old tote road that paralleled our garden near the woodlot. For years I'd thought it was called a toad road because I couldn't hear well and my family didn't have time to enunciate.

"You'll need to get at least a hundred hay bales in. You got room for that?" She eyed the low, oddly shaped barn behind me, her hair clinging to her rough shiny cheeks.

I nodded, unable to find words, even those as primitive as "uh huh." I couldn't stop looking at Dakota's gentle brown eyes, the blaze beneath her forelock. I couldn't stop my hands from caressing her neck. I had no idea how I'd get the hay.

"Grain her if it gets too cold. Fifty pounds of sweet feed should last you a while."

I agreed, not knowing what too cold was.

"Dakota moves pretty fast. Be ready." Then Paula turned and walked the way she'd come without saying bye or even telling me when I'd have to babysit her son. Halfway down the driveway she bellowed words I couldn't understand.

I started in surprise and nervousness, my heart picking up speed. What had I done wrong? Her dog ran by me in a blur of muscle, and I exhaled in relief. Then they were gone.

In the sudden quiet I could hear the whine of the Eagles singing "Hotel California," indicating my parents were anywhere but inside with my two sisters who still lived at home. Not having appeared while the dogs were barking, I assumed they must be deep in the gardens or the woodlot. I took off the damp blanket and western saddle that were too big for me and dropped them with a thump onto the ground before using the play gym ladder as a mounting block and slipping onto Dakota's sweat-ruffed back. I relished the warmth of her fur, the reality of it against my naked legs. I lay across her neck, not to hang on like I had many times with Donny years before, but to hug her. Coarse strands of reddish mane rubbed my cheek and chin. In seconds I loved her with all the power I had to love.

Thin and bony, her spine pressed the seam of my shorts uncomfortably against my crotch. She tore at the grass as if she were angry at it. I pulled on the reins to raise her head, and she trotted a few steps forward then threw her head down to the grass. I struggled to get her head up and squeezed my thighs against her sides tighter, directing her across the yard to the road that continued beyond my house, past the cemetery, past everything that usually sent jolts of get-away energy into my legs. Dakota snorted and settled into a fast walk that kept me searching for balance on the ridge of her spine.

I let the reins hang loose, and she grabbed at the leaves of bushes as we passed, her bit clanking against her teeth. I felt newly alive, as if I heard the sounds of the birds, the tree groans, and the breeze in the trees for the first time. I especially loved the sound of Dakota's hooves on the gravel and her breath blowing through her nose. I felt like an Indian, a girl and her horse alone in the woods, but not really alone. The coyotes, coy dogs, bobcats, deer, moose, and smaller animals were all around me, unseen. There were rumors of bears.

With each hoof step past the low-lying junipers, choke cherry bushes, young maples and pines encroaching on the narrow gravel road, I felt the grip of home loosen. I began to feel something I can describe only as possibility, a release in my chest that made me breathe more deeply and fully.

I rode the three miles—seemingly endless acres of thick woods on each side of me—onto a dirt road into the next town, rocking gently side to side, lost in Dakota's rhythm. That Saturday I traveled the farthest I'd gone, the farthest from home without my family that I'd ever been. This is freedom, I thought, the woods stretching out into the world around me. This is what it must feel like to be free.

I returned to my family's conversations that beat time with the seconds of the day, always ending where they began, nothing ever resolved or forgotten. I thought I would know what insanity truly was if I spent one more minute listening to my mother complain about the daughter-who-holds-grudges longer-than-God who had married a dumb-stupid Frenchman, or another who behaved like a whore, or another who had amounted to nothing, or how neighbors had refused to wave as they passed. Around and around, like the rides on the bus to school, always starting over as if we'd never gotten to where we really needed to be.

THERE WAS A DAY I RODE DAKOTA WHEN I MET A TEENAGE BOY. Walking alone on the dirt road where I entered the next town over, he waved at us to come closer.

"Want to ride with me?" he asked, blocking the sun with his hand as he looked at my face. His brownish-blond hair sparkled in the sunlight. "It'll only take a second for me to saddle my horse. I live over there," he pointed to a crumbling house and barn down the road past a field that hummed with grasshoppers and crickets.

"Sure," I said, although I'd never ridden with anyone. I followed him down the road and across the field and waited while he went into the house to tell his mother. In a few minutes he came out, followed by a heavy older woman in a housedress and stretched moccasins that gaped at each side of her pale, veiny feet. Instantly I recognized the clenched teeth behind the pinched lips, the jerky motions that spoke of barely held rage. The boy—he might have been fourteen—shrank to thinness beside his mother's aggressive bulk. Staring up with a narrow hand suspended like a visor over his forehead to where I sat on Dakota's back, he avoided my eyes easily, the sun an excuse.

"Ma says she has to saddle Betsy herself. Can you wait?"

The woman looked over at me, her short hair tight to her head, her doubting eyes assessing my cut-off jean shorts and old T-shirt, my bare feet, the soles and toes brown with dirt. *What could she tell by looking?* I thought. *Did I look like a bad influence on her son?* I felt myself cave inward. I wanted to hide from her searching eyes, avoid an adult's disappointment.

"I don't have time for this," she said to her son, her mouth biting each word, separating them as if she were speaking to an intellectually challenged child. "I have things to do too, you know. Why do you need to ride with this, this"—she looked around, as if seeking the air for a correct descriptive—"this girl, anyway?"

She stomped out to the unpainted, grayed-out barn, slamming doors, tossing the saddle onto the wooden bleached planks, not seeming to care about the saddle's tree. I can still see the sun on the boy's hair, the light caught in his brown eyes, but after that everything is a dull gray except for Dakota's chestnut coat and the green grass. I remember sliding off my mare's safe back and leading her away from the open barn doors to graze, wishing I hadn't followed this boy, whose name I would never remember.

"Don't just stand there," his mother shouted. "Get the curry comb. Can't you do anything right?"

I moved farther away to where I could hear only the rise and fall of the voice but no words. Why had I agreed to ride with him? What was I doing here in a yard with strangers? I rode to enjoy Dakota's company away from bad tempers and judgment. Why had I felt a pull toward this boy?

At my side Dakota ripped big chunks of grass from the earth, snorting in loud accented bursts as she moved her nose over the square of lawn we stood on, reminding me that she was all I needed.

Finally the boy appeared on his horse. I noticed that he had shoes. His bare legs, although dirty like my feet, were covered in thin, short hairs as if he were sprouting. His mother led him like a baby. Humiliation has no limits. I maneuvered Dakota away to a bowed, weatherworn picnic table, stood on the bench, and slipped my bare leg over her back. Smiling in my direction, the boy rolled his eyes, seeking a shared connection with me to dispel the tension.

"What did you just do?" his mother's voice rose acid and dangerous up the octave.

How many times had I heard those very words spoken in my house?

My insides tightened as if readying for assault. I could see the mother's spit spray out toward her son, hear the rasp left by cigarettes.

"Do you dare mock me in front of this tramp of a girl you found?"

I had known the label was there between us, waiting to exit the woman's mouth and land on me. Before I could prepare my seat, my handmade reins, Dakota spun on her hind legs and took off at a gallop across the field, back toward the old gravel road. Her legs pumped and her hooves pounded. She ran away with me hanging onto her neck just like when I used to hang onto Donny. After my first month with Dakota, I'd stopped using her bridle. I preferred bareback with only a halter and ropes for reins, with no bit in her mouth so she could graze and drink without restriction. Never had she been a runaway like Donny. The boy would think that I too was against him.

My heart thumped in rhythm with Dakota's legs. She didn't break to a trot until we reached the woods divided by the road. Sweaty, her lungs heaving, Dakota blew out dust into the air through dilated nostrils, and I wished suddenly that I too could let go in one great release of breath. I unhooked my arms from her neck and sat up. I let the ropes hang loose, and Dakota's head dropped low like a well-trained western pleasure horse as she walked. Remembering Lady, I hoped she wasn't thinking about rolling.

The boy never caught up with me, and I never went back. I hardly ever cried anymore, having given that up with the dolls I pretended were chimps, but my face was wet. I felt exactly like the tramp the boy's mother saw. What part of my appearance announced me as a bad girl? Did the boy think I had teased him? That I had run away on purpose to further humiliate him? I missed the possibility of his presence even as I craved solitude, even as I felt sorry for him. I missed him because I realized anew that despite living in a large family, if not for Dakota, I was alone. Daisy, desperate to get away from her tied-out existence, would flee from me as soon as I let her loose. Where I wasn't Daisy's pack, I was Dakota's herd.

Although I'd pledged to take care of Dakota, promising everything I had to give, she took care of me. As we retraced the road back, both of us breathing heavier than when we'd started out, I was sorry that the boy didn't get time away on the horse that his mother had furiously saddled. I was certain his mother had turned to him and said triumphantly, "See, I told you she was up to no good."

17

Predators

As FALL APPROACHED AND THE DAYS GREW SHORTER, FEAR AND anxiety preyed on my mind each evening in the dark barn alone. I could hear the coyotes yip, howl, growl, and fight with one another, as if they were right outside the walls. When I told my mother that I was scared, she said I'd known what I was getting myself into when I'd asked for a horse. "Stop reading so many Stephen King books," she suggested, as if that would fix everything. "They're filling your head with nonsense."

But if my head were already filled, stopping the books now wasn't going to do any good. My mother was stressed herself, had her own worries, and I felt sorry for her even as I was sorry for myself. One sister, the hair-twirling-pretty one, was fifteen and skipping school, smoking pot, and sneaking around with boys. Another was sixteen with a baby due in a few weeks, and two of my mother's other daughters were on the edge of divorces. Grandkids lived with us more than they didn't. That she'd allowed me to keep Dakota another year during the chaos of raising the last three of her daughters was miraculous, and I was as grateful as a twelve-year-old going through puberty can be. I earned money to pay for Dakota by babysitting just as I'd promised, but it was never enough. I needed more babies to sit.

In October I got lucky. A hunting buddy of my brother's told me he had a toddler and wondered if I'd be willing to sit for him. It was late afternoon, and he followed me out to the barn, carrying the water buckets I'd prepared for Dakota. Suddenly brave in the dark with this strong man beside me, I led the way across the frozen lawn through the descending opaque black to where Dakota waited expectantly. This man who made me feel brave leaned against the stall door and watched me shovel horse manure into a wheelbarrow. *Don't leave, don't leave, don't leave,* I commanded him silently, remembering to add a please by the third time the triplet chant passed through my brain. He must have heard my silent plea because he stayed, asking questions every so often.

"Do you clean your horse's stall every day at about this time?"

"Does anyone ever help you?"

"So you're out here all alone?"

"Every day," I said to the first, "I wish," to the second, and "Unfortunately," to the third. However, I added, out of loyalty to my mother, "But it was my decision to lease Dakota, and I promised to do all the work."

"I'll help you when I can," he said companionably, and suddenly I felt the great weight of fear and the dread of early evening darkness lift from my mind.

"You'd do that?"

"Sure, no problem," he patted Dakota's chestnut nose and smiled at me. "It must be scary out here for you. Are those coyotes or coy dogs I hear?"

"Both," I squawked, pleased he had caught on so quickly to my problem. As we walked to the manure pile, with him pushing the wheelbarrow, I told him that it wasn't just the wild animals, but the Stephen King books I'd been reading had also given me ideas about what sorts of things waited in the dark. And sometimes it was like Dakota heard something too, and even the dogs wouldn't stay in the barn with me. I decided not to push my luck and tell him about Margaret.

He smiled, not condescendingly as if he thought I was a baby, but as if I was right to be worried, which scared me even more. We returned to the barn, and his brown eyes reflected the light from the bulbs that hung from the low cobwebbed ceiling, his wavy blond hair reminded me of Bo Duke from the new show I watched, *Dukes of Hazzard*. Strands were speckled with pieces of hay from the bale he'd opened. He slung his arm over my shoulders as I closed Dakota's stall for the final time and turned out the lights.

"Nothing will get you while I'm around," he said, and I couldn't believe my good fortune.

H E PICKED ME UP TO BABYSIT AT FIVE ONE SATURDAY AFTER-noon, dressed in jeans and a leather jacket. If my blustery-and-favored brother was the country version of Fonzie, this man was a blond can-do version: the way he dispelled the illusion of monsters waiting in the barn's shadows, the way he distanced the coyotes' voices, the take-charge way he, in a few months, would plow a path to the manure pile, and the way he smiled at me as if what I had to say was interesting made him seem like my hero.

My mother told him to have a good time, and off we went, the truck's tires crunching as he backed down the gravel driveway, the leather of his jacket creaking "I'm cool" with his movements. We arrived at his house after thirty minutes, during which I told him point by point the plot of *The Stand*, spending extra time on de-tailing the devilish Randall Flagg and his opposite, Mother Abigail.

He laughed and said it sounded long but like a book he'd read if he had the time, and then with a quick look in my direction that reminded me of my mother's woeful brown-eyed spaniel, Tippy, said, "I wish I could talk to my wife as easily as I can to you."

He then told me about his overweight, moody wife. Having grown up with five sisters and a burdened mother, I assumed ill tem-per was an innate female characteristic and wasn't sympathetic as much as surprised that he didn't know this himself, being twenty-six. We went into the living room to wait for his wife to come home with his daughter. We sat on his couch, not faded and stiff like the one at my house but upholstered in a soft material with colorful flowers that looked to strangle one another with their tangled stems. He exhorted me to never, no matter how much I wanted to sleep, go to bed angry with a partner. At our house all of us went to bed angry all the time.

"To be honest," he said, continuing his conversation from the truck, "I only stay here because of my daughter. I'm miserable, and some days I think it can't be good for my kid either. Her mother's so moody, always mad about something. It's a real drag."

I'd overheard my brother tell my parents that his friend was rich. I knew angry moody well, but I assumed wealthy people were neither of those things because they could have all the chocolate and dogs and horses they wanted. Nonetheless, I offered sympathy because I really was sorry for him: "That sounds hard." I might have even placed my hand on his leather-jacketed arm, a female soothing instinct surfacing for the occasion.

"I hate it here now," he said.

I studied the room that was cluttered with candles and hanging crucifixes. Where were the books? Whenever I heard people were rich, I pictured them atop heaps of gold coins surrounded by books and animals, like Scrooge McDuck in the Warner Brothers book I colored with my niece.

"I don't love her," he said, lowering his voice as if it were a secret, although where I came from, if you didn't like people, you announced it to everyone. "Not anymore."

I considered saying he might like his wife more if he could get her to vacuum and throw away some of the sparkly candles and plastic flower arrangements. "It's a simple request," my mother would say. "It's not like I'm asking you to move a mountain. Just pick up your room." He needed to talk with my mother about all this, not me.

"I've been happier lately though," he said. "Do you know why?" His breath, thick with a hot smell I couldn't identify, closed in on my face so that I could see the roots of his beard and a small pimple on his lip that was possibly a cold sore. "You get them from fibbing," my mother had told my sisters often enough. For years I'd heard "coal" sore, assuming the raw skin was like a burn. If I'd never gone to school, many of my words would have lacked ending consonants.

My nose struggled to find an opening of clean air, just as my brain struggled to understand what he was saying, what he was doing. I edged away to breathe. I shook my head no.

"I know you're young, but you seem so grownup." He squeezed my shoulders with his fat arm. "I'd like to be your boyfriend."

He likes me? I thought, bewildered, nervous, and curious as to what would come next. *Actually me? Not my hair-twirling-pretty sister?* I didn't want to look at him. His beard and stink were too close. The room was too small, too Jesusy. Then it occurred to me that I had misheard or misunderstood.

"What do you mean?" I asked for clarification.

"I mean I really like you. But I want you to keep what we do just between us until you're older, until I can talk to your parents." He smiled, a sad smile, and pressed his thigh against mine. Surely I would suffocate even as I felt sorry for him, even as I couldn't believe someone liked me. I thought briefly of Shaun Cassidy waiting at home on my bedroom wall. I'd been imagining our accidental meeting a lot lately—me on horseback, him playing a guitar and singing in a field.

My helpful-friend hugged me, and my body fought the contact, muscles tense. *Stop it*, I told my limbs. *You need the money for grain, he stayed in the barn with you and said he would again, he might even buy you chocolate and soda.*

"What do you want me to do?" A strong New England work ethic flowed in the blood that pumped through my veins.

He whispered into my right ear: "I'd like you to stroke me."

Partially deaf from repeated ear infections and my mind wandering through varieties of daily work, again I wasn't sure if I heard correctly and didn't know if I should say, "what?" or "pardon?"

My helpful-friend stood and unzipped his pants. My mind couldn't believe what my eyes saw.

He held his penis out to me as if it were a gift, and worry of breaking my mother's rules settled into my brain beside niggling curiosity and new information. His penis was considerably larger than his thumb, and I suddenly needed to tell my hair-twirling-pretty sister that her theory was wrong.

"Touch it," and he took my fingers and placed them around his swelling skin, moving beneath me like the sheep used to and Tippy did if my hand was near but not patting them.

I knew I was being bad, breaking several rules of where my hands belonged, but this man had saved me from the barn, carried heavy buckets of water, pushed loads of manure, had just told me how sad and miserable he was, which made me sorry for him, and now he'd chosen me to confide in. Me. He didn't think I was too young or a baby, scoffing in disgust that I may have anything of value to offer. He didn't have better things to do, mysterious work things that pulled his attention away from my words. He stood there holding his penis and looking down at me as if I were important, as if I was all he needed in the world to be happy. My mother would be furious if she saw me now, but I was miles away from her eyes and her police-dog-sniffing nose. Snippets of night barn scenes played in my brain. I could almost hear the coyotes howl. I needed my helpful-friend, and now he needed me.

His penis was surprisingly velvety, almost like Dakota's nose. In seconds it proved as unpredictable as the bullshit-artist-ass-Skipper's behavior, and the tiny mole near the top expanded like a spreading stain.

"Squeeze harder and move up and down," my helpful-friend whispered. "You're doing it exactly right. You're doing great."

I wished he wouldn't whisper because I needed to hear the instructions clearly, but I caught the tone of praise and felt a glimmer of pride that someone was pleased with my performance.

He began to groan softly, and his eyes closed, just as his penis and face changed color.

"Keep going," he commanded.

In seconds, it seems, as my adult mind replays this scene, I went from sitting on the couch wondering if the flower design was his idea to holding his penis in my hand and being told to go faster. My twelve-year-old mind wondered why everything I did became a job that I was always ready to quit before the job was actually finished.

"Don't stop. Don't stop."

Without any warning I could detect, his penis squirted into his underpants, stopped, and squirted again as if it couldn't make up its mind. Surprised and slightly distressed because I had no idea from my time spent staring at half-naked men in Sears and Roebuck catalogues that penises did this sort of thing, I jumped back to disassociate myself from trouble. There was the sound of car doors slamming and he hobbled away, a white drip hanging from his thigh.

"Say nothing," he said not unkindly over his shoulder on his way to the bathroom, jeans around the knees.

As if, I thought.

Plump with tired brown hair, his wife entered. A blond two-foot-tall kid hung from her hand. She eyed me as if she knew I'd just touched her husband's private area, similar to how my mother looked when she suspected I was the reason there weren't enough chocolate chips left to make cookies.

"You're the youngest sister? The one with the horse?" she asked abruptly—rather rude, I thought, for just having met me.

"I guess."

"What do you do when he visits?" She hooked her chubby, short thumb toward the bathroom.

"Nothing"—my practiced answer to questions asked in this tone.

"Does he visit with just you or with your parents?"

"I don't know. Both, I guess." Then I pretended an interest in her daughter to distract her, squatting down to eye level. "What do you want to do tonight?" I asked enthusiastically, all the while thinking like I'd done enough and should call an end to the day.

My helpful-friend poked his head into the room, avoiding my eyes. "You ready?" he asked his wife, and then retreated before he found out.

It would be years before I remembered her questions, realized she suspected, and then be furious that she hadn't said anything to my parents. I didn't see him again until he drove me home two hours later.

"Are you hungry? We could stop for a pizza."

Real pizza? I couldn't believe it. I had never had real restaurant pizza. My stomach growled. I'd had plain boiled macaroni for supper hours before. I was tired but suddenly awake, like part of the actual world. I nodded yes. I felt shy and a bit worried. What if I ate too fast or forgot to keep my mouth closed while I chewed? I had never eaten in public before, and I didn't want to embarrass myself by my need to taste.

Lost in my worry, I saw we'd arrived at a nearly empty parking lot. The clock on my helpful-friend's console glowed 10:30. I was never allowed to stay up so late.

"What do you want on it?" he asked after we'd found a booth inside Pizza Hut.

"Just cheese," I smiled nervously at the waitress when she approached the booth. She was not chewing gum and had no order pad, which was confusing. I stared up at her stiff feathered bangs, thinking how much they looked like my hair-twirling-pretty sister's hair and nothing like mine when she said, "Do you know what you want yet?"

Instantly, the nouns dogs, horses, candy, and money tumbled through my mind before I realized she meant for supper. My heart thudded, bringing hot blood to my face at the realization that she was waiting for me to speak, her blue eyes were not unfriendly but not friendly either. I'd seen ordering done on *Happy Days*, but I had never spoken to a waitress or a store employee of any kind. Except for my helpful-friend and my siblings' boyfriends, I'd never spoken to an adult who wasn't either family, the mailman, or a teacher. Even at the doctor's or dentist's office, my mother spoke for me.

"We'll have a large cheese pizza and two large Pepsis," my helpful-friend said, his voice instantly directing the waitress's attention to him.

Relief spread like a warm blanket through my chest, relaxing muscles I hadn't realized were tense. My shirt stuck uncomfortably to my armpits, and my waitress fear was replaced by the fear of stinking.

"I've been thinking about you," he said, leaning over the table slightly, his voice low. "About this afternoon. To be honest, I can't think about anything else. I'll be up tomorrow after work. I'll tell your mother I need you again for babysitting."

My mind hadn't gotten past the Pepsi and pizza. I looked around to see where the waitress might be.

Forty-five minutes later, back in the truck, I wanted to lie down and hug a stomach that felt like it would burst from the pressure of grease and gas, much like the wolf's stomach must have felt after the mother goat filled his stomach with seven stones and sewed him back up. My helpful-friend reached over and placed a ten-dollar bill in my lap, squeezing my thigh gently before returning his wide hand to the steering wheel. I remembered the strippers and vinyl seats that my blustery-and-favored brother had forever connected in my mind and wondered if anything as high as a ten-dollar bill had ever stuck to their skin.

"That's for babysitting."

The ten, I thought, would buy fifty pounds of horse grain. My mind couldn't take it all in. My allowance was a dollar, and that was a recent increase from fifty-cents, and I hadn't seen it since Dakota.

We reached the four corners before the last half-mile up the hill to my house. My helpful-friend didn't turn onto my road but instead parked off to the side so that branches reached out to touch his truck, scraping and squealing in the black that surrounded us. He pulled me over beside him.

"I loved what you did earlier. Want to try it more?"

There was more?

He unzipped his jeans, and I understood his question had been hypothetical, similar to when my mother asked if I wanted to sweep or collect wood. He pushed my head down and told me to open my mouth.

"I think I love you," he said, caressing hair I hoped didn't feel dirty because I was allowed to wash it only once a week and could never remember to brush it. He curled his fingers in the long strands. "Someday I'll marry you," he said as his hand gently pushed my head farther down.

I tried not to think of the steering wheel pressed into my shoulder, the odd brown mole I'd seen earlier, or the last time he'd peed. If I allowed myself to picture these things, to think them through, I would gag and throw up. I had no choice but to disappear inside my head to a special place I reserved for getting yelled at or for sitting in the dentist's chair, a place of existing without feeling. Not once did the word "no" seem a possibility.

BY AGE TWELVE I'D LEARNED BAD WAS SMOKING POT, LETTING boys stick their hands up your shirt or down your pants, sticking your hand down a boy's pants, or sticking your own hand down your own pants. Bad was kissing a boy unless he was your fiancé, touching a boy on even his leg, allowing a boy to touch your leg, accepting chocolate or jewelry from a boy, or visiting a friend of any gender and saying the mother was a good cook. Bad was drinking beer puddles out of the neighbors' bottle collection or trying to smoke cigarette butts ferreted out of trash cans. Bad was stealing food from a store or from the kitchen cupboard or Tampons from the closet or saying "hell," "oh my God," "piss," "suck," "boob," "crap," "fart," or using any word that referred to male and female genitalia or any sensual and sexual act. Bad was taking the last slice of bread, drinking the last bit of milk, snapping gum, coughing, menstruating too often or not menstruating enough, throwing up, burping, passing gas, diarrhea, and peeing voluntarily or involuntarily anywhere other than in the toilet. To miss the toilet was very bad. Bad was getting up during the night or not getting up early enough in the morning. We were the human version of crated puppies. Bad was using more than two inches of water for a bath, sneaking more than one bath a week, or throwing away food your mother made. Bad was lying. The penultimate bad was divorce, the ultimate having a baby before marriage or having a baby with more than one spouse.

"You better not let Mamma catch you doing that" vied only with Mamma catching you doing that.

The youngest of six girls, I knew that necking was trampy and that good girls always kept their clothes on. Letting a guy see or touch your breasts got you smacked with a broom. No parent or older sister had explained sex or puberty to me. Although by twelve I'd heard the words "penis" and "vagina" in school, the actual parts and their functions were as unfamiliar to me as candy bars after school. When the sex education teacher pointed to a medical illustration of a vagina, I didn't believe that all girls had them and was surprised and frightened when, that night, I sat in the tub and discovered I did. It was like having a hole in my stomach. My body flushing with heat in the three inches of tepid water where I bathed and washed my hair, I worried that something would get inside and harm me if I wasn't vigilant. The first fear was soon replaced by the second fear of having touched myself in an area where nothing but a washcloth was meant to go. I worried about the consequences.

When my helpful-friend told me he loved me, followed by, "I'm going to get a divorce," I felt as if I were testing the waters of very bad and slipping dangerously close to worst, the line that separated good from evil. Divorce was scandalous. It would mark the divorcee and divorcer for life as losers, and worse, if they remarried, they might be tempted to have intercourse with yet another partner, and seconds were the sin of excess. From servings to spouses, everyone should be satisfied with just one.

TWO NIGHTS LATER, IN THE WICKER ROCKING CHAIR, MY LOOKOUT spot, I waited. My mother opened the entry door, my father followed behind her.

"I need to tell you something," I rushed before anyone could leave for the cellar or the bathroom. My father went to the fridge, took out a stick of cheddar cheese, and cut off a chunk. My mother collected mugs for tea, careful not to bang the cupboard doors. My father disliked noise that wasn't his own, such as the screaming whine of the table saw and the deeper howl of the chainsaw, both tools that sent waves of black into my mind.

"Well, I haven't got all night," my mother said. "What are you waiting for?"

My stomach trembled in panic as the words about my helpful-friend gathered at the back of my throat. Voice shaking, I blurted, "After I babysat last night our helpful-friend told me he loves me, wants to marry me when I'm eighteen. He's going to get a divorce."

"Poppycock," my father said, which sounded like puppycock.

At the same time my mother said, "Oh, piffle wiffle."

"I don't have time for this bologna," my father muttered and opened the cellar door to descend into privacy. "Tell me when tea's ready," he yelled up.

"Daddy's right," my mother said. "Stop making up stories." She turned away to fill the mugs with water.

I had made up many stories in the past. Once I'd told her there was a tiger in the woods and that's why I'd been twenty minutes late for lunch. The tiger had turned out to be a rusty culvert half buried by leaf and branch debris, but I'd sworn to her it was a tiger. Another time I'd insisted that a school friend had given me a Kit-Kat when actually I'd stolen it from a store. I'd been so consumed with guilt over my theft that I had later gone back and left a handful of pennies and nickels in the rack when my mother wasn't watching. Then, still sick to my stomach because I began to worry that a customer, not a cashier, would take the money, and certain I was going to hell, I had run crying to my mother and told her what I'd done. She'd been hoeing dirt around her plants in the garden, and when I told her she'd listened, her hoe quiet.

After I'd finished she said, "I think you've learned your lesson. Just don't do it again," and went back to her work. The weight of guilt and fear had evaporated instantly at her words as if she were the Pope and had blessed me.

"It's true," I insisted about our helpful-friend. "Honest."

"Now, don't you go making trouble for others by including them in your tall tales. You know how you let your imagination run away with you. Look at what you tell me is waiting to get you in the barn. There's nothing there, and you know it."

My stomach trembled at the reminder of what could be in the barn's dark corners. We both had been surprised by the snakes that went in there during the summer to escape the heat. I didn't dare tell her what my helpful-friend had asked me to do. She had turned back to boiling water, and the conversation was over. The guilt that had sat in a corner of my brain all day grew in size like the Grinch's heart when he heard the Whos of Whoville sing.

MY HELPFUL-FRIEND INCREASED HIS VISITS TO ALMOST DAILY. He arrived most afternoons at 4:30. For the first fifteen minutes or so he chatted happily with my mother. He teased her, gave her small gifts of food, helped her with chores, and, that winter, he plowed her driveway and a wide path to the barn and manure pile. He went outside to the barn with me, carrying buckets of water across the yard and then hay bales from the room where we kept it next to Dakota's stall. "Is there anything else you need?" he'd ask, smiling. "What else needs to be done out here?"

So I did whatever he asked me to do because I thought I should be fair and was grateful. I needed him to be with me in a barn where I was certain that predators, having nothing to do but prey, waited patiently to catch me alone.

With my helpful-friend standing at the stall gate watching, the same place that my blustery-and-favored brother had years before told me to stand so that Donny wouldn't hurt me, I chucked manure into the wheelbarrow without feeling the need to turn and see what was behind me. With this man in the barn, nothing could get me. As I shoveled, Dakota munched hay that she dipped into her water bucket like a lady dipping her cookie in tea, and he listened to me talk.

"People don't need so much meat," I said one afternoon. "They really don't. There's no need to kill and slaughter so many animals. Animals know when they're going to die. If you are what you eat, people who eat meat are eating pain and terror." I recognized how my father's words about "no need" exited easily out of my mouth.

My helpful-friend's eyes were intent on my face, kind when he said, "I never really thought of it that way."

"What do you think it'd be like to be a deer grazing in the field, look up for a second at a strange noise or smell, and then, boom? Deer don't die instantly, you know. My brothers follow the blood trail, and sometimes they never find them. The animals suffer."

"I don't like hunting," he said, "but I love you."

And as the black-as-pitch night pressed heavy against the cob-webbed windows at my back, I thought that I loved my helpful-friend too.

When he wasn't there I raced to the barn in over-large boots, spilling precious well water. I slammed the planked door against the impenetrable inky darkness that reverberated with the howls and yips of coyotes, and my body felt wound up, ready. Any strange sound sent my blood pounding hard through my body and my feet racing to the door. Gone were the years when we had sheep, cows, pigs, and chickens. Gone were reasons for anyone but me to go out into the barn after dark.

DIVORCE PROCEEDINGS BEGAN, AND MY HELPFUL-FRIEND DIDN'T need me for babysitting, but he told my mother he did. He went on plowing her driveway and doing her favors. Moving into a motel room about ten minutes from my house with no other place to go but work, he waited outside my school or at the bus stop, and he drove to my siblings' homes on the nights I took care of their children.

I wondered over and over again how my mother couldn't know when she usually knew so much. "Oh, piffle wiffle" repeated itself in my brain when my helpful-friend asked me to touch him. "Puppy-cock," my father's voice thrummed in my thoughts when my helpful-friend promised that when I turned eighteen he'd marry me. There was no one to tell me different.

SOMETIMES WE MET AT A SISTER'S IN-TOWN APARTMENT. I BABYSAT for several siblings.

On my birthday my helpful-friend arrived with a wrapped box after I put my niece to bed. Surprised, I worried we'd get caught and began to think up the lie that would have to be told.

"Now that you're thirteen, I can tell my friends I'm dating a teenager," he said, as if this were the most ordinary thing in the world. "This birthday makes all the difference."

Yesterday I'd been twelve; today I was a teenager. He had given me a chamois shirt for Christmas, and this day the box held a silky maroon sweater.

"Try it on," he said. "I want to see you in just the sweater."

I undressed, and before I put the soft fabric over my head, he pulled me to the couch. "You're getting a little chubby," he said. "You should watch that."

I would hold this sentence in my brain for the rest of my life. Suddenly I didn't like him, forgot I needed him for the barn. He was the one who bought me all the pizza, the candy, the soda. Besides, he was the one who was fat; his large stomach cast a shadow on his feet. Like any thirteen-year-old, I sulked.

"Let's just see if we can do it," he said.

"Do what?" I said flippantly, hugging myself with my arms to hide my fat from his eyes. I really didn't know.

He took his pants off and led me to the secondhand couch that was snagged tweed, pressing me back. I felt his penis, hard, bumping between my legs. I was surprised by the heat, by how heavy he was. Maybe he was the devil. Because my mother was right—I did let my imagination run away with me—I thought not of Bo Duke but of Randall Flagg, and I began to get scared.

"Just hold still," he said and pushed. I tensed and wiggled away. He adjusted himself and pushed again, harder. I shifted as if he were the wrong side of a magnet. Suddenly he was abrupt and announced, "It's not going to work," as if I'd failed some test. In seconds he dressed and was gone.

If this was sex, it wasn't worth all the yelling that had gone on in my house for the last thirteen years.

Two days later my mother found my helpful-friend's sweater gift.

"Where'd you get this?' she said, holding it up in front of her, where it shimmered in the light coming in the window.

I almost said Randall Flagg gave it to me for my birthday, but instead I used his real name.

"When? I didn't see him."

I was the youngest in a family of proven thieves and liars.

"Just before he left two days ago."

Her lips pressed into a line, she folded the sweater, and placed it on the table where she was folding laundry.

"He shouldn't give you gifts like that," she snapped. The sweater proved to her what I already knew: I was no longer the good child, and the weight of the changed identity stifled me. I never saw the sweater again.

IN FEBRUARY MY HELPFUL-FRIEND, WANTING ME TO MEET HIS friends, took me to an apartment late at night after pretend babysitting. He leaned his back against the wall while talking to a man who sat in an armchair with a woman on his lap. There were only a few lamps, giving the apartment a reddish Stephen King novel glow. Beer bottles cluttered the end table near them, and I wondered how someone could drink so much and not have to pee. I stared in wonder—much as I'd stared at the chimpanzee wiping poop on his cage bars two years before—as the woman placed her hand on the man's jean-covered penis. She rubbed him slowly, rhythmically. He pressed upward into her, and my helpful-friend smiled, as if a woman caressing a man's erection through his jeans in the company of friends was normal. I couldn't help but notice they were breaking all my mother's rules, and being a lookout for so many years had taught me that even my sisters knew that you hid to do these things.

The adults laughed and talked, and I began to wish I'd brought reading material, but then my helpful-friend pulled me to stand in front him, gripped my hips and pressed his pelvis into my bottom. I could feel his hardness against me, and in the truck an hour later, he would pull over onto a dirt road and tell me that he had been so aroused pressing himself into me in front of his friends that he almost came. I remember not entirely understanding, feeling both powerless and powerful.

EACH DAY I WENT TO SCHOOL AND PRETENDED I WAS THE TYPE of child who would never touch a man until marriage. Fear that I would be found out pushed me to work harder at schoolwork, pushed me to be friendlier. If I got As and had many friends, then no one would ever know the truth.

My English teacher said, "Well, how nice. You're nothing at all like the last sister I had," and the shame rose because I was exactly like her. Voted the most popular, the most likely to succeed, the best artist, awarded a certificate for outstanding achievement in English— nothing could ease the mountain of lies I teetered on.

One Sunday in March a relative of my helpful-friend visited my house. She sat beside me on the couch where I was memorizing Greek gods and goddesses for school. Sitting there, reading about the troubles of the gods, such as Hera being cheated on, the unfairness of it all, caused fresh anger to writhe up from my gut into my brain, making me think my head would split open, only instead of Athena, all my secrets would escape and smother me.

"Do you enjoy all the babysitting you do?" this visitor asked.

Possibly she was simply being polite, thought I'd say, "yes," and finish my homework. Maybe she had a friend who needed a sitter.

All I could think was, she knows my helpful-friend, and before she could lose interest and leave, I blurted, "He makes me do stuff."

Instantly she sat upright from her previous relaxed slouch and grabbed my arm, "What sort of stuff? Tell me," she said, intense.

Tears and words exploded at once, and I told her everything.

"I'm so sorry," she said, pushing my hair away from my wet face. "So, so sorry."

I cried harder.

"I want you to know I'll take care of everything," she said in a soothing, capable tone. "This isn't the first time," she added. "He can't seem to control himself around cute young girls."

Through my agony, my relief morphed to hurt then to jealousy that I wasn't special.

My mother suddenly stood in the living room doorway, arms akimbo, glaring, "What's going on?"

"Nothing," I said. *Everything*, I thought.

THE NEXT DAY MY HELPFUL-FRIEND WAS OUTSIDE THE SCHOOL building. Sometimes he liked to pick me up and drop me off at the end of my road where the school bus would, and then come back later to visit. That gave him thirty minutes of free time with me because I was, in my mother's mind, on the bus. I was surprised to see his truck. I'd assumed these rides were over.

"Let me drive you home, and then we'll sit for a bit," he said, his forearm resting on the rolled-down window of his truck. I knew what "sit" meant.

Neither of us spoke. I was sullen, my schoolbooks lined square on my lap, thinking about the others I'd learned about. He joked and squeezed my thigh in an attempt to get me to talk. Now a teenager of several months, I sat a stereotype of rebellious silence, rolling my eyes each time he looked at me.

Up the last hill, down on the other side to the four corners where he always turned off to park, my parents' station wagon sat big and authoritative. First, relief hovered in my consciousness: they were there to save me. But then I saw their expressions through the windshield, their rage aimed at me. Slamming the car door, my father walked to the passenger side of the truck.

"Get into the car!" he ordered. I did, trembling, wondering what he would say to our helpful-friend, what our helpful-friend would say to him, but my father only waved across the hood at our friend, and when I turned back helplessly my helpful-friend no longer looked like Bo Duke or a blonde Fonzie but like a bearded Squiggy as he maneuvered his truck into a horseshoe turn and drove away.

I walked to the station wagon and sat on the vinyl seat, waiting for the fallout, with my books in my lap. Now would be a good time for the Apocalypse, for Jesus to save me, if saving me was His priority.

The half-mile drive up the dirt road bristled with tension, but the screaming didn't begin until we entered the house. Through the entry door and into the kitchen we walked single file. Tippy didn't greet us but slunk under the table. My father threw his cap on the fridge with a violence that sent it skidding over the other side into the next room where it fell to the floor.

"You slut," my father boomed and threw a paperback at me. Not one of my Stephen King books, because those were the property of the library, but a Harlequin romance with a large-breasted, half-dressed woman held by a chiseled, half-dressed man on the cover. The book was my mother's, and what was in it broke all of her rules.

"I tried to tell you!" I shouted. "You didn't believe me!"

"You didn't tell us," my mother said. "We found out through his parents. He has enough problems with his divorce. He doesn't need you making things worse," she sobbed. "How could you do to this me? Now how are we going to face him?"

I shifted my gaze from my father to my mother and back again, knowing I had officially joined the ranks of my siblings.

THE NEXT YEAR, AT THE END OF EIGHTH GRADE, I WENT TO A wedding reception that my helpful-friend attended. He'd been at the wedding service too, but I'd hidden beside my mother, thinking back to the days when I'd thought of her as the person who would protect me from the snakes that my tough-yet-admirable sister brought into the house and dropped on the middle of the table. She was the one I'd run to if my siblings wouldn't let me play with them or if they were mean.

The marriage ceremony hadn't made me dream of my own wedding; it had made me dream of freedom and horses. "Do you take this man to be your lawfully wedded husband? To honor and obey?" was not part of my fanciful script.

"Don't do it," I wanted to yell to my sister-in-law-to-be, but I'd now seen six weddings, and not one of the participants had said, "I don't," like a woman might who didn't want to be told what to do or what animals to own.

I was not going to promise myself to any man. I was not going to be secondary. Once I finally had control over my life I would not give it up.

"You are not to go near him," my mother snapped in an angry whisper when we were at the church, and when she saw my helpful-friend's truck in the reception parking lot she repeated the order, adding, "Just behave yourself and don't cause any trouble."

They went in ahead of me, smiling and shaking hands, speaking with their helpful-friend as if he were still helpful. I'd brought a boy from school as my guest. I felt sick. With pictures of what we did in my mind, I wondered if my helpful-friend's girlfriend knew, if they did all the same stuff. I noticed she was chubby and felt sicker still.

Walking up to me as the band played, he took my hand and pulled me aside, and I thought my guest looked like a little boy, and then realized he was.

"I've missed you," he said. "How have you been?"

"Fine." I didn't know what to say or where to look. I was afraid my mother would see and yell, call me names in front of everyone.

"Dance with me."

Just like the year before, "no" didn't occur to me, and he hugged me to him in a waltz. I could feel the shape of him through his thin slacks. When the song ended, my boy-guest was gone. I found him in the parking lot.

"Why'd you ask me to come with you if you like that old man so much?" His voice choked in his throat with accusation as he stared at me, waiting for an answer I couldn't give because, hard as I thought, I had none.

18

Rocket Man

UNTIL THE SUMMER BEFORE NINTH GRADE, INFECTIONS PLAGUED my right ear, hammering away at the sensitive tissues like a clapper on a bell. Outside noise couldn't be heard over my whooshing heartbeat and the ringing tones inside my middle ear. I was half-deaf, turning my head at people like a curious puppy. When my mother accused me of hearing only what I wanted, she was right.

In July green fluid had begun to trickle again from my ear, and my mother had taken out the usual eardrops that the doctor prescribed for all my earaches. I got in the usual position—left ear to the table, hair pushed back, right ear facing up, ready to receive. She squeezed the bottle three times to release three drops that rolled leisurely into the canal, where they blazed three separate fire-like trails deep into the center of my head. I shot up from the chair and hopped around the room, clutching my ear. A sudden bitter taste filled my mouth.

"What did you do to her?" my father, who disliked jumping of any kind, demanded.

"Nothing! I did it the same as always!" my mother said, clearing herself of blame.

"This isn't right. Take her to someone else," he ordered, and because I had caught his attention by making a racket, after eleven years of sham diagnoses and constant infections, my mother scheduled an appointment with a specialist.

I CLIMBED THE STAIRS TO THE SPECIALIST'S OFFICE THAT WAS located in the town my family judged as being full of stupid Frenchmen: the City-over-the-Bridge. I worried that if they knew this about the people on this side of the bridge, why would they choose a doctor from here to fix me? I worried that he was chosen for his discount prices. Each step up the stairs and into the small waiting room brought me closer to what I knew was torture. With my heart pounding in concert with my ear, it was only seconds before I heard my name called. A short thin man with a slight stoop led me to an exam room that held the dreaded chair. My stomach clenched anew with fear because this specialist couldn't afford a receptionist. He spoke little and not to me before picking up his otoscope and looking in. He whistled, sighed, and muttered, reminding me for an instant of the tiny wizard who steps out from behind his big voice in *The Wizard of Oz*.

"There's no eardrum," he said, shaking his head at my mother. "I can see right to the bones in her middle ear."

"I had no idea," she said to declare her innocence.

"There is no eardrum," he repeated as if he thought she'd said, "I did not hear." He stared at her and then announced, "You have been medicating her middle ear."

"How was I to know?" my mother asked suddenly, forgetting I'd complained of earaches all my life.

He looked in my left ear. Then back to my right. I drew away each time he approached. "She'll have to have antibiotics and then surgery."

"What will surgery do?"

"Give her a new eardrum."

I thought of Jamie Sommers in *The Bionic Woman* and hoped he meant that. He pointed to pictures on the wall of people with red radiating lines coming out of their ears, and I hoped he didn't mean that.

The tympanoplasty was scheduled within the week because I needed to heal before ninth grade started. My mother dropped me off at the hospital on August 16, 1981, the day before surgery, and by evening I'd exhausted all the imaginary pictures I could make out of the swirls and knots in my hospital room's wooden door. None of them were ponies or chimpanzees but rather scary deformed faces. My mother had allowed me to bring an Archie comic book, but nothing else in case it got stolen. Thieves were everywhere.

The next day at 5:30 a.m. a nurse wheeled me from my room. Then people surrounded me and there were bright lights in my eyes. They strapped my wrists to boards that extended from the bed, taped various objects to my chest, and covered me with blankets. The room was cold like when my parents were sure there would be a frost and we covered all the pumpkins and butternut squashes. Panic blossomed in my stomach as I struggled to squelch my need to move. My fists curled and my leg muscles tensed. I didn't know if I could control the sounds I felt rising at the back of my throat. Then the small wizard-like man entered, and the activity increased. A masked man placed a plastic flexible container over my nose and mouth.

I struggled against its suffocating weight and smell. I held my breath.

"Breathe," the man ordered, in the tone of someone who thinks he shouldn't have to say something so obvious. I took a little breath, fought nausea, and held it again.

Then a woman took my hand; her skin was cool and dry. "It's going to be alright, honey. Just count to three slowly." She stroked my hand. "You won't remember a thing. You're going to be fine."

Who wouldn't remember this? I thought just before I knew nothing.

My mother arrived solo on the third day to take me home. "You know how uncomfortable hospitals make your father," she defended his absence.

TWO WEEKS PASSED. "HOLD STILL," THE DOCTOR ORDERED. HE reached toward my ear with long thin tweezers.

I moved.

"Don't move," he said, yanking me back toward him.

He pulled blood-soaked packing out of my ear like a magician who pulls infinite scarves from his sleeve. He seemed immune to the hatred of a fourteen-year-old girl with filthy matted hair.

When he finished he ordered with what sounded like glee: "No scuba diving, no snorkeling, no surfing, no hiking up Mt. Everest, no parasailing, no flying."

I would return for a hearing test in a month, he said sternly, expecting improvement, as if it was something I could control if I were a good patient and practiced.

I BEGAN NINTH GRADE WITH A COTTON BALL GLUED INSIDE MY ear opening with Vaseline. For weeks my mother had washed my hair in the kitchen sink each Sunday night while I held a washcloth over the right side of my head to protect my ear. My hair hung one-quarter greasy and three-quarters clean eight weeks into school. I sat in homeroom attempting an escape into Thomas Bishop's world imagined by Shane Stevens in *By Reason of Insanity*. Changing identities seemed brilliant to me. The goo from the Vaseline pasted a small section of hair into a dark clump against my temple, which drew all eyes. "Look, look, look," the greasy hair called. "And, hey, since you're looking, slide your eyes down to her homemade shirt and her five-dollar cloth sneakers."

NINTH GRADE HAD A "MULTIDIMENSIONAL UNIFIED ARTS PROGRAM." I asked the guidance counselor, whose pants rode high around his waist, if I could repeat shop class or take art or home economics to fulfill the requirement. He said it was time to expand my horizons. *There is only one horizon, and it's unexpandable*, I thought, but I didn't want my guidance counselor to know I had a smart mouth. I didn't explain the concept of infinity or lines and how they pertained to the horizon; instead, I explained the importance of finishing what you start. My wooden lamp from the previous semester's shop class didn't have its wires. Not aware of what type of family I came from, he said, "I'm sure your father will be happy to help you complete your lamp at home."

"Chorus will satisfy it," he said, his eyes on my ragged jean jacket, torn not to look cool but because I was the third member of my family to wear it.

"I can't sing or play a musical instrument," I argued, following him up and down the school corridors to make sure he understood that I had no musical ability.

Raised to think a house should be silent of all noise but parental yelling, I valued quiet. When two of my sisters used to have giggling fits, I was on my father's side when he tied them to the kitchen chairs and said, "Now let's see if you think that's funny!"

Even though the surgery to repair my ear had taken place in mid-August and it was now the end of the first semester in December, I tried to use pain as an excuse.

"Chorus will hurt my ear," I told him, pointing to the right side of my head in case he didn't know where my ears were located. "A person needs a reliable eardrum to sing but not so much to sand wood."

"Staying on key isn't that important," he said. "Just take it. It'll be good for you and build character."

School made as little sense as my father when he said, "what have you" all the time when we had nothing.

In shop class I'd been surrounded by boys. And teenage boys, if you're a teenage girl, are the kindest of the human species. Chorus, I assumed, from growing up with brothers who carried shotguns, not aspirations for opera, close to their hearts, meant girls, and girls were as mean and unpredictable as geese and honey badgers.

I ENTERED THE POORLY INSULATED SCHOOL GYMNASIUM THAT second semester, just twenty days before my fifteenth birthday, to the sound of a male voice singing Billy Joel's "Piano Man." I sat down in an icy metal chair on the dark stage among a gaggle of girls, with *Cujo* in my lap, ready to save me if I needed to escape from the discomfort of not knowing anyone. Pretending I was busy reading, not left out, was my time-proven method of survival.

"Sing us a song, you're the piano man," the boy's voice drew me in.

I stared at him, tilting my head to hear more clearly. I noticed his brown curly hair that flopped at odd angles, his long face and large mouth and the way his eyes closed with the emotion of the words, and it occurred to me, in a heart-thumping, face-flushing instant of visceral reaction, that I wanted to marry him more than I'd wanted to marry Shaun Cassidy.

As soon as he finished the last series of sorrowful la, la, las, a plump girl, one with blond hair waving down her back like a real-life Marcia Brady who could manage the hundred brush strokes a day, asked him to sing another song as we waited for the chorus teacher to finish instructing art down the hall. I had to fight the urge not to leave my seat to shove this shiny-haired girl and tell her the pianist was mine.

I listened carefully as he sang Randy Newman's "Short People." In my home I heard only AC/DC, Led Zeppelin, Aerosmith, Bad Company, Foreigner, and, when younger, Janis Joplin and Neil Diamond. The curly-haired pianist noticed me staring, and he stared back, his eyes a dark brown, almost black, and wise, like he knew everything.

"Short people got nobody to love."

My stomach flipped. I was short. How could he know I had nobody to love? Again my stomach flipped, a sensation I associated only with the possibility of candy.

The song ended, and I set *Cujo* aside and forced myself to stand in spite of the trembling that had begun in my gut and was quickly spreading to my legs. One foot in front of the other, like Kris Kringle teaches the Winter Warlock to do in *Santa Claus Is Coming to Town*. I walked over to him, the simple act of forward motion awkward. My insides zinged and zanged off each other in cahoots with my untrustworthy outsides. I hoped the curly-haired pianist wouldn't see me shaking.

Why hadn't I seen this person around school before? My voice, usually at the ready with questions, judgment, and insults, didn't feel like mine, "Who are you?" I'd learned from my year of stuttering that it was best to ask important questions first.

He wore an orange chamois shirt and jeans. I hoped he wasn't a hunter, but if he were, I'd change him.

"Who am I?" he asked, emphasizing the "I" as if I'd been rude.

I usually walked away from people who responded to my questions with questions of their own; it broke down the whole information gathering process. He slid over on the piano bench, inviting me to sit beside him, and my legs gave way. I noticed his jeans were faded but clean. No one could place this piano-playing boy in the riffraff or hooligan group. I was relieved that my thighs were smaller than his when spread out on the bench.

His hands weren't nicked with cuts and hard calluses, but they weren't soft or feminine either. I stuck my dry red ones under my hamstrings. I couldn't groom Dakota with mittens on or pat her warm nose, no matter how cold it was outside. His hands looked, I thought, like the kind of hands that would never kill an animal.

He said, "I'm Eric," and I looked from his perfect hands into his brown, almost-black eyes, and I heard my subconscious say, "He looks a bit like a chimpanzee."

"I'm Helen," I began, thinking Heidi might sound better.

"I know who you are. I saw you in French before I dropped it."

The girl with the freshly brushed blond hair leaned over the top of the small upright piano and asked sweetly, "Eric, could you play a boogie? I just love your boogies."

I didn't know what a boogie was, having never heard the word except in instances of washing a toddler's face.

I was glad she was fat.

"Sure," Eric said, proving immediately how good-natured and agreeable he was. I imagined him doing whatever I asked.

When I began to stand he pulled me down. "Stay," he said, and despite what my mother said about me always doing the opposite of what anyone asked me to do, I stayed. Eric played, and his muscular thigh brushed against mine as he thumped out the beat with his foot and pounded his fingers over the keyboard. My thigh didn't want to move away as it had with my helpful-friend.

I had never met anyone like this boy before. Even as everything about him reminded me of a chimpanzee-like human and my mind zoomed in frazzled new directions, something else about him settled me.

The chorus teacher's exhausted voice interrupted my confusion. "Everyone take your seats," she said, followed by a big sigh, her fingers paint-stained blue and green.

"Can I call you?" I asked Eric, frantic not to lose what I had just found.

"I would love that," and he removed a pen from his shirt pocket and wrote his number on my hand. For those few seconds I felt like I could do anything.

The blond girl took a stack of sheet music from the teacher and handed them out to the other students. "Can I do the solos?" she asked.

I began to hate her.

THAT JANUARY DAY I WALKED HOME FROM THE BUS STOP WITH nerves eating away at my stomach in indecision. Was it too soon to call him? Would he think I was forward? Would he think I was annoying? I didn't know what to do, how to begin. All I had were questions. I didn't talk on the phone much, not like my sisters had before they'd moved out. Only my hair-twirling-pretty sister still lived at home, and she spent her time at work or her boyfriend's house.

I walked slowly up the dirt road that was covered in a thick layer of ice, oblivious to the neighbor's old German shepherd, who barked lackadaisically at me as I passed. My mother wasn't home, having driven my father to work so she could use the car later to drive herself to work as a temp employee at the post office. I entered the quiet house, patting Tippy's nose, now streaked with gray below her rheumy eyes, on the way through the entry. Even though I'd wrestled with the decision to call, I walked directly to the phone, as if my body had known exactly what to do all along.

My heart beat so loudly in my ears and chest that I worried about a possible heart attack. I picked up the receiver and dialed, my stomach gripped with anticipation.

"Methodist parsonage," a man answered on the other end. I remembered Eric saying, "Don't hang up if my father answers. He's a minister."

"Is Eric there?" I asked softly, afraid if I spoke in my real voice that this minister man would know I was forward and once had a helpful-friend.

"Just one moment, please," he said, and I marveled at the courtesy.

"Hello?" My stomach cartwheeled. "It's me," I said.

"I could tell. Thank you for calling me."

So polite. Who was this family?

"I'm glad you sat with me today," Eric continued. "Do you like to sing?"

I wanted to lie and say I loved it, say, "I'm a musical superstar," and add that I could do the solo if he wanted me to, but each untruth that arrived creatively to my throat died before it moved to my tongue. It was as if I was under one of the truth spells that Endora put on Darrin every few episodes to prove he was a mortal schmuck.

"I might if I could do it," I answered. "I never had lessons or anything. I'm not musical at all unless you count knowing the words to all of Lorne Green's songs." There was silence. I thought he was disappointed. Having little to offer in the way of talent, I added, "I can draw just about any album cover, though."

He laughed, not a little chuckle, but a sudden big laugh, like a pleased chimpanzee. "Doesn't Lorne Green do Alpo commercials? You're very funny," he said.

That was worrisome. I scrambled to say something that would demonstrate my serious nature and that I was an advantageous person to know. "I have a horse."

Again, silence. I hastened to fill it. "I have a dog too. I'd like to have a goat."

My mother arrived home just as I was desperately thinking of something else I owned.

"Who are you talking to now?" she asked, like I was already in trouble.

I worried that Eric would hear her and assume I talked copiously.

"Get off the phone and go do something useful," she added firmly before shutting the bathroom door with a forceful clunk.

"I will soon," I said as agreeably as I could so that Eric wouldn't know I had a smart mouth. Stretching the cord the longest it would reach to where she wouldn't see me when she came out, I sat on the stairs around the hallway corner.

"Is that your mother?" Eric asked. "I could call you back later if you have to go do something."

Was he looking for an excuse to say goodbye? I suddenly didn't think I could stand it if the line disconnected us.

"No, it's okay. How long have you played the piano?" Question one. I planned to keep the questions under ten.

"Since I was nine. I wanted to play the bass guitar like Peter Tork in The Monkees, but we had a piano. I hope to get a degree in piano performance after I graduate."

"The Monkees?" Question two. I didn't dare ask about college. The thought of him moving away was more than I could bear.

"You don't know who The Monkees are?" He laughed.

"No, who are they?" Question three. The Monkees sounded like something I should know about. I suddenly got the idea that Eric might have a connection to actual guitar-playing monkeys and jumped to the conclusion that I might get an opportunity to hug one.

"They're a band. They have a television show. 'Hey, hey we're The Monkees'?" he sang questioningly, as if to jog a specific memory he thought everyone should have.

I scanned my brain: *Bewitched, The Brady Bunch, Gilligan's Island, Happy Days, Laverne and Shirley, My Three Sons, Grizzly Adams,*

Emergency, The Six Million Dollar Man, The Bionic Woman, Chips, Dukes of Hazzard, Little House on the Prairie, The Waltons, Star Trek, Bonanza, Gunsmoke, Charlie's Angels, and, lately, a lot of *General Hospital* because my hair-twirling-pretty sister and my sad-tittering sister loved soap operas. I think Laura was kidnapped somewhere and Luke was trying to find her. The obstacles for Luke and Laura were endless. No sign of *The Monkees.* "What's it about?" Question four.

"Each episode they sing and the plot is a comedy sketch."

"Oh, like *Hee Haw?*" I didn't like *Hee Haw.*

Silence, then "No."

I swallowed, searching my brain for an intelligent question: "Do you watch anything else?" Question five.

On his side I heard the polite deep voice of his father: "Eric, this is a business line. Other people may be trying to reach us."

Crap, I thought, *a wasted question.*

"I have to go, but I'll call you back. What's your number?"

I said it as fast as I could and then tried to be silent to give him a chance to recognize that I could listen too, hoping he wouldn't think like my mother did, that I talked a blue streak.

"Got it," Eric said. "Thank you. I'll call you back as soon as I can."

And the phone calls began, hundreds of hours, both of us "talking up a storm," my mother complained, both of us needing the phone lines to connect us.

An old red van rattled up the road and into my driveway. I'd never asked a boy to visit before who wasn't from the neighborhood, who didn't know my family or how we lived. Tension clenched my insides into a knot, the what-ifs accumulating as quickly as flies on the bug tapes that hung in the barn and cellar. I hadn't been able to eat anything all day.

Eric's father didn't get out but rolled down his window and said, "Well, you certainly live out in the sticks, don't you?"

Afraid of this man with blue eyes and a graying short beard and mustache, I didn't answer but nodded to confirm the obvious and stared at Eric, who stared at me. His father backed down the driveway, and worrying that my mother would embarrass me, I delayed going into the house by taking Eric to the barn. On the way across the yard he shied away from Tippy, who walked slowly beside us, and he kept an eye on Daisy, who barked at the end of her chain.

Once inside the gloomy, low-ceilinged barn, he kept his hands in his CB ski parka.

I led him to Dakota's stall. "This is Dakota," I said, holding onto her nose to make the introductions.

Eric removed one hand from his pocket to pat her before plunging it back. "She's a horse," he said.

"She is," I answered, giving her a kiss as I tried to process the expression on his face. I opened the stall door and stepped down beside her. "Come in and see her," I encouraged.

Eric walked cautiously down the one step and stood close beside me, keeping his feet away from the manure and Dakota's feet. He took my cold bare hand in both of his, holding it firmly with his warm fingers.

"Your hands are so cold," he said. "You should wear gloves." His concern for me overcame my worry that he didn't appear to love horses and made my throat tighten like I might cry. I released Dakota, who blew out gusts in between bites of hay. Each time she snorted, I saw Eric tense.

"I really like you a lot," he said, his voice low, his eyes moving rapidly from the horse to me. "I was wondering if you'd like to go out with me."

I worked to steady my voice, although my insides were leaping around like fleas on a dog. "I think so."

Then he kissed me, releasing my hand to hold the sides of my face like I'd seen the men do on the covers of my mother's Harlequin romances.

I'd been kissed by few boys and by only one man. With them I didn't like it much, tried not to struggle, tensing up as my upper body curved backward like an expert limbo player. All I could think when lips touched mine was how long since they'd eaten a piece of chicken or a pig. I'd envision the tendons and muscles gnashed between the molars that lay behind the busy lips, and all I wanted was to get away. In my mind's keen and judging eye their tongues would be covered in bristly papillae like the cow tongues my mother boiled for my father's sandwiches. I'd fight not to gag.

When Eric kissed me I forgot to think about meat.

Afraid my mother would come out to the barn and catch us, I brought Eric to meet her.

"This is Eric, the boy from school," I said.

Busy feeding my eighteen-year-old sad-tittering sister's toddler son, she looked up briefly and then back to the plastic bowl of mashed banana.

"The one you tie up the phone with so that no one else can use it?" she said.

"Nice to meet you," Eric said to her back.

I pulled him out of the kitchen to the living room, where we sat on the couch, knowing that my mother could hear everything we said.

My hair-twirling-pretty sister bounded down the stairs and walked into the living room. Her bangs were feathered Farrah Fawcett–style, whereas my hair hung in my eyes because I'd rather read in the morning than use the curling iron. Her eyes twinkling and her smile mischievous, she was prettier than ever because she had found the man she was going to marry. She was seventeen, her summer wedding date set, the third sister to get married before age eighteen.

"Are you the boy Helen won't get off the phone with?" she asked. "Why do you want to talk to her so much anyway? All she does is read and play with her stupid horse."

Eric laughed but didn't seem taken in by the charm my father and other boys couldn't resist. "I love talking to her," he said. "Wish I could more."

"Whatever," my hair-twirling-pretty sister said. "You're probably just as queer as she is."

ON SATURDAYS AND SUNDAYS MARRIED CHILDREN AND THEIR kids would arrive one after the other as if on a pilgrimage to return to the homeland. I tried to keep Eric away from the kitchen, where most of the drama took place. I sat with him on the couch and tried to block the sounds of voices with records he brought—The Beatles' *White Album* and Elton John's *Goodbye Yellow Brick Road*—songs and artists I'd never known existed. I had to listen hard to the soft distant voices coming out of the speakers because my parents insisted the stereo made it difficult for them to think.

At supper one night, about a month after Eric stood in Dakota's stall and kissed me, the bullshit-artist-ass-Skipper, his shirt unbuttoned, his gold necklace exposed in the curling hair of his Skipper-like chest, slammed his fist onto the supper table as if he'd suddenly been challenged to imitate the giant from "Jack and the Beanstalk," shouting, "You want to know what those sons of bitches told my kid? That the sun's a star. Unbelievable! What are we paying teachers for anyway? Too goddamn much!"

My father said on cue that teachers were overpaid, adding, "There's no need of that. They have whole summers off and they barely work as it is the rest of the year. They should get summer jobs."

Then no one spoke again. The clatter of forks and knives against plates and bowls dominated. I ignored the bullshit-artist-ass-Skipper. Ignoring ignorance was the key to good digestion if there wasn't a book handy.

"Well, actually the sun is a star," Eric said logically before I could alert him that logic had no place in my house. "All stars are suns and all suns are stars."

My mouth opened and I might have gasped. This curly-haired pianist had no idea how to stay out of trouble.

"Oh, they are not either," the bullshit-artist-ass-Skipper shouted, grease shining on his chin and the corners of his lips from the bone he sucked. "You don't know what the hell you're talking about. Everybody knows the sun is a large ball of gas. You're just as stupid as the rest of them."

Rest of who, I wondered, if everybody knows.

Then he turned to me, asking, "Where'd you pick up this bozo, Helen?" as if I were some hooker on a street corner.

Eric sat there at the table, his fork suspended above his pork chop, looking from one face to the other. Words erupted before I could talk myself out of them: Why did the first person that Eric met have to be the family hanger-on? Where were my quieter family members such as my sister-who-holds-grudges-longer-than God or my heart-of-gold brother-in-law? "The sun is a star and it is a ball of gas, so shut up and eat," I snapped.

"That's enough of that, Helen," my mother said, warning me. "Just mind your own business."

"It is my business," I said belligerently. "What there's no need of," I separated the word "need" from the others, "is," I pointed, "him."

The bullshit-artist-ass-Skipper skidded his chair away from the table and stood up. He pounded his leather booted heels back and forth on the kitchen linoleum as he walked, "Are you going to let her talk to me like that?" he yelled at my mother. "Damn kids don't have the sense God gave them." He stopped his pacing to point his piece of fresh pig skeleton at me. "You kids don't know a goddamn thing. And I'll tell you another thing. You'll never amount to anything if you don't learn some respect."

I took Eric's hand and pulled him away from the table into the living room, switching on the goose-shaped lamp that sat on the television. Black night seemed to beat at the windows both outside and inside the house. I wondered how the glass had withstood the pressure for so many years. We sat down on the couch, listening to the bullshit-artist-ass-Skipper's voice fill the rooms.

"Just calm down," my father said. "Why you letting kids rile you up? You know they don't mean nothing by it."

Eric turned to look at me in the dim light of the room and asked, incredulity outlining his syllables, "How do you live with this?"

"I read a lot, especially Stephen King. Have you read any of his books?"

"I've read them all. I read *The Shining* while we camped on North Haven and was afraid to go into the woods."

"You should have been afraid to go into a hotel."

"I'm not sure Stephen King books could be the reason you seem normal though. There's nothing normal about what he writes."

My chest flooded with happiness because he'd read Stephen King, and I tried to overlook the "seem normal" when he could have said, "are normal."

"You don't understand," I argued. "Everything King writes is about real people and real fear. That's what normal is."

OUR HOME LIVES WERE SO DIFFERENT THAT WHEN ERIC ASKED me to be his girlfriend, I was afraid he would abandon me. His parents were separated. He played the piano when he wasn't listening to albums and spent considerable time alone despite his two siblings. He was the oldest and I was the youngest, but outside our families we were both isolated. I waited for the moment he would say, "You're bizarre. I need to stay in my world and you need to stay in yours." I was so confident he would reject me with each new thing he learned about me and my house that I was careful to unfold sibling and parent history slowly, careful to show my solidarity with him.

"Those cussed Japs," he heard my father say. "Not worth the ground they stand on."

"Those coons better not look at me if they know what's good for them," he heard the bullshit-artist-ass-Skipper say.

"What do you mean you play the piano?" my blustery-and-favored brother asked on his way through the kitchen to go outside and cut, chop, or fix something. "Are you a fairy?" And he held his arm out and allowed his hand to flop helplessly.

"No one believes in dinosaurs," my holier-than-thou brother said. "The earth is only fifty-seven hundred years old. Helen doesn't need you confusing her more with lies."

Instead of being frightened of the cemetery up the road from my house, scared of Margaret's ghost and whoever Mr. Cootsy was, Eric said, "Dead people are not the people you should be worrying about."

"WHAT ARE YOUR PLANS AFTER YOU GRADUATE?" HIS DAD ASKED on my first visit.

At a loss, I scanned my brain: what did I want to do? 1. Leave home. 2. Be with Eric. 3. Have dogs. 4. Eat candy. "I want to be a writer," my mouth said to my surprise, and I wondered if I was telling another tale.

"What have you written?" he asked, genuinely interested.

"Nothing much," I said, having written a lot actually—hundreds of stories about animals and hundreds of journal entries. But I couldn't think how to answer because I'd just learned who I wanted to be.

"I'd be happy to read anything when you have something to share," he smiled, then walked across the kitchen on the way to his study, the heels of his loafers tapping the floor gently.

"It's amazing to me how little you know about the world," Eric said. "It's hard to imagine someone not knowing all The Beatles' songs but knowing all the popular lyrics of Led Zeppelin, Aerosmith, and Janis Joplin."

"Maybe I heard them and just didn't know what I was listening to." I defended myself. "I'm not good at paying attention."

"Plus, you've never been to a Burger King other than to its restroom, but you've been to Florida twice. It's just odd; that's all."

What most surprised him was that I'd never purchased anything from a store. I was afraid even to go into a convenience store by myself if it meant I had to interact with the cashier. Even if Eric gave me a five dollar bill and the Clark bar cost fifty cents, I worried I might not have enough money, that the rules would suddenly change and I would be called stupid.

When Eric asked if we could ride bikes back and forth to his house, I had to tell him I'd never owned a bike except once as a first grader.

"I have other things I can do, though," I explained argumentatively, and I began to list them. "I can plant and weed. I know how to can and freeze corn and peas. I can dig holes and put up fence. My parents taught me a lot."

"How to be a farmer," he said. "Do you want to be a farmer?"

As I SLEPT I WOULD DREAM ABOUT ERIC HUGGING AND KISSING another girl whose face was hidden but whose family was perfect city folk. They played the piano together, and I thought I'd suffocate from shame. A smart person would have been nicer to Eric when she woke up, having learned something from the dream, but my response was to be angry, as if he'd really betrayed me.

"You're going to find someone better," I accused when I saw him in the morning at school. "Someone who plays the piano like you do. You'll love her!"

He smiled at me patiently like a superman who uses kindness in the face of adversity instead of lifting impossibly heavy things.

"No, I won't," he said confidently. "I won't fall in love with anyone else. Plus, it'd be way too complicated to have two pianists in the family. How would either of us ever practice with just one piano?"

"You'd figure it out," I carried on because I had learned from my mother never to let a subject drop. "And once you do, you'll discover how great it is and forget all about me!"

"You're being silly," he said, laughing. "After meeting you and your family, nothing could make me forget."

Anxiety and worry gnawed on my insides and grew and then gnawed and grew some more. I tried to make him jealous by talking to other boys. I threatened to break up with him. *You're nuts,* I told myself, even as I did it. *He's the best thing that's ever happened to you. You didn't escape crazy after all.*

Instead of leaving, Eric asked me to marry him. We were both fifteen, so I said yes easily, just like when I wanted a horse. I never considered all the years that lay ahead and all the unknowns. His father laughed at us in his good-humored patient way and said it would never be. We were kids, and kids didn't know what they wanted.

Once Eric and I decided on marriage, age eighteen skipped even farther out of reach. Frantic to be with him, I stopped being with other people. Now that I had this person who spoke a language I understood, I couldn't hear enough of his words. I couldn't see enough of his face. I couldn't waste any minutes that could be spent with him. I didn't understand that people thought I was abandoning them, that they might be hurt.

Leah, a friend for several grades and annoyed that I no longer invited her to ride Dakota, said loudly in the school parking lot: "Eric, did Helen tell you she was a home-wrecker and a heart-breaker?" And she moved past us to stand in a gaggle of girls and laugh.

My heart boomed in my ears and heated blood reddened my face. It was March. We stood close to the school to block the wind. Eric looked at me curiously, stuck his hands in his jeans pocket, and leaned against the brick building.

"What does she mean?"

I wanted to say that Leah was making things up, but the words refused to come. I still wore my hair-twirling-pretty sister's hand-me-down denim jacket and her Barefoot Trader jeans that exposed my knees to the raw gusts. People talked in tiny groups around us, and it felt like they and the school were spinning in some elaborate clog dance, which could have been a symptom of my malfunctioning Eustachian tube.

"Leah's talking about someone I knew before I met you."

"Who?"

"A family friend, but I didn't wreck his marriage."

Eric frowned. "He must have been old."

"He was twenty-six. I babysat for him. Sort of."

Eric looked confused. "What do you mean, sort of?"

"He used babysitting as an excuse to see me. He asked me to do things." I didn't want to say what things.

"What things?"

"I can't tell you here," I said, although the actual reason I couldn't tell him was that I didn't know the words for what my helpful-friend had asked me to do, and it was time to go inside to homeroom.

All through the next few classes I worried about what Eric was thinking. I rehearsed in my mind how I would describe what happened during those five months, how my helpful-friend had offered pizza and Pepsi and, most of all, protection against the coyotes and coy dogs howling like they were outside the thin plank door, waiting. I never knew what cast those black shapes across the barn floor and on the walls. I thought up as many excuses for my wrongdoing as I could, hoping that Eric's fear of dogs would work in my favor.

But he was a pastor's kid, a PK. I assumed, with each new thought of how to describe my relationship with my helpful-friend that a minister's son was pure goodness, and he would recognize the folly of associating with badness. Would he want to marry a girl whose father had called her a slut just before he threw a book at her head? Would he want to be her boyfriend?

At lunch we met outside again.

Everything I'd planned to say couldn't find its way to my tongue. "I don't know how to explain," I said, and I realized I was trembling. It was as though my brain had no control over anything my body did.

"So what sort of things did he ask you to do?"

I lacked the words. I couldn't say "dick" because I wasn't sure whether that was slang for penis or a bad name to call someone. I couldn't say "penis" because I'd been taught the word was evil, and just thinking it made me feel like a tramp. I'd never said it out loud. I still thought BJ was a television character who had a chimpanzee called Bear.

"He asked me to put my mouth on him"—I searched for safe words—"on his crotch." I was so embarrassed just to say these sentences that I didn't think I could ever tell him everything.

"You mean he asked you to perform oral sex?" Each word rose higher than a question was meant to go.

"Oral" I knew meant mouth, and "sex" here seemed generic, so I said, "I think so. And he asked me touch him until, well, you know," but not knowing then what I do now about teenage boys, I wondered if he really did. Before he could judge, I added, "But I didn't want to and I didn't like it." And instantly my mind wandered to whether or not I would like it with Eric, and I felt new shame for thinking such a thing about a preacher's son.

"And you were only twelve?"

I nodded, then added, "Well, I turned thirteen." I paused considering how much to divulge after a lifetime of being secretive. "And he said he wanted to eat my cherry," I looked up at him quickly to see if he knew what that was, because I still didn't.

"Did your parents press charges?"

"What?"

"Did they go to the police?"

"Are you serious? Why would they do that? They were furious, but they wouldn't want me to go to jail. And they wouldn't want the publicity."

Eric stared at me. Silent. Here was the part where he would say I could still be his friend, but nothing more. The wind sent my hair spinning in concert with the dried leaves that never got cleaned up from the fall. Students talked and laughed around us. My eye caught Ray, a boy from homeroom, leaning against the building to the right of us. He had one leg up on the bricks to brace his body, a Herman Hesse book open in his hands.

I envisioned Eric lecturing me on right and wrong and then me kicking him and stomping off into the school in a grand exit. I always fantasized about fabulous leave-takings—the drama, the final perfect sentence, and then I'd be gone and people would be impressed but sad and regretful they'd treated me poorly. I searched so deeply for an excellent comeback to his imagined rebuke that when he spoke, I jumped. The teenagers bunched in a group near us came into focus.

"You bet, I'm right," a girl shouted sassily to a thin boy who tried to look like he didn't feel the goose bumps and wind-beaten skin that covered his bare arms. "I could kick your sorry ass at arm wrestling any day."

I focused on the Grateful Dead skull with American eagle wings on the back of the girl's jean jacket. Sections of the wings were missing as if the material had been washed too hard. Eric's voice was tight with anger. "Your parents should have been furious at their friend. Not at you." He emphasized "friend" in a snotty tone. "You were a kid. He's the one who should have gone to jail."

Like a gymnast somersaulting off an apparatus, I tried to twist what I knew in my mind to consider Eric's perspective. How could my helpful-friend be the criminal when he'd been so good to me? Done so much work? I'd willingly done what he asked. He'd never said, "do it or else." I wanted company in the barn, and to get it, I was agreeable. It was obvious I hadn't explained the relationship to Eric correctly. I'd known I was going behind my parents' backs. I had known it was wrong to put my hands and mouth where I'd put them. When I was twelve I was still me. I wasn't a baby. For years I had lived by the keep-your-hands-to-yourself rule. No one had fooled or tricked me. No, Eric was wrong. I could have refused to have gotten in the truck. I had heard good behavior, right behavior yelled in the doorways of my sisters' bedrooms and now mine late into the night for years. My mother made sure we all knew that sex was bad under any circumstances until a woman married a man.

"What are you thinking?" he asked.

"I'm thinking that I wasn't clear." I pulled hair away from my face and tucked it into the back of my jacket so it'd stop blowing in my mouth. I shivered with a chill that seemed to sink into my bones. "I need to explain better when we're not here." I gestured to the people around me, the school.

Relieved that Eric wasn't going to reject me, I stopped saying out loud that I didn't agree. I was too shamed by the events to want the words in the air between us. It wouldn't be the only thing we didn't agree on. We had long discussions on politics and ethics when we walked to his house after school.

Eric's acceptance and his continued surprise at my family lessened the darkness I carried with me. My house was set high on a hill, almost as if it were on a different planet, and it was hard to distinguish between what was real and unreal, even for those who'd lived there all their lives. Ghosts were as much a part of my family as the living members. Eric recorded cassette tapes of songs, ones he wrote and ones he learned off Elton John and REO Speedwagon albums. I went to sleep each night listening to his voice, thinking he was like a rocket man, exploding me out of the darkness I had lived in for such a long, long time.

19
Caught

ERIC PEDALED THE THIRTY MILES ROUND-TRIP TO MY HOUSE ON his Miyata 1000 seven days a week in the summer and, during the school year, on weekends. If there was too much snow on the roads, he walked. On foot, instead of forty-five minutes, the journey took three hours. Thinking we'd stop, slip into the woods, and have sex, my mother wouldn't let me meet him. She was right. Swarms of square-tails and mosquitoes, rocks and branches would have been inconsequential. I would have forgotten to look for snakes.

When he was with me time sped to a pace I could not catch. I feared it passing and watched the clock with scared eyes. When he left, time returned to the sloth-like crawl I'd lived with for fifteen years. As I saw him go, I behaved like Donny searching for Lady after my brother sold her, running the fence line in a mind so cluttered with panic that there was no room for reason. I'd try not to watch him disappear around the bend of the dirt road because no one likes to feel bereft, but I couldn't stop myself. Tinier, tinier still, then he was gone much like Mike TeaVee, the naughty television-watching boy in *Charlie and the Chocolate Factory*, and I'd start to count the minutes until he would call to say he was home safely, because I worried he would vanish as quickly as my hand-knit mittens did near Spunky the goat.

"You just saw him. Why do you need to talk on the phone?" my mother would say, exasperated, with her short hair in pink curlers, her hands strong and large, capable.

"You can't tie up the line for so many hours," Eric's father said to him quietly.

The parsonage phone connected people in need to their pastor. In addition to writing sermons and visiting sick people, pastors act as therapists.

Eric accepted his father's rules without comment and walked to the phone at his mother's greenhouse, a business she owned three miles from his house. His mother no longer lived with him and his father, and the greenhouse was closed for the winter. Even ministers got divorces. There was no heat, and I could hear how cold he was and felt guilty for being warm. Or he would walk two miles to a pay phone in town. He would tell me when to call so he wouldn't have to waste his dimes.

"What could you possibly talk about for so many hours?" my hair-twirling-pretty sister would ask, truly wondering. "I need the phone."

"Lots," I'd answer. Then I'd get off so she could make her call, listen closely for her to say goodbye, and get back on as soon as she left.

"What were you practicing?" I'd ask Eric, knowing that's what he did each second he could.

"The Gershwin Preludes I've been working on, but also an arrangement of a Beatles' song for a bit."

"I want to hear what you've done so far. Can you record the Preludes?"

"Sure. What are you doing? Did you study for your ancient history test yet?"

"Uh huh, and now I'm reading *Jane Eyre*. I'm at the part when Jane faints on the doorstep of the Rivers' house and St. John finds her. I think she will have to get back with Mr. Rochester soon. I don't think Charlotte is as honest about life as Thomas Hardy. There'll be a happy ending. Her sister and Hardy seem to understand the real world better."

"Do you want me to see if I can find a movie of *Jane Eyre*? I rented *Tess of the D'Urbervilles* for after school tomorrow."

"That's going to be very sad."

"Probably, but it'll be interesting to see how much they include from the book."

"Will we have enough time to stop at the library? I want to get *Jude the Obscure* and check the Stephen King section for anything new.

"We can, but I bought a copy of *Jude* for you. It's in my backpack. I'll bring it to school tomorrow."

My gratitude and love could not be measured.

ONE JUNE SUNDAY WE STOPPED AT A CONVENIENCE STORE. NEW to biking, I braked too late on the wet tar and slammed the Schwinn's front tire into the side of the building. I fell off the seat onto the cross bar and realized a pain in my crotch that I hadn't known since I was eight, when a teenage boy on bus number two had kicked me there to amuse his friends. I stayed outside with the bikes while Eric went into the store to buy drinks. My thigh muscles quivered from the strain of pedaling eighteen miles at get-away speed, and my side was bruised from hitting a mailbox several roads back. We were sneaking away for a few hours to swim on the private beach outside a vacant camp that belonged to friends of Eric's family. I'd told my mother we were biking to Eric's house, emphasized that his father would be there to make sure we behaved. I was getting to be a seasoned liar. But we had to pedal fast if we were to get back so that no one would find out we'd left.

I felt free. Not the free like when I rode Dakota and everyone knew I was in the woods around the farm, but the sort of free where you're away, and even if someone tried to find you, they wouldn't know where to look.

Eric appeared and gave me a can of Ramblin' root beer before drinking long from a Mountain Dew. I appreciated the can. As new to soda as I was to biking, I still couldn't drink from a bottle without my teeth suctioning tight against the opening.

"I wish I didn't ever have to go back."

"I know."

"How will we ever get through?" A question I asked him and my-self each day. "I don't even have Dakota."

When I thought about Dakota a lump formed in my throat. I'd free leased her for two and a half years before her owner, Paula, de-cided she wanted her back. Within an hour's notice of the call Dakota was gone. I hated not seeing her in the yard and barn. I hated Paula for taking her from me and knew Dakota would be happier with me because I gave her treats and spent so much time with her. I didn't consider how Paula felt about Dakota, that she might have missed her. I felt empty and sad, but it was nothing compared to the sadness I would feel two years later when my mother would tell me that Dakota was dead, hit by a car after she ran through her fence into the road.

"We will," Eric said. "You'll see."

Then we were back on our bikes, eight more miles, on curvy Maine roads toward the lake, my mind churning, trying to figure out a way for two fifteen-year-olds to be together without parents. School wouldn't be out for a few weeks, so the next day meant up at 6:00, on the bus by 6:30. The monotony was almost unbearable. Parents and adults made it their business to keep us apart. It wasn't just that they suspected sex and wanted to prevent it; they'd decided it wasn't healthy for two people to spend so much time together.

"You shouldn't settle on the first boy that comes along," my mother lectured, although my father had been her only boyfriend. "Those marriages don't last. I think seeing Eric at school is plenty, and I'm sure Mr. Peppe doesn't approve."

"You should date other girls," Eric's father said in a serious tone. "You're too young to decide who you want to marry. You should see what your choices are before you make a decision. It's not good for you to spend so much time with the first girl you find."

When Eric told me this, I assumed his father didn't approve of me, that his son could get a better deal, as if deciding who you mar-ried was like buying a car: you researched one dealership after an-other to find the perfect model.

Our psychology teacher took us aside: "Humans are social animals. It's not good for you to invest so much in one relationship. Talk to other kids." When he chose captains for psychology games in class he made each of us a leader so we couldn't choose the other for a teammate.

"Good for you," I would repeat to Eric in the school hallway. "I'm not good for you, which is the same as I'm bad for you, which is the same as I'm bad."

"That's not what they mean at all. You're the best thing that's ever happened to me." I would try not to think, *liar*.

Our creative writing teacher said, "Put some space between those desks and stop looking at each other. It makes me uncomfortable."

Three students we didn't know, two girls and a boy, blocked us at the bottom of a school stairwell. We'd seen them there before, and they'd stuck their feet out so we had to step over them, laughing and poking at us as we passed to go up the stairs to our classes. Each day they went a little further until one morning they refused to let us by. Two girls in jean jackets and pants so tight they couldn't move except in tiny steps. Every part of their female genitalia was defined. For years I'd heard my mother rant about how disgusting it was for girls, especially grown girls, to wear pants so tight that nothing was left to the imagination. Without hesitation, just for the deep indentation of the jean's seam defining their crotch, I judged them bad girls. That they stuck their arms wide to each side to block us, something you could do as a student only if you had no books, made them appear stupid. The boy stayed in the shadows with a sneer on his pimple-covered face. He didn't have any books either.

"You two make us sick. Fucking losers."

When the girl spoke she curled her lip, showing her yellow teeth. I was glad I'd chosen sex, not cigarettes, as my teenage vice.

"Let us by," Eric said, quiet like his father.

"What are you going to do about it? I'll beat your little girlfriend up. Then we'll see who's so smart."

"No one's going to beat anyone up," Eric said, although I could hear the uncertainty in his voice. "We don't even know you. Why would you care about us?"

"Because we don't like you. And that's good enough reason."

A bell rang, and other students began to move around us to go up the stairs. Unable to hold back a crowd, the girls moved to the side. I took Eric's hand and went up the stairs with the tide.

"Saved this time, but you just wait," the girl with the yellow teeth called after us. Her spaghetti-like hair reminded me of Sheila the bus driver's. "You'll be sorry I ever saw your ugly faces."

I was the sister of one of the toughest people I knew. I'd done a lot of free babysitting for her, but I didn't think she'd refuse me even if I hadn't. I asked around at school and found out the students' names. My tough-yet-admirable sister lived close to the high school. Still muscular, still daring, she met the students-of-the-stairwell unannounced in a parking lot at night.

"You'll leave my little sister alone or we'll just see who gets beaten up. If I even hear of you laying one finger on her, you'll be the one who's sorry you ever looked in her direction. You fuck around with her and you fuck around with me," she threatened. She might have even grabbed the girls—I don't know. My hair-twirling-pretty sister who'd accompanied her reported the conversation to me.

When I saw the students-of-the-stairwell the day following their introduction to my tough-yet-admirable sister, they didn't look me in the eye. No one ever threatened me or Eric in high school again, and I never loved my tough-yet-admirable sister more. Or my hair-twirling-pretty sister, who could have decided to stay home but didn't.

On our bikes, we were together. This far from parental authority, we could do anything. Eric turned onto the narrow wooded road that curved to the small seasonal camp that he'd been to with his mother and her friends. Set back from the private water frontage, the small, locked, cottage-like cabin dripped with light rain. It reminded me of my aunt's camp, my first fantasy escape place, and for a few minutes I allowed myself to fantasize about living there with Eric, reading books and playing the piano. That's where my fantasy fizzled. How could we get a piano all the way out here?

Ignoring the rain and rawness of Maine spring weather, we swam naked in the lake. We knew we'd have only a few hours before we had to turn around and bike home. Our skin tight with goose bumps, we thrilled at the closeness. I knew I could never love anyone as much as I loved this person, who chose to spend his time with me, when before he met me, he'd used every second he wasn't in school to play the piano and write music.

We went for a walk in the woods—not the thick, dark woods dense with trees, vegetation, and wild animals that surrounded my house but rather the open woods of random pine and birches that city people call the forest, as if they expect to stumble upon witches' cottages, dwarves, and woodland fairies.

"Tell me what you're thinking," Eric said. He held my hand. Despite the chill of swimming, his hands were still warm.

"I'm thinking that some disaster will strike and we'll never be together for real. It seems impossible, like your father might be right. How will we be able to afford to go to school full time and live in Portland?"

"I know what you mean," he stepped over a log, and twigs snapped beneath his feet. "I'm not saying it won't be really hard, but it'll be easier than the waiting."

Wave upon wave of frustration rolled across my brain into my limbs. It began to rain harder, as if the clouds echoed our moods. We sat on the ground beneath the leaky canopy of trees and talked, the water streaming through the branches above us. Night was coming on. I could see it creeping through the sparse woods languorously like a stretching cat. As the shadows lengthened, my body seized with the dread of leaving Eric and returning to the emptiness of home without Dakota.

"What if we didn't go back? What if we hid away?" I asked suddenly, grabbing his bare arm to make my point.

"We can't hide away," Eric said. "We have no money, no place to go."

"But we could try," I pleaded. "Every time I'm with you it's harder and harder *not* to be with you." My mind railed against me: *you're trying to convince a PK to hide away with you.* "Please?" I asked, hanging onto him as if he were the person with all the power. "Can we stay?"

When a naked girl exhorts even an intelligent boy to do a stupid thing, he usually does it.

WRESTLING OUR DAMP CLOTHES OVER DAMP SKIN, WE GOT ON our bikes and pedaled the eight miles to the convenience store. After we bought a loaf of bread and peanut butter, we inserted one of our last dimes into the pay phone and called my friend from homeroom who had introduced me to Herman Hesse books. We gave him our parents' numbers and asked him to tell them we were safe but not coming home. It was my idea to call people so that no one would worry. I didn't want my mother to think I was dead. Then we got back on our bikes and rode the winding miles to camp.

My quivering leg muscles protested the hills, and my overused seat bones fought contact with the padded vinyl triangle beneath them. The rain continued, dripping and splashing down from the trees and up from the bike tires. I could see very little in the dusk that had turned to darkness, but I could hear Eric behind me. I'd never worn a helmet to ride Dakota, but Eric insisted I wear one to ride a bike. I disliked the weight of it on my head, how it twisted and flattened my hair, but now it offered protection from the rain, keeping water out of my eyes. My lungs struggled to take in oxygen, and they were raw with the effort as I shivered, my bruised side aching.

Back at the camp in the soaking rain, Eric secured the bikes beneath a camp overhang and snapped the old wood frame around the simple lock on the rustic door with his strength and weight. The words *breaking and entering* swam through my consciousness. I shoved them aside. *We were finally alone. Really alone.* After eating our peanut butter sandwiches, we went to bed in the loft. I'd ridden my bike over thirty miles, Eric had ridden his forty-five, and with the emotional stress of running away, exhaustion lay close beneath our anxiety.

I didn't want to sleep, was afraid to lose a minute with Eric, but my eyelids refused to obey and dropped shut. My last thought was, *there's no way this will work.*

BANGING, FEROCIOUS POUNDING IN THE DISTANCE, SPLINTERING wood, two harsh male voices—I know instantly we are caught. No longer do camps seem like the perfect place to run away. Boots thud and heels stomp against planks: "This is Sheriff Munsey. I'm coming up."

A scene from an action movie flashes through my brain, in which police officers break doors open with their shoulders and thrust their bodies, guns pointed high and straight, ahead of them. Now more than any other situation I've ever been in I wish for some mind-bending Stephen King–character-power. If only I could start a fire with the intensity of my thoughts or at least make the sheriff see dead people. If vampires were real, now would be a good time for several to appear.

I try desperately to wake Eric but cannot. I am frustrated, angry with him that he refuses to move.

Nothing supernatural or otherworldly slows the sheriff. He clomps up the narrow ladder competently to the loft; his flashlight beam dances in spurts of color along the walls and ceiling as he climbs. Responding to some primal urge that I must do something, I dive under the twin bed beside the one I've been sleeping in. Just before I exit the warmth, I whisper-shout, "Hide!"

Even as I leave the bed I feel shame for abandoning the one person who has risked trouble, risked everything. Before he met me he was good, praised for his remarkable responsibility, demonstrated by a paper route at such a young age. He never drank, smoked, or used drugs. He watched out for his siblings, not like I did so they wouldn't get caught but rather so they wouldn't hurt themselves. Whereas I was told by various adults that I would amount to nothing, Eric was told that if he kept working, he would go to Julliard or the Eastman School of Music. Not only was I bringing him down, but I was leaving him alone, blissfully unaware, in this moment of surprise capture by Sheriff Munsey.

Eric doesn't hear me, but the sheriff does, and he shines the light under the bed, where I'm pressed naked against the floor, gravel and cold plywood digging into my breasts and hipbones.

"Well, no one's ever hidden under a bed before," he says, and his chuckle will play in my mind whenever I think of this night in the future. To him, this is just another night, nothing personal that he has to own. He watches me crawl out, and I notice that he doesn't leave as I dress. Eric is awake now, slipping on his jeans and T-shirt. I can't tell what he's thinking. I can't see his face well in the shadowy loft. I'm afraid he's decided that loving me is not worth what is about to happen, that this isn't what he had in mind when he asked me to be his girlfriend three months ago in Dakota's stall. I see all our plans—our life in Portland, working and going to school—weaken and pop as if they are no more than a cartoon bubble.

I walk ahead of him to the ladder. My bare feet are silent. He's already put his Nikes on, and they thud against the bare boards. The sheriff's boots are loud; they rasp and clunk. I left my old cloth sneakers downstairs. I feel as if we are walking to our execution. I need to pee and wonder how long I'll be able to hold it. Is it permissible to mention? There is an outhouse, but will I be allowed to use it? Maybe they will think I am using urine as part of my escape plan to run off into the woods. A part of me thinks this is possible. If I pee in a car, it won't be the first time.

We climb down the ladder to the small living and kitchen area. Eric's dad is there. He talk-shouts to his son: "Do you have bread-crumbs for brains?" I instantly picture evil stepmothers, witches, and children trying to save themselves.

I'm sure the two men think "tramp" and "bad girl" when they look at me and "poor guy, he didn't see it coming" when they look at Eric. Neither of us answers because, like so many questions, the asker doesn't expect any.

"We've been badgering your friend Ray and his family for hours. I am so disappointed. Get outside and put the bikes in the van," his dad continues.

Eric leaves, looking back at me with worry in his brown eyes, and his father follows him out, his loafer heels clicking softly on the plywood camp floor. I'm alone with Sheriff Munsey.

"Let's go."

I pick up my sneakers and walk outside. It's stopped raining, but there are no stars. The ground is soggy beneath my feet. I hope none of the wetness is worms or slugs. I forget I'd planned to ask him to wait so that I can use the outhouse, because now I envision worms on the soles of my feet twisting themselves to get free. I get into the police car. I'm so scared, I can barely think.

"You can sit in the front if you want to," he tells me.

His words confuse me. I'm already halfway in the back and think it will look silly to open and close doors to switch seats. I'm embarrassed, but most of all I'm afraid of what is waiting for me at home. I'm relieved there are no lights or sirens or German shepherds. As soon as my bottom touches the seat, I begin to imagine all the kinds of people who have sat on this vinyl. Suddenly I obsess it's leather, the skin of a cow or deer corpse.

Thieves. Wife beaters. Murderers. Drug dealers. I suddenly don't want my bottom to touch the upholstery. I don't belong here. I know it with all that I know. This is all wrong. I want to leap out of the car. Roll. Disappear into the woods.

"Why'd you run away?" he asks. "Is home life that bad?"

I never discuss my life with anyone except Eric. Instead, I try to distract people, keep them out of my head. I worry now that I might be forced by law to talk on a personal level.

"I don't know."

"Is there violence?"

I wonder if he asks this because of the bruises on my thighs and sides from running into the mailbox and the store earlier that day. I wonder if I can get in trouble for denting someone else's property. Being the daughter of a post office maintenance technician, the thought crosses my mind that everything to do with the mail is sacred. This person's mailbox might be yet another crime to add to my record.

"I don't know, I guess."

"Bad?"

This question tells me that some violence is good.

I say nothing.

"I'll speak to them."

I don't know how to tell him that the physical violence is not my mother, the person who will open the house door shortly. He won't know about a sister who has a toddler I saw her push to the floor. Coming home from school one afternoon, I picked his small body up and raced outside, hugging him to my chest, my sister shrieking, "It's none of your business what I do! He's mine!"

The sheriff can't do anything about the fact that my mother has tried to help her, given her everything she has to give, but still cries in great hiccupping gulps as if her heart is broken, and it's because she loves her daughter but also loves her new grandchild as if he were her own son. She cries to my father, to me: "I just don't know what to do. What can I do?"

I can't tell him about the bullshit-artist-ass-Skipper, who bellows and slams his fists into furniture and people, how I saw him chase my hair-twirling-pretty sister up to the garden, screaming, "I'm going to kill you!" How my father tried to calm him down but couldn't. "Come on now. That's enough," he'd said, and I could see he was really scared. My father said to my mother: "He's sick, honey. It's not his fault." My mother cried so hard she could barely breathe. It wasn't until my heart-of-gold brother-in-law showed up unexpectedly and calmed everyone down with his strength of character that she stopped crying and could breathe again.

There has never been a day when I didn't wonder how different all of our lives would have been if this family hanger-on, who had scoffed I could never be a veterinarian or anything else real because I was a girl, had never hung on at all.

The sheriff will not know that my holier-than-thou brother called Eric's parents and told them to keep their son at home, that he is ruining me more than I am already ruined. I can't tell him how my mother is embarrassed because, in her words, I cavorted with a man more than twice my age when I should have known better—*did* know better.

I can't tell him how I don't have a reason to go back because Dakota is gone, and the emptiness of the barn and the pastures overwhelm me, make my muscles so tired that I doubt I'll have energy to walk into the house. I won't allow myself to bring self-pity into the air because my mother has given me more than she has given any of her other children. I am the one who is hurting her now.

"I'll be fine," I assure him. "You don't need to say anything."

He ignores my words as if I haven't spoken and asks, "How's school going?"

This question can't be answered either. I know he is just making conversation, passing the time, but to reply honestly I'd have to tell him about the algebra class I'm failing because I am not the detective my mother is. I can never find the missing X. I'd have to tell him about the biology class where I'd refused to dissect any animal because it was wrong. Students have books, pictures, models to show them what is inside an animal. Dissection, unless you are on your way to a medical degree, is a waste of life, and it reinforces to people who already don't value their pets that animals' lives are worth nothing. My biology teacher had smiled his smug smile and given me a B for the semester. I'd have to tell him about the boy I know who attempted suicide and who lost most of his eyesight, about another boy who died in a motorcycle accident, about the bullies, the bus rides with the pot smokers and the drinkers. It may be a question of only three words, but school is eight hours of my day, five days a week. It would take at least an hour to explain how school was going, even if I just skimmed the surface.

"Fine."

He's silent. All I can see are tree-shaped black outlines, quick open spaces around houses, and then more tree-shaped black outlines passing outside the window. The tires swoosh through puddles, and time is punctuated when Sheriff Munsey turns on the wipers. I notice his blades swipe smoothly, almost silent, whereas my parents' windshield wipers make an unrhythmic eee-aww sound as if the water has bumps in it.

Would I hurt myself if I jumped? Could I get far enough away before the sheriff realized I'd left? I plot my escape and remember suddenly how I used to imagine bouncing out of the back window of the station wagon. *Would I ever ride in a car and not think of escape?*

The clock in the car says it's 12:30. I have to be on the bus in six hours.

I realize I'm shaking, my whole body is trembling, and I can't stop it. I try to recall if a sheriff ever drove any of my eight siblings home, given all the bad things they did. I almost laugh. With eight brothers and sisters ahead of me it had been almost impossible to do things first. Now I have.

"I'll talk to them," he says again. He sounds tired too.

I want to ask him questions. I want to keep him away from my life.

"Do you have children?"

"No, but I have parents and three sisters, so I know how it can be." He pokes a card through the grate divider that separates the back from the front seat. "Call me if you need to. That's my direct line at the station."

He turns onto the road that leads to my house, slowing down as his car hits the unsteady dirt. The road was recently graded, and it pulls at his tires, making it difficult for him to drive without weaving. I picture my mother standing at my lookout window, watching the lights bounce unevenly through the trees. Panic edges its fingers into my brain, my scalp tingles, and the inside of the car wavers. I can't get enough air.

Now, I order myself. *Open the door now and run for it.*

I do nothing.

In the driveway he opens my door like a gentleman. Once we are in the house the two dogs bark and sniff at his uniformed knees. He's lucky he doesn't have a clipboard; Tippy always checks. My mother is in her nightgown and housecoat, and my father is sleeping. I think suddenly of Eric's dad at the camp, his worried face, and I note that my parents went to bed.

The sheriff and my mother stay in the entry talking. I drop my wet sneakers to the floor in the corner and go to the bathroom. Even in my misery, considering what's to come, I experience relief.

When I come out the sheriff's gone, and I miss him. I want him to tell my mother he has three sisters and he knows how it is.

"How could you do this?" my mother begins. "You've embarrassed me in front of the police, in front of Mr. Peppe. I expected better from you." I notice she doesn't seem to care what Mrs. Peppe will think of her. She's been trained to worry only about the opinion of men, trained to believe they are the superior gender.

But I expected better from me too. We're both disappointed about the same thing.

"I'm just so tired," I say.

She thinks I mean from lack of sleep, but I mean from everything.

"Then go to bed," she says. "Just get your trampy self to bed." Her tone passes across the divide of victim to judge. I hear almost word for word the directives and names she once called my sisters. *I'm no different*, I think.

"I don't want to see your face again until morning. I've had enough of you tonight," she shouts. "All that worrying over nothing."

I go upstairs and she follows, slamming her feet into each step after me.

"I thought you didn't want to see me again tonight," I want to say, but I watch my mouth.

Until 2 a.m. she lists all the ways I disappoint her. I cannot tune her out by lying on my good ear because she's too close. It's obvious she is trying to not wake my father.

When she leaves I sleep as if I'm still awake. Then I am awake. Rocks hit my window from outside. It's 4 a.m. Running downstairs, I see my mother at the door and Eric on the porch. While I've been in bed, he's walked the fifteen miles in from town. More guilt layered on like a rotten onion. I see Eric in front of me, but the distance is as great a divide as when the continental plates split.

"Are you okay?" he asks, trying to see me around my mother's large house-coated body. He's pale, red eyed, haggard. In the dim light I see his clothes are wrinkled and dirty. I've brought him to this. I cannot understand, cannot fathom why he loves me, but I love him more. I think it's impossible there can be this much love.

"She's fine. Now go home," my mother says, as if he were no more than a stray dog.

None of us in this family have ever been fine.

"I'll see you at school," he says and goes slowly down the driveway, back twelve of the miles he's just walked, to the doorstep of the school where I will meet him. All I can think about is the next time we'll be alone. I plan the minutes. I think of his words in the woods that afternoon, what seems almost a lifetime ago: "I'm not saying it won't be really hard, but it'll be easier than the waiting."

There's this place in the woods not far from the parsonage where we go to be alone. We escape to our special place whenever we can, sneaking off as little as thirty minutes and as much as sixty before an adult has demanded we be somewhere. Eric's hidden a trash bag in a tree. Inside are a sleeping bag and a small tarp. We sit below the trees and talk, laugh, and are silent, always within the cage of clock time, a cage we test frequently out of frustration and anger. Every part of my mind and body is exhausted except the part that drives me to be with him. We'll get away again. No one can stop us.

20

The Starting Line

In bed on my back, I stared up at the ceiling and the outline of the seventies-style light fixture that sometimes looked like a monster with a twisted face. I breathed in the dark, held it in my lungs, fought the black weight of trouble that hovered in my consciousness. Sixteen years old. Three days late, the cause could be anything—stress, poor nutrition, too much bike riding—but I knew somewhere in my brain where people know these things. I thought I'd guarded against the odds, protected myself, but true safety from teenage pregnancy is possible only for virgins.

"And I'm gonna keep on lovin' you," Eric's voice floated from the cassette player on my nightstand. He'd learned the REO Speedwagon song off the record when I was away with my parents in August.

Immune to bullying and begging, time had refused my plea to bring age eighteen closer. "'Cause it's the only thing I wanna do." I placed my hands beneath the sheets on my flat stomach, expecting to feel the terror knotted there with the fertilized egg, a tangled lump within my gut like a breeding ball of snakes.

I was careful to keep my hands away from my breasts, my crotch. I'd been amazed that Eric knew no fear of his own body. He never used a washcloth in the shower like I did. He wasn't afraid to touch his own skin.

"Don't assume the worst," Eric had said in school earlier that day. "Just wait and see. You could still start."

Sometimes his encouraging words made me want to shake him. He didn't know trouble like I did. Trouble and I were old friends, and I was about to take our relationship to a whole new level.

IT WAS NOVEMBER, CLOSING IN ON A YEAR AND A HALF SINCE Sheriff Munsey had driven me home. Eric and I had spent every second we could together, outwitting adults each day, being sulky and rude when apart. To help with Eric's missed piano practice, his mother and her new partner moved a secondhand piano into my house. It was so heavy that my father installed support posts in the cellar, and it was so old and beat-up that he refinished it. Eric taught me to play simplified Scott Joplin rags and pieces out of *John Thompson's* piano method book. He showed me walking bass patterns and then improvised boogies on the treble, but never when my father was home; then the need for quiet reigned. If I practiced too long when my mother was in the house, she would cover her ears and shout, "Just stop it! I can't think with all that noise!"

Several minutes later she would say, "I'm sorry. I know you're trying to learn." Life, since I alone lived with her as the last child, was different. She wanted to spend time with me and had questions of her own. She had her own regrets, I learned. Many about how she wished she'd had more time, more money, more patience, and more education.

My father muttered and grumbled when, without permission, Eric bought me two parakeets who screeched at the wild birds outside the windows, even when I covered them. He also bought me two baby goats who, on the side of the house where my father slept, bleated early in the morning for attention. "Can't I have any peace?" he would yell, his hair askew and his eyes small with weariness. Cleo and Daffodil's answer was to butt him in the backs of his knees when he wasn't looking. I made the goats a stall inside the barn, but they wanted attention, so they chewed the wood frame around a window until they had a clear place to stand and bleat facing the house. If no one answered their calls, they chewed their stall's two-by-fours and supporting beams. I came home one afternoon to find they'd escaped the barn and eaten their way through my mother's flower gardens. They came running to me when I appeared around the corner of the house, where they had been dining on porch railings, their little white knees brown with dirt from kneeling in the gardens. I squatted on the ground and hugged them, knowing from the flattened gardens and the gnawed railings that it was in their best interest for me to find them a new home. Cleo rested her head on my chest, lazily munching a piece of my shirt, while Daffodil stood behind me with her front legs on my back. When I got up to take them back to the barn, part of my ponytail was missing.

I was sad to lose the goats to common sense, and I worried that the woman who bought them wouldn't love them like I did. Eric brought me a spaniel-mix puppy to replace the hole the goats left in my life. We named him Joplin. He was a good dog, smiling with his mouth when he saw me after school, following me everywhere. But he stole deer meat when my father was cutting it up. My father tried to get it back, but only once. After that no one bothered Joplin when he had something he wanted.

Eric bought me two hamsters, which lived in an aquarium in the dining room until they escaped and gnawed the telephone wires and electrical cords and chewed a hole into a stuffed chair for nesting material. I was never able to catch them.

The rabbits were my idea. I'd needed to save them all from the slaughterhouse. Ira Gershwin, an angora I'd bought at the Cumberland Fair when I walked up to his cage, and he bowed his head to be petted. It is true that rabbits multiply rapidly. Gershwin's former owner offered me a guinea pig as well, and I was too polite to refuse.

For my seventeenth birthday Eric would convince my mother, who secretly loved all my new pets, especially Joplin because of Tippy's recent death, to contribute to the purchase of a flute that would take me hours and hours of screechy, out-of-tune practice to perfect my embouchure. My mother suggested I take over one of the small bedrooms on the far side of the house as my practice area. I was no longer the only one in the house who wanted me to be eighteen and gone.

No one shared those few weeks of silent agony with me except my partner in crime, the boy I planned to marry, the boy who asked each time I saw him: "Did you start yet?"

"Don't you think I'd tell you if I did?"

Eric whispered as he hugged me: "We're in this together."

I wanted to believe him, but nausea bit at a foreign emptiness in my stomach, and fatigue embedded itself into the fibers of my muscles. When I looked up at his smiling face I knew that "in this together" meant something completely different for him. His clothes wouldn't get tighter, he would walk past any adult and not turn heads, and he would not cause people to consider the immorality and dangers of teenage sex at the sight of him. He wouldn't fall asleep during classes, his body worn out from playing host to an embryo.

I couldn't keep my eyes open in geometry because my brain decided it was too much work to figure out the angles, the proofs. This was not information I needed anymore. Balking, turning inward, my hypothalamus told me what I really needed was to eat a hamburger. Being a vegetarian, I vomited.

"You're going to be okay," Eric said. "You'll see."

He wiped my face, placing the strands of throw-up dampened hair away from my mouth. I couldn't see what he saw. I was too exhausted from feeling everyone's unspoken criticism. Guilty, never again innocent, stupid, knocked up—the gavel banged within my mind. I wanted nothing more than for people to think I was intelligent and better than the bad people. I returned from school to Joplin, who treated me like a hero because I could open the refrigerator. I wanted to live with two dogs, my two parakeets, fifteen rabbits, a guinea pig, a horse, and Eric. Maybe a donkey.

Desperate to eat, I opened the fridge a lot.

"Why are you frying all those potatoes?" my mother asked as she pointed accusingly at the cast iron pan. "Why are you eating so much?" She stared at my stomach, my breasts. Could she see they ached? Her voice got harder and her eyes got smaller. "What's going on here? Tell me."

I couldn't answer. If I didn't eat the potatoes, I would throw up. I couldn't shove them in fast enough, yet they didn't seem to touch the empty recess that was my stomach—so much effort to fill it, then one slice too many. I threw up, noting with fascination how little I chewed.

"Are you pregnant?" Assessing me like she would a pound of ground meat that was the right color but smelled wrong.

Not "Are you sick?" Or even a polite "What's wrong?"

She assumed that I'd turned out bad based on a pan of wasted fried potatoes, possibly because waste of any type sent her flying off the handle. My hair-twirling-pretty sister had had sex as a teenager, when she was younger than I was, but she didn't get pregnant so could pass as good.

"I don't know," I said, opening a can of baked beans and putting them in the microwave, moving with my back toward her.

"How did this happen?" her voice and face pale and rigid with emotion.

"I don't know." My knowledge on the subject was shaky. What little I knew was the result of someone in the school administration thinking reproduction should be taught as part of the curriculum.

"You don't know?" she yelled in disbelief, the volume escalating. "How can you not know? Why, I thought you knew everything, little miss butter-couldn't-melt-in-your-mouth-know-it-all."

I removed the baked beans from the microwave but didn't sit to eat them. There was no time. I had to get the beans into my stomach as fast as I could.

"You're no different from your sisters," she continued on, her words sounding to me like the wheeking of my guinea pig, Penny, if she heard the rustle of plastic. "Didn't you learn anything from watching all their mistakes?"

"You're not alone," Eric had said, but he wasn't getting yelled at.

"What's your father going to say about all this?" my mother asked as she broke into my self-pity rant, which brought on sudden and overwhelming fatigue. I needed to be left alone so I could vomit privately.

"I'm sorry," I said. And really I was when, seconds later, I kneeled on the bathroom floor and threw up all the kidney beans. It would take a huge effort for me to wash my bowl in the sink so that I could start over to fill the emptiness.

DAYS PASSED AND MY FATHER SAID NOTHING. HE DIDN'T LOOK me in the eye. I was invisible. My mother took me to the gynecologist, keeping me out of school for the November 16 appointment. It felt wrong, almost painful, not to be in class. A schoolgirl version of a vampire, I wasn't supposed to be outside of brick buildings during the day. The office nurse weighed me in at 116 pounds. She took my blood pressure. I peed in a cup, and seconds later I put on a paper gown. My mother stood nearby, her face stiff, her mind unyielding. The doctor knocked gently and entered.

We begin:

"How are you today?"

What do I say? Do I show regret at my condition? Proper mortification? Apologize?

"I need to ask a few questions before we get started."

Locked in embarrassment and fear that he will ask something that will get me in even more trouble, I wonder if I can lie. Is the exam table like the witness stand?

"Date of last menstrual period?"

"September 28."

"Do you smoke?"

"No." But if I did, would I admit it in front of my mother?

"Do you drink?"

"No." But again, if I did? . . .

He laughs. "You're the first pregnant teenager in here who doesn't smoke and drink."

Awkward—should I take this as a compliment? Does this mean some part of me is still good? Is love that leads to intercourse equivalent to a bad habit? He can see how difficult this is with my mother standing there.

"Do you know who the father is?"

Suddenly I am grossly offended. Is this a roundabout way of calling me a slut?

"Yes," I say firmly, possibly rudely.

"And that would be?"

"Eric Peppe." I see him write the name down on his clipboard. Even if I don't marry Eric, my medical record will always read, "Eric Peppe, father of baby."

Short silence, then surprise: "Oh, Eric Peppe, I know him."

He says "Peppe" as if the last name is French for grandfather: "Pep-pay." I don't like Eric's last name and think that we might be able to come up with a better one when we get married.

"He teaches my daughter piano. Talented young man."

I smile carefully. How do I respond? With pleasure at the connection? Will he remove his daughter from lessons, from Eric's bad influence, or am only I the tainted one? What are the rules of this doctor-patient relationship and my teenage pregnancy status? I don't know the protocol, and I wish there were a book I could read to discover the answers.

Polite talk over, the exam begins:

"Lie back. Scoot closer to me. A little farther. Yes, that's it."

My legs are spread wide, my feet in stirrups. I've never been to a OB/GYN, to a doctor of any kind except for my ear and my teeth. My first pelvic exam is everything I've been taught never to do in front of a male. Hot blood pulses in my face—blood, the life force my uterus withholds for another life. I try to remember when I last took a shower.

The doctor, low voiced, no enthusiasm—is that judgment I hear? Disappointment? "Your uterus is enlarged. The urine sample is positive. You're about nine weeks along, I'd guess."

My mother's anger escalates as if she hadn't actually believed I was pregnant until someone with a speculum and white coat said the words. We'd all thought I would do better.

"How could you," she began as we left the office, "talk to that doctor as if you are a married woman expecting your first child? You embarrassed me in front of him in there, acting like I'd never taught you right from wrong. Don't you care anything at all about how I feel?" She slammed the car door and shifted to reverse.

I leaned my head against the window, feeling the need to eat again, as nausea began to worm its way back into my stomach. I suddenly craved a hot fudge sundae—any sundae actually, the mixture of syrupy warmth over cold ice cream. I wanted to stop at Goodwin's Dairy up the street. I began to plan how to get a sundae with Eric after school. "I do care. I'm sorry."

My mother backed out of the parking space and maneuvered the maroon sedan into the street. I watched women on the sidewalks intent on their own lives as we waited at the lights. They were probably thinking about lunch or an appointment or work they needed to do at home. They might even be on their way to eat a hot fudge sundae. They might have one for dessert every day at this time. Had any of them been pregnant as a teenager? I envied them—their independence, their ability to walk in the street, change direction, get whatever they wanted to eat as soon as their stomachs demanded it. If they had jobs, they could call in sick, leave early, ask for more hours, and always go home at the end of the day to a life of their making. Likely none of them had vomited within the last twenty-four hours. I wanted to be them, any one of them, it didn't matter which. They were all outside of this car, outside of my life.

"And what do you have to say for yourself?" my mother asked, pausing in her lecture-rant.

I didn't know. I hadn't been listening.

My stomach growled, and I rubbed it to ease the hunger pains. A new emotion flitted into my mind when my hand came in contact with my abdomen. My mother detested how her daughters-in-law—any women actually, everywhere and anywhere—touched their stomachs when they were pregnant. She would yell about how silly they were, how melodramatic. "There's no need of women behaving so ridiculous," she would snap.

"Nothing," I answered, and I moved my hand to the door armrest.

"That's just what I figured," she said triumphantly. "Just like your sisters. Showing not an ounce of gratitude for all your father and I have done for you."

She drove up a hill that seemed to go on forever. The car's engine strained, then shifted deeper. I felt part of the struggle, like I might not make it up the hill. The high school spread out before us at the top, and I got out of the car as quickly as I could, kissing my mother good-bye so as not to make her angrier. I walked to the main entrance at the front of the brick building and allowed the school to suck me back into the schedule of its day.

I moved ghost-like down the empty corridors. I felt the strange emotion from the car, when I'd touched my stomach, take hold and plant itself. I opened the door to geometry class as quietly as I could and slipped into my seat beside Eric.

Mrs. Levesque nodded at me and continued to explain a proof that I had no way of ever understanding: "If one of the givens is point C and the midpoint of AB, your statement would read 'AC = CB,' and your reason would be 'definition of midpoint'," her voice droned.

Eric looked over at me.

"I am," I said, and for a reason I still cannot explain, we both smiled.

He reached across the area between our desks and squeezed my cold hand.

EACH AFTERNOON I MET MY MOTHER'S DISAPPOINTMENT AT THE door. Our conversations were careful: nothing about pregnancy, babies, my relationship with Eric, or my discomfort. I kept my hands away from my stomach. I was too busy trying not to throw up the last thing I ate to speak much at all. I wore my fear of being found out at school like Harry Potter wears his invisibility cloak. In September the guidance counselor had chosen me to be one of the two peer facilitators in my high school. I spent one period a day explaining the college application process to other juniors. I had been on the college track myself, and now I didn't know what my future held. My plan had been to marry Eric, move to Portland, and earn a bachelor's degree, majoring in English.

No one told Eric that he'd ruined his future. He was a pianist, talented, winner of competitions, gifted and smart. Except for the scrawl of his name on my chart, he was still all of those things. He chose to tell his father at Goodwin's Dairy in the City-of-the-Library, and I wondered if anyone else recognized the irony of "good" and "wins" blinking in neon across our booth table. His father's eyes widened toward me at the news, with disbelief and disappointment.

"How did this happen?" he asked, staring directly at me.

Everyone had predicted pregnancy, warning, "If you're not careful, you'll get pregnant, and that'll be more trouble than you'll know what to do with," yet now they were all asking how it happened?

"Well, what are you going to do now?" he said, still staring at me, the pregnant one.

"Whatever we need to," Eric said, and I was grateful for the "we."

"What do you mean 'we'? This is her problem, and she needs more than you can give to help her."

He stared at me without drinking the coffee his hands held as if the cup were anchoring him to the table. "You are too young to have a baby. What about going to college, being a writer? How are you going to do that now?" He didn't raise his voice. He didn't have to.

My mouth dared me to take another bite of hot fudge sundae. I touched the spoon, and my stomach decided that was far enough. Eric could see the forces taking sides, gaining strength. I swallowed, clamped my teeth together, and averted my eyes. He covered the ice cream with a napkin and pushed it to the opposite side of the table. In that moment I knew what real love was and knew I'd love him forever.

Eric's father reached across the table and took my hand, rubbed his thumb along the side of it. "I know this is hard," he said. And I wondered if he really did.

THE NEXT DAY ERIC'S MOTHER ACCEPTED THE NEWS AS IF SHE'D been waiting for it.

We stood in her small kitchen. She leaned against the counter, her arms crossed over her substantial breasts, her short black hair at attention all over her head. "It's unfortunate," she said to both of us, "but I'll do what I can to help. How are you feeling?"

"Okay," I said, tears gathering force. She didn't make any suggestions or ask how reproduction happened. She invited me to Thanksgiving.

I'M PREGNANT, I THOUGHT WHEN I WOKE UP. I'M PREGNANT, I thought when I went to sleep.

My stomach swelled, but not noticeably to outsiders. It could have been all the potatoes sitting there in one great lump like when Lady, Donny's pasture companion, had looked when she'd eaten them for all those years instead of grain.

One morning I didn't throw up and was surprised. I tested the change by picturing myself eating macaroni and cheese, ice cream, or an egg salad sandwich. These thoughts passed the gagging test. I no longer craved meat. I seemed to be in control again. As the day aged, an ache began in my right side. By nightfall the pain nagged persistently at my attention.

Early December, the time when teenagers are thinking ahead to Christmas, my mother took me to the OB/GYN, and Eric insisted on coming.

The nurse weighed me. I'd gained four pounds, which surprised me, considering how much food my stomach had forcefully rejected.

The doctor ordered an ultrasound and we drove to the hospital. The doctor's concern and kindness unsettled me and irritated my mother: no one should treat me nicely, as if I were a real woman having a real baby. My name was called, and the three of us traipsed into the small room, heads down, silent.

There was a fetal sac but no heartbeat.

"It's still early," the doctor decided. "Too early to know anything for sure. Everything else is within normal limits. Let's give it another week and get you back in here."

First I was late, and now I was early.

"But the ache?" I asked.

"I was concerned that the pregnancy was in your fallopian tube, but the tubes look normal. It's likely gas pain," he said. "Pregnant women experience a lot of gas." He sent me home and said to come back for a second ultrasound in a week.

"Pregnant women." I was having difficulty adjusting to my new identity, one that included vomit, weight gain, and gas.

Time slowed to a trickle. I'd been crossing the days off in the Bronte women journal Eric had bought for me the year before, and I had another year and a half to go before marriage, but these last pregnancy weeks had seemed the slowest of my life. First, the uncertainty, the waiting to know if I was pregnant; second, the waiting for a conclusive ultrasound to recheck the heartbeat; and third, what would happen when I knew. If I'd had a magic lamp when I first saw Eric playing Randy Newman's "Short People," I would have asked that genie to add four years to my age. Now I didn't know what to ask a genie.

THE NEXT WEEK ARRIVED, AND WHEN I LAY ON THE EXAM TABLE alone with the radiologist at my side, my sweatpants pushed down to my hipbones, the cold gel on my abdomen, I didn't feel excitement for Christmas or a new year.

"Got any Christmas plans?" the technician asked.

"Not really," I said in a voice coated with fatigue.

"Looks like it will be white," he said, his tone cheerful but his face blank as he slid the wand over my slightly rounded stomach. Back and forth he rubbed, pressing down, lifting, then pressing down again. Searching, I thought. A wave of sadness rolled across my mind. I didn't know what to do with it, how to respond to what the chemicals in my brain wanted me to feel. He wiped my stomach with a towel.

"Stay here," he said. "The doctor will be in to see you shortly."

I lay there, my legs, even my toes, still, not daring to move despite my instinct to flee. I needed to get off this narrow table, away from the lamps above me, the machines to my side. I had no place to go, but I had a place I could feel calling me just as I'd imagined Waterboro must have felt that summer day so long ago when his little legs paddled so furiously to get him far away.

The doctor knocked and entered, avoiding unnecessary preamble. Maybe he reserved pleasantries for the legitimately pregnant women.

"You have what we call a nonviable pregnancy, a blighted ovum," he said, almost monotone. "In other words, your pregnancy is terminating itself."

Like the road I live on, I thought. *A dead end.*

"The fetal sac should be removed immediately," he continued, "by dilatation and curettage, more commonly known as a D and C. If it's not removed, you could suffer a painful miscarriage over the holidays. And we wouldn't want that, now would we?" He patted my leg. "I'll speak to your mother." Then he left, leaving me there on the bed, trying to figure out what it was I had lost.

"Well, that was a close call," my mother said, pleased, almost giddy, when I exited the exam room. "I hope you've learned something from all of this."

ON DECEMBER 21 I PUT ON A JOHNNY IN THE HOSPITAL DAY surgery, and the nurse led me to a semiprivate room. My mother had left after signing forms but would return in a few hours. Eric arrived as she was leaving, entering the room with two packages of

Reese's Peanut Butter Cups to look forward to postsurgery. He also had a biography of George Gershwin. Stephen King's newest book, *Christine*, was in my lap, face down and open flat so as to hold my place. From this angle it looked like a seagull, the type I drew in one swoop of a line, a small wave cresting in the sky to illustrate a distant bird flying so high and so far that no detail was expected.

"Isn't it cool how books look like birds and they fly us away from the place we're in?" I picked up *Christine*, flapping its covers toward him. "Books seem silent, but there are worlds of noise in them, and even when you come to the end, they're not over. You begin them again and find something new each time." My voice wavered and I set the book down, afraid I was going to cry, afraid of the loss I didn't understand, afraid of the surgery, the bright lights over my head, the mask, afraid of the feeling of suffocation, nowhere to go but inward, like when I read books.

Eric rubbed my cold hands between his secure warm ones. "Want me to read to you?" he asked. "It might help you relax."

I gave him *Christine* and picked up the Reese's Peanut Butter Cups. I loved the soft crinkly sound of the orange wrapper, and I tried to concentrate on the chocolate-coated peanut butter that was so close. Sweetness would spread through my mouth and happiness through my chest when I bit into the firm candy and savored the chocolate's reliable goodness. I put them carefully in my jacket pocket with my gloves.

We continued the wait for surgery, Eric's voice taking me from the hospital and my situation to the life of another troubled teenager and an incomprehensible, independently minded Plymouth Fury. If fury wasn't incomprehensible and surprising, there would be less fear.

Why, when I had feared pregnancy so much and pleaded with the pregnancy gods to make it go away, was I sad that it was over?

My mother had drilled the difference between good and bad into my head like a woodpecker with an obsessive-compulsive disorder, holding me up for comparison to my sisters even before I reached puberty. One day I would realize that having sex at fifteen might not have been a wise choice, but it did not make me a bad person, just as having sex hadn't made my sisters bad people. We were all just struggling to find love and attention and room to breathe in a home where parents had no time to examine the reasons behind our behavior or theirs.

One day I might understand the sadness, the sense of loss that wasn't acceptable for sexually active teenagers to voice out loud because, from a sensible adult's point of view, we should have been cheering our good luck.

WE WAITED. WARM AND FIRM, ERIC GRIPPED MY FINGERS LIKE he wouldn't let go. Then a nurse came in, and I tried not to think, *she's judging me*, when she said to Eric, "We'll tell you what happens so you don't wonder how she is. You can wait for her here."

Then she touched my hand gently, smiled, and said, "We're ready to start." And it occurred to me that I'd been ready to start all my life.

21

When Pigs Fly

My mother had nine children, the first six a year or so apart, three boys and three girls. After a respite my mother had three more children, all girls, designated forever as the "three youngest" regardless of how old or leathery we grow. This last group arrived more slowly. I am the youngest of this second set, separated from my next chronological sister by almost three years. My mother probably thought the possibility of a ninth child had faded to none. To ensure against a tenth, the doctor performed a tubal ligation at the time of my birth.

The older six brothers and sisters accused us three youngest of not knowing real work, the hard kind. We knew baby work for the babies we were. From where I knelt in the garden, my back and neck cramped with strain, my skin cooked to a light brown by the sun, fingernails stuffed tight with dirt from weeding, a cloak of mosquitoes fighting for my blood, I might see my blustery-and-favored brother holding a pitchfork, hurling cow manure into a pile that stretched into the thick woods with extended families of snakes and hot smell. Or he might be digging a hole; my family dug many holes when the ground wasn't frozen, not an easy thing to do when the backyard is ledge and the front yard a mass of weeping willow tree roots. My parents waited each year for the thaw, anxious to complete work that snow and ice had delayed.

Fence posts, cables, pipes, trash, stumps, trees, flowers, vegetables, and animals all required holes, sometimes wide and long enough to be called ditches, others deep enough to be called graves.

Shovels broke, spade handles snapped, post-hole diggers scraped without clasping dirt, and hoes clunked in our effort to break the earth. "Is that good enough?" one of us would dare to ask only inches into the dark ground, our arms bloody from overscratched bug bites, our toenails crammed with dirt.

"Less complaining, more digging," my father might respond. Or, because we never ate what died on its own: "If you bury the ram in a hole that shallow, the coyotes will dig him up, and there'll be pieces in the dooryard. Mamma will be fit to be tied."

The ping, that telltale clang of metal hitting rock, triggers chemicals to gather in a knot of stress, muscles to bunch in frustration. The worst clunk is when the hole is almost deep enough, when you've almost made it. The I-can't-believe-it-after-all-this-work feeling sinks into your gut before you try to determine the size of the rock. Can you go around it? Get it out? Will this be your lucky hole? And then someone might comment, "It's hotter than all get out," which means nothing regardless of how you arrange the words. Or that person could repeat for what felt like the millionth time, "It's hotter than Hades out here," and conjecture about digging to China, which is confusing to a child after you've just mentioned hell.

I promised myself I'd never dig another hole after I left home. I worried I would unbury a snake, a nest of coiled muscled lengths suspicious of my intent. As I jumped onto the spade's metal edge with my bare feet, wobbling atop the earth, black flies taking advantage of my neck while my hands were busy, I decided I'd never dig when I got to direct my own life. I would refuse to own a shovel, a hoe, or even a rake. Once out of the house I wouldn't have calloused hands or splinters from wooden handles.

WE DUG, WEEDED, HARVESTED, CANNED AND FROZE VEGETABLES, cleaned stalls, cut up animals, carried and stacked wood, mowed yards, vacuumed out heating registers, and scrubbed floors and walls, but we also got to jump rope and play house in the woods. While we rode horses and "gallivanted around the neighborhood," my parents continued to work. They never rested but for a cup of coffee or tea. I asked my mother once: "When will all the work be done?" And she was silent for a moment, her face drawn, before she answered, "The work will never be done." Then she threw the ball to me a few times before returning to her task, often ones set before her by my father, who always had renovation projects in progress.

There was a small plastic pool that my aunt bought for us when she visited from California. My father allowed us to fill it with about three inches of water once a week in the summer, a risk because, if the well ran dry, which it often did, we had to carry water from a quarter-mile away. The three youngest sat in the pool, slapping away the dead grasshoppers, beetles, and moths that floated amongst the grass clippings, and we drank frozen slushy Kool-Aid like the princesses my siblings said we were.

There was a handmade log swing set in the yard, and if you sat there long enough, bucking your body to make the swing go, a parent might come along and push you high, almost over the top, making your viscera lift and resettle. I don't know where my father got two gigantic wooden circles that he leaned together over a wooden base to form a playhouse for the three youngest, but I enjoyed reading in there until a family of snakes took up residence beneath its floor.

In the evenings, after all the work was done, if my father was at work or busy in the cellar, my mother might play Gin Rummy, Fish, Casper the Friendly Ghost, or Scrabble with me while my sisters tittered or fought upstairs. She would jump rope, play half a game of around-the-world at the basketball hoop, and start craft projects. Being the youngest, I had her to myself more than my siblings ever could or did. Until I was four she rocked me at night and sang about Tippy's ears cut long and her tail cut short, until one night my father told her she sounded like a cat he'd stepped on; then she never sang again, not even at birthdays. Instead, at night she read me picture books and helped me sound out words. One of my treasured possessions is a recording of her helping me read a story about a cat and a mouse. Her voice is quiet and calm, so I know it was a good day.

She recently said, a year or so back, "It was so unfair the way your oldest sister would rock and take care of you when I wanted to, but there was always so much work, and if it wasn't that, your sisters and brothers gave me so much trouble. I missed too much of your childhood."

This made me consider trouble differently: instead of us being afraid of getting into it, she was given it.

Once, later on a visit, my mother suddenly said, "I wish I'd known what I do now about molestation and what it all meant. I didn't know about that sort of thing back then, and I feel bad. I just didn't know how to handle it, and I'm sorry." After she left I considered the number of times she'd said, "didn't know" and tried to remember the context of her life when my helpful-friend spent so much time with me. She'd had a pregnant daughter in the house and then that daughter's child. She was the one who got up at night with the baby because my sister needed her sleep to finish high school. And then there were all my other siblings in various phases of distress who needed her attention. At that time I never wondered if she got time alone with my father or if they were content with each other. What I didn't know about her easily equaled what she hadn't known about me.

I WAS INCAPABLE OF TWISTING MY THOUGHTS TO THEIR PERSPECTIVE during the years I lived under their control. Why did holes always have to be one spade-full deeper? Or vegetable rows so straight? There were infinite "have-tos" especially when you needed a parent's time. My mother might say, "I can't bother with you right now. I have to get supper started," or "I have to mow," or "I have to help your father." I felt fury when my parents shouted and complained over what I thought was nothing but they thought was something. This makes me feel guilty now, a bit sad, in the same way that I feel when I think back to how I hated the neighbor's sable German shepherd, who nearly strangled herself on her chain in her snarling rushes to get me, while at the same time I felt sorry for her.

With saliva swinging against what looked like stacks of teeth below curled lips, this shepherd was caught up in the emotional zone of attack and destroy. However, despite a hate that was grounded in terror, I felt empathy. This dog lived on a chain her entire life. How different was her life from my parents'? They were trapped by nine kids who got married and had kids they dropped off. Their home was too much work and they had too many bills and children, as restrictive as the dog's, whose home was a circle of yard and the dirt beneath a porch. I never saw anyone play ball with her, pat her, or take her for walks.

I HAVE A FEW PICTURES OF MY PARENTS BEFORE THEY HAD KIDS—only a few because so much was lost in house fires. In these sepia-toned photographs, my parents are cutting into their wedding cake or standing close after the ceremony. They are young and laughing, without a notion of what's ahead of them, possibly feeling triumphant that they overcame all the obstacles and married. It's likely they thought they had time to do many things before they started a family. Stephen King's character Jake Epping observes, "If I'd known what the future held for me, I certainly would have gone up to see her. I might even have given her the kiss that had been flirting in the air between us for the last couple of months. But of course I didn't know. Life turns on a dime."

NOT LONG AGO I VISITED MY BLUSTERY-AND-FAVORED BROTHER'S home where he now farms pigs. I walked down back behind his large and newly remodeled house with Eric's and my daughter. We rounded a John Deere tractor, and the wooden boards of a pigpen stretched out of sight into the woods, where about a hundred pigs wallowed in mud, rooted through the bushes, and rested on rocks, their fat sides rising slowly and peacefully. Sows snuggled with nursing piglets in the various shelters and in scooped areas beneath the trees.

"You wouldn't believe the stories," my blustery-and-favored brother said when he saw me watching the mothers with their babies.

His arms were black with dirt, and it was difficult to determine where his deeply tanned skin began. His T-shirt was thin from washing and use and the many stains that decorated the material like inkblot appliques. His hair was thinner than ever, and a few teeth were absent in the lineup, but his smile was wide and his eyes shone with pride.

"These pigs are so crazy smart, it's frickin amazing. During that big rain storm we just had that sow over there built a shelter out of twigs and branches for her babies." He pointed off to the woods. "She made the piglets stay under it and lay down beside them to block the cold and wind. Frickin pig's smarter than your dumbass brother."

I didn't need to ask which brother he meant. As we peered through the trees to see the sow, other pigs snorted and squealed at each other, communicating things we'd never understand fully.

"Animals are amazing, that's true," I agreed, knowing as I said it that we would always differ on their purpose. "Can I hold a baby?" I asked, thinking of all the piglets of my past, specifically Waterboro from long ago. "Will the mother let you go in and pick one up?"

"She won't bother me none," my blustery-and-favored brother answered confidently, pleased that I was interested in his stock, and he climbed over the board fencing to the shelter where half a dozen piglets raced to avoid him. His boots sank into the mud with a squishing sound, and when he lifted a foot to step forward, the hole quickly filled in as if he was never there. Their mother looked up and went after the dirty-jeaned leg as it passed her snout, and I felt only admiration and love for my blustery-and-favored brother as he pushed by unconcerned and returned to me with a wiggling and squealing pink piglet. I held the baby close to my chest so she could feel my heartbeat and allowed her to put her snout and head into my hair. My daughter, the same age I was when I was given two tiny chicks, reached up and patted the tiny muscular side.

"She's adorable," I said, as if congratulating a parent on his new infant. I scratched her back and touched her pink nose, and after she quieted, I handed her back before her squeals could renew and motivate motherly reaction. My blustery-and-favored brother took the baby and rubbed her head affectionately.

"This pig's mother isn't as good as the sow down back. I tell you, that pig's so smart, it's some frickin crazy. Unreal." He shook his balding head as he leaned over the boards and set the baby down. "No one believes me when I tell 'em."

"I believe you," I said, my arms feeling suddenly empty without the baby. It was a cool afternoon and I hugged myself. "Yet you still eat them." He was well known for his pig roasts.

"Not her. She'll be here for a long time." He scratched the tremendous back of an adult hog who grunted, shoving another mud-covered pig out of the way to get closer. He chuckled. "These pigs are delicious. All they eat is real food, none of that corn garbage." He looked at my daughter, who was staring at a pig in front of her, her nose wrinkled. "You like your mother, or are you not so foolish? You must eat meat. It's good for ya."

My daughter's nose unwrinkled slightly as she said, "Well, maybe if you washed it first."

Her blustery-and-favored uncle burst out laughing. "Where'd you get her anyways?"

We turned then to leave because I had to get back, just as anyone who has grown up on a farm has to always get back. The work pulls, and as my mother said once, it never ends. We walked up the hill to my Tacoma truck that had a cap with screened windows for my black German shepherd and boxer.

"What's 'c-h-c-l-a-t-e' mean?" my blustery-and-favored brother asked, referring to my license plate. "Don't tell me you still eat that stuff?"

We hugged and said our good-byes. As soon as the truck doors slammed, my daughter observed, "He sure does love his pigs, doesn't he?"

I considered her question. Minutes before, I'd stood holding a baby animal that I knew would be slaughtered and yet I hadn't run with it to safety. I'd listened to my blustery-and-favored brother talk about the pigs' intelligence and I hadn't felt the need to explode against how he could shoot and slaughter animals he'd just told me would build shelters to protect their babies from rain and wind. I'd broken a number of promises to my young self. I wait now more than I ever did as a child. I photograph animals for hire and for fun, and I sit, kneel, or stand patiently on the edges of fields, in door-ways, and sometimes from a window, waiting for animals to show me who they are, to act free and real. I broke those promises to my-self just as shovels break the earth.

I run my own life now, yet I dig holes: small ones for vegetables and flowers, larger ones for trees, and sometimes even ditches for underground wires. I push my spade into the ground and hope the dirt will move smoothly, easily, that there will be no pings or clunks, no obstacles, but they're impossible to escape—no one is that lucky. With each hole, I pause, with the shovel loose in my fingers, con-sider if I need to keep working, and continue on. I understand that ground must be broken for anything to grow.

My blustery-and-favored brother once said that skin and vinyl stick together like dollar bills to a stripper. I think skin and vinyl stick together like memories to our brains. Sometimes they hurt when you peel them away, but you must to go on with your life, un-stuck. I looked into the rearview mirror one last time before answer-ing my daughter's question, the first of what would be many as we drove back to Portland. "Yes," I said. "Your uncle does love his pigs. He really does."

Acknowledgments

To my children, Morgan and Alex, who helped me find the humor and who continue to forgive me for parenting blunders. To my daughter-in-law, Katie, who often asks, "Would you like some time to write this afternoon?" and then will ride bikes with Morgan to the playground. To Doreen Metcalf, a horse and dog trainer, who after reading the chapter "Pecking Order," said, "I'm surprised you didn't get killed. Your family knew jack shit about horses." She taught me how to ride without hanging on to anything. To three of my siblings who helped me clarify events and who support my need to explore my childhood: my hair-twirling-pretty sister, my sister-who-holds-grudges-longer-than-God, and my blustery-and-favored brother. To Russell Peppe and Pauline Kenniston, who read the chapters as I wrote them and who cheered me on. To Jackie Peppe, who paddled canoes and rode horses with Morgan so that I could write. To Anita Jones, who offered the use of her remote cabin so that I could do nothing else but swim and write. To Debra Marquart, who encouraged me to examine my childhood memories around food and who then read hundreds of pages with unflagging enthusiasm, all which began PCS. To David Mura, who continues to encourage me to ask questions and to think wider. The day he e-mailed, "I believe in you and your writing" was the day I revised Chapters 12 and 17 to reflect a deeper honesty. To Suzanne Strempek Shea, who encouraged clarity by asking her own questions and by offering her constant support. To Wendy Strothman, my savvy and patient agent, and to Merloyd Lawrence, my wonderful and insightful editor, who understands my love for animals and my need to keep them alive. And thank you to Lori Hobkirk for putting up with all of my questions and edits. Lastly, I owe my sanity to Stephen King, who, although he doesn't know I exist, gave me a place to go for eighteen years, and to Jane Goodall who taught me that everything is connected and anything is possible.

About the Author

HELEN PEPPE began writing stories, mostly about animals, on scraps of butcher paper when she was knee-high to a horse. All of her furry characters lived happily ever after. When she was shoulder-high to a horse, at age fourteen, she learned to research publications before submitting manuscripts when she sent an essay about her rabbit's death to *The Christian Science Monitor*. The editor wrote back within two weeks to say she loved the story, was sorry for the loss, but couldn't publish it because rabbits don't have souls. Helen's first published story, nonfiction, was about a young woman sitting in a concert hall imagining herself outside with the squirrels.

After undergraduate work, she delayed writing to devote twelve years to raising and homeschooling her son, but when she had a second child, Helen realized there wasn't enough time left to wait another twelve years before getting an MFA in writing. As a student, Helen again wrote short stories and personal essays and worked as a professional photographer, specializing in horses and dogs. She now teaches writing by illustrating craft through her photography. Her work has appeared in anthologies and print and digital magazines, and she has won several literary awards. *Pigs Can't Swim* is her first book. One chapter, "The American Eagle," was a finalist for the 2011 Annie Dillard Creative Nonfiction Award. Helen lives in Maine with her husband, Eric, her children, her dogs, cats, rabbits, guinea pigs, and her horse. Her website is www.helenpeppe.com.